# Tomorrow's Dinner Cooked Tonight

## 72 Complete Menus for Easy Entertaining

MICHAEL LOGAN & LISL POPPER

*With a Foreword by*

Mapie
Comtesse de Toulouse-Lautrec

*Illustrated by*

GINGER TILLEY

PETER DAVIES : LONDON

Peter Davies Ltd
15 Queen Street, Mayfair, London, WIX 8BE

LONDON   MELBOURNE   TORONTO
JOHANNESBURG   AUCKLAND

Reproduced and printed by photolithography by
Morrison & Gibb Limited, London and Edinburgh

# Contents

## Menus 1 - 72

## AUTHORS' NOTE

All the recipes in this book are designed to serve 6 people.

# Foreword

Mapie, Comtesse de Toulouse-Lautrec
Author of *Good French Cooking*

Michael Logan is a happy man—happy because he has been wise enough to arrange his life to suit his tastes. An American who has chosen to live in France—though *not* in Paris or one of the other great cities, with its noise, crowds and traffic jams—he has settled in the country, in a most beautiful and peaceful corner of the *Département* of the Yonne.

His charming eighteenth-century house looks down from its hilltop on a scene which Claude Monet would have delighted to paint, its principal feature being one of those canals, typical of this part of France, whose banks are lined with shivering poplars. From time to time a lumbering barge or a light pleasure craft passes by, adding a human touch to the calm countryside though never disturbing it with noise or haste. Let us be thankful that such tranquil places still exist in the world for those who know how to appreciate them. It is hard to believe that the great motorway from Lille to Marseilles, with its ceaseless burden of traffic, runs within a few miles of the house, yet it means that Michael's many friends are within easy reach of him, and of nature in its unspoiled beauty.

Perhaps there was another reason for Michael Logan's choice of location. The *Département* of the Yonne lies between the provinces of Champagne and Burgundy: two names that have carried the glory of our wine throughout the world. Moreover, Burgundy is gastronomically one of the greatest of the French provinces. It produces superb cattle (the famous Charolais), succulent and abundant game, exquisite fresh-water fish, delicious fruits and vegetables. Over the centuries, in this region civilised for so long past, men and women have evolved a wide and varied selection of recipes. What more is needed to ensure happiness than peaceful surroundings, frequent visits from friends, and good cooking?

Michael Logan is a born cook who likes nothing better than to go into his own kitchen and prepare some of his best dishes for his friends, dishes drawn not only from Burgundy but from all over the world.

An old French proverb says that no one can be at the stove and the mill at the same time—you cannot be in two places at once. Michael cannot be in the kitchen preparing a sauce and still be in the sitting-room enjoying the company of his guests. It is because of this that, in collaboration with his friend Lisl Popper, he has drawn up the menus which are presented in this book. They serve a double purpose: they allow the cook to be with his friends as much as possible and to gratify them with his culinary talent. Lisl Popper has ably helped in this task. She is both a gourmet and a business woman, with little time to spare for kitchen chores. The object of this cookery book, therefore, has her warm support and the benefit of her wide knowledge of Central European cooking, based on her Austrian upbringing. And so Michael and Lisl have pooled their resources and produced a cookery book which combines time-saving and talent.

From the recipes it will be seen that the main preparation can be carried out the day before. Some of the dishes, prepared in advance, are served cold, but every menu includes at least one hot dish which may be left overnight and reheated the following day, before serving, without losing any of its quality. In fact, some of the dishes are even improved by this treatment. The essential thing is to choose them with intelligence and discrimination, and I am sure that you are going to agree with me that this is exactly what our friends have done.

*Translated by B.L.*

# Introduction

The hostess at a dinner party today seldom has the chance to shine both as cook and conversationalist. Too often the arrival of guests is the signal for panic and confusion behind the scenes; too often, when the guests are supplied with aperitifs the hostess promptly performs a disappearing act, accompanied by the sounds of feverish activity from the kitchen.

This book has been prepared for those who like talking to their friends as well as feeding them. All the menus can be prepared the day or evening before the dinner or supper party, yet none of the dishes will loose its flavour. We have borne in mind the inexperienced cook, and generally only one course of each menu requires more than a minimal amount of time and effort to prepare. On the other hand there are plenty of little-known and exotic dishes for the more ambitious hostess.

We have tried to provide menus that are well balanced and attractively put together; they range from haute cuisine for a formal dinner to more traditional solid fare for an informal supper. In all cases complete freedom of choice is ensured since hors d'oeuvres, main dishes and desserts are indexed separately.

Finally, we would ask you to remember twelve useful hints:

1. Before shopping, it is worth making a careful list of all supplies needed. It is also useful to list all the things that have to be done on the evening of the dinner before the first guest arrives.

2. Cocktails can be mixed beforehand, champagne cooled. Glasses and appetizers should be ready on a tray, with ice in an ice bucket.

3. Never cover any food before it is cool.

4. Never put hot food into the refrigerator.

5. Any food which is to be reheated in a soup, gravy or sauce should always be cooled or kept cold in a cool or cold larder.

6. Dishes that require reheating should be removed from the refrigerator or cold larder for an hour or two before they go into the oven or on the stove. (Note that food for reheating can be kept just as well, if not better, in a larder as in a refrigerator.)

7. Any dish containing eggs must always be reheated in a double boiler.

8. Game and poultry may be carved in advance, reconstructed, wrapped in a towel or in foil, placed on a platter and kept cool until serving time.

9. Salad should be washed, dried, arranged in a bowl covered with a plastic lid and kept in the refrigerator. Salad dressing can be mixed well in advance and kept in a covered glass jar.

10. If you serve roast beef, lamb or pork underdone and some of your guests prefer it well done, have some boiling gravy at hand to pour over the underdone slices and all your guests will be satisfied.

11. A spacious, thermostatically controlled hot tray will prove an invaluable aid to serving any hot dishes.

12. A coffee tray can be prepared in advance (unless you are using Cona coffee). Make the coffee beforehand, pour it into the coffee pot, and keep the pot hot in gently boiling water.

# 1

## MENU

*Fish Chowder Logan Version*

*Lettuce Salad, Rice*

*Grapefruit and Strawberries*

## Fish Chowder Logan Version

1½ lb. halibut or cod cut into 1-inch pieces

4 lb. sea bass cut into 1-inch pieces

4 large onions

4 large potatoes

6 medium tomatoes

salt and pepper

8 oz. tomato juice

1½ level tablespoons whole pickling spice

fish-heads, bones, or any small fish ⎫
1½ pints water ⎪
8 oz. dry white wine ⎬ for fish stock
bay leaf ⎪
parsley ⎭

2 lobster tails, frozen or fresh

5 tablespoons Worcester sauce

8 oz. brandy

juice of 1 lemon

¼ lb. butter or less according to taste

4 tablespoons olive oil

▶ Ask the fishmonger to skin and bone the halibut or cod and the bass.

▶ To make the stock use fish-heads, bones and any small fish. Add 2 peeled tomatoes, a bay leaf and some parsley. Cover with 1½ pints of water and 8 oz. dry white wine. Cook slowly in a large saucepan without the lid, until the stock is reduced to 1½ pints.

▶ Put 4 tablespoons olive oil into a large deep fireproof earthenware casserole. Peel the potatoes, cut into ½-inch cubes and arrange them in a layer on the bottom of the pot. Place the fish, cut into 1-inch pieces, on top of the potatoes. Sprinkle with salt and freshly ground pepper. Cover with the onions, sliced very thin, and the 4 remaining tomatoes peeled and left whole. Sprinkle again with salt and pepper and pour over the tomato juice. Put in whole spice tied in square of cheese-cloth or muslin and add strained fish stock.

▶ Simmer very slowly for one hour, stirring occasionally with a wooden fork, being careful not to break fish or tomatoes. If an electric stove is used, put an asbestos mat under the casserole.

▶ Let the fish chowder cool and then store it in the refrigerator.

▶ Next evening reheat and let soup simmer for another half-hour. After 20 minutes, add unfrozen lobster tails cut into 1-inch pieces.

▶ Just before serving add the juice of 1 lemon, 5 tablespoons Worcester sauce, 8 oz. brandy and $\frac{1}{4}$ lb. butter. When the butter has melted, the chowder is ready for the table.

▶ Serve in the earthenware casserole with individual earthenware bowls of rice for each guest.

## Lettuce Salad

| | |
|---|---|
| 3 heads lettuce | $\frac{1}{4}$ teaspoon salt |
| 5 tablespoons olive oil | $\frac{1}{8}$ teaspoon black |
| 1$\frac{1}{2}$ tablespoons wine | pepper |
| vinegar | $\frac{1}{8}$ teaspoon Dijon |
| | mustard |

▶ Discard outer leaves of 3 heads of lettuce. Separate the leaves and wash in cold water. Drain and shake dry. Store in the refrigerator wrapped in a towel.

▶ In a jar with a screw top, shake until well mixed 5 tablespoons olive oil, 1$\frac{1}{2}$ tablespoons wine or cider vinegar, $\frac{1}{4}$ teaspoon salt, $\frac{1}{8}$ teaspoon black pepper and $\frac{1}{8}$ teaspoon Dijon mustard. Put aside. Shake well again before using.

## Rice

| | |
|---|---|
| 12 oz. long-grained rice | 2$\frac{1}{2}$ pints boiling water |
| 1 dessertspoon salt | juice of 1 lemon |
| butter | |

▶ Bring to a boil in a deep pan 2$\frac{1}{2}$ pints of water and 1 dessertspoon salt. When boiling rapidly, pour in 12 oz. long-grained

rice. Stir. Boil rapidly for 15 to 20 minutes. Drain in a colander. Pour over cold water until thoroughly chilled. Drain, shaking the colander until all water has gone. Store in a buttered, ovenproof dish.

▶ To serve. Dot with butter, sprinkle with the juice of 1 lemon. Reheat in a pre-heated moderate oven 350°F, Reg 4 for 15-20 minutes. Stir occasionally.

## Grapefruit and Strawberries

| | |
|---|---|
| 6 grapefruits | 6 oz. honey |
| 2 punnets of strawberries | |

▶ Cut the tops off 6 grapefruits so that you are left with a wide opening. With a sharp-toothed curved grapefruit knife, cut around the edge, until you feel the fruit is separate from the skin. Now cut in quarters so that you can remove them without spoiling the grapefruit shell. Put the shells into a plastic bag. Remove the membranes from the sections of grapefruit, saving as much of the juice as possible. Put in a bowl. Pour over the honey. Cover and put the bowl and the bag of shells in the refrigerator to chill.

▶ To serve, hull and wash strawberries, mix with the grapefruit sections and fill the shells.

# 2

## MENU

*Kipper Salad*

*Boeuf Strogonoff*

*Apple Aspic in Sauce*

▶ Wash and dry 2 heads of crisp lettuce (cos lettuce if available), wrap in a towel and put in the refrigerator to crisp. Peel 4 hard-boiled eggs and cut into quarters. Peel 4 tomatoes and cut into eighths. (If you pour boiling water over the tomatoes, leave for 10–12 seconds and then drain; you can remove the skin without difficulty.) Wash 1 green pepper, cut off the top, remove the seeds and cut away the white membrane. Slice into thin strips about 2 inches long. Wash and remove the outer skin of 4 shallots and cut into smallish rounds (but not chopped). If shallots are not available use 4 small onions.

▶ Combine all of the above ingredients in a salad bowl, pour over the following dressing, and mix well.

*Salad Dressing*

▶ Put 2 oz. wine vinegar, 6 oz. olive oil, ½ teaspoon salt, good pinch of pepper, dash of paprika, and 1 egg yolk into a jar with a screw top. Shake until thoroughly mixed and pour over salad; you can beat the dressing in a bowl with a wire whisk if you prefer.

## Boeuf Strogonoff

| | |
|---|---|
| 2½ lb. fillet of beef | 1½ cartons (7½ oz.) |
| 1 oz. butter | sour cream or |
| ½–1 tablespoon | double cream with a |
| cooking oil | tablespoon of |
| 1 medium-sized | lemon juice |
| chopped onion or | 2 teaspoons of Dijon |
| spring onions | mustard |
| 1 good pinch of | 2 teaspoons of |
| ground black | cornflour and |
| pepper | 1 tablespoon single |
| 1 level teaspoon of salt | cream for thickening, |
| | if required |

▶ Cut the beef into 2-inch pieces ½ an inch thick.

## Kipper Salad

| | |
|---|---|
| 3 kippers | 4 tomatoes |
| 2 heads crisp lettuce | 1 green pepper |
| 4 hard-boiled eggs | 4 shallots or small |
| parsley | onions |
| | salad dressing— |
| | (see recipe below) |

▶ Place 3 kippers in a pan and cover with cold water. Heat to boiling point, drain and dry. Remove the skin and any bones, cut the fillets into not too small pieces.

► Using half the butter and the oil, melt the butter in a sauté pan or a saucepan and add the oil. When hot, fry the meat, a few pieces at a time, on a high heat to brown the outside and keep the inside of the meat still rare or red, 2–3 minutes or less on each side. Keep the cooked pieces of fillet warm and add a little water to the pan so as to add to the meat juices and dissolve any brown residue left by the meat. Tip this liquid over the meat and use the pan to fry the onion in the remaining butter and oil.

► When the onion is soft, mix in 1½ cartons of sour cream, simmer a moment and then add the mustard and mix well. The sauce can be thickened at this point with the 2 teaspoons of cornflour slaked with the tablespoon of single cream. Reboil. Season the beef with the salt and black pepper and put together with the sauce in a covered flameproof casserole to cool and then refrigerate till next evening.

► When ready to reheat and serve, put the flameproof casserole on to the flame and reheat, though without coming to the boil. Unless great care is taken, the meat will be well done, rather than rare, and the dish is not good when overcooked.

# Apple Aspic

| | |
|---|---|
| 3 lb. cooking apples | 2 teaspoons gelatine |
| 1¼ lb. granulated sugar | 5–6 oz. glacé cherries |
| ¼ pint water | 4 tablespoons dark rum |
| 1 tablespoon lemon juice | |

► Peel, core and quarter 3 lb. cooking apples. Cut into thin slices lengthwise.

► In a heavy enamelled saucepan put 1¼ lb. sugar, ¼ pint water and 1 tablespoon lemon juice. Bring to a boil stirring until the sugar is dissolved. Add the apples to the syrup and boil over moderate heat, stirring frequently so they will not stick. Cook until they are transparent, 20 to 30 minutes.

Soak 2 teaspoons gelatine in a tablespoon of cold water for 5 minutes. Dissolve over a bowl of hot water. Coarsely chop 5–6 oz. glacé cherries and add to the apples. Remove from heat and add 4 tablespoons of dark rum.

► Rub the inside of a 2-pint cylindrical mould with oil. Cut a round of greaseproof paper to fit the bottom of the mould, set it in the mould and oil it lightly.

► Spoon the apples into the mould and chill in refrigerator overnight. Serve with the following sauce:

## Sauce

| | |
|---|---|
| 4 egg yolks | 12 oz. rich milk |
| 3 level tablespoons castor sugar | 1 teaspoon vanilla extract |
| 1 teaspoon flour | 4 tablespoons single or double cream |

► Beat 4 egg yolks with a wooden spoon, add 3 level tablespoons sugar and continue beating until smooth and creamy; add 1 teaspoon flour. Scald 12 oz. milk and add to yolk mixture little by little. Return to the saucepan and cook over a low heat, stirring constantly until it thickens and coats a wooden spoon. Do not let it boil. Remove from heat. Stir in 1 teaspoon vanilla extract. Let it cool, stirring it from time to time to prevent a skin from forming. Put it into a bowl, spread a thin layer of 4 tablespoons of cream over the top, cover and put with the Apple Aspic in refrigerator to chill.

► Before serving, unmould and beat the layer of cream into the sauce.

# 3

## MENU

*Lettuce and Almond Soup*

*Moroccan Chicken*

*Fried Carrots*

*The Guards Trifle*

## Lettuce and Almond Soup

| | |
|---|---|
| 4 small heads lettuce | 2 small onions |
| scant 2½ pints chicken stock | ½ teaspoon dry mustard |
| ½ lb. ground almonds | ¾ pint thick cream |
| 2 teaspoons sugar | toasted almond shreds |

▶ Combine in a saucepan 4 small heads shredded lettuce, 1¾ pints chicken stock, ½ lb. ground almonds, 2 teaspoons sugar, ½ teaspoonful dry mustard, 2 small onions sliced thinly. Simmer for five to ten minutes until the lettuce is wilted.

▶ Blend until smooth in a liquidizer or put through a very fine sieve. Add ¾ pint chicken stock, ¾ pint of cream and chill.

▶ Serve in chilled cups garnished with toasted almond shreds.

## Moroccan Chicken

| | |
|---|---|
| 2 small chickens | 1½ teaspoons saffron |
| 3 tablespoons olive oil | 3 teaspoons cinnamon |
| 2 lemons | small new potatoes |
| ½ pint chicken stock | salt and pepper |
| 3 small cooking apples | |

▶ To be prepared in advance, ask the poulterer to cut up 2 small chickens as for a fricassee. Heat 3 tablespoons olive oil in a frying pan, fry the chickens, a few pieces at a time, until golden brown on all sides. Put the pieces as they are browned into a warmed dish which has a cover.

▶ Cut 2 lemons into thin slices, removing any pips; scatter the slices over and around the chickens.

▶ Peel, core and cut in quarters 3 small cooking apples; arrange them around the chickens.

▶ Mix ¼ pint hot chicken stock with 1½ teaspoons saffron and 3 teaspoons cinnamon. Pour over the chickens. Salt and pepper.

▶ Cover the chickens with a piece of tin-foil the size of the dish. Put the cover on the dish and place in a previously heated moderate oven 350°F, Reg 4 for about 30 or 40 minutes. The chicken must not be quite done. As it is cooking, add some of the remaining ¼ pint of chicken stock if it seems dry.

▶ Put aside to cool, leaving it covered, and when sufficiently cold place in the refrigerator until the next day. (This can be done the same morning if you prefer.)

▶ Reheat slowly in the oven 350°F, Reg 4 for another 20 minutes or until the chicken is done when you test it with a fork.

▶ In the meantime peel and boil small new potatoes, drain them and arrange them around the chicken before serving.

# Fried Carrots

| | |
|---|---|
| 10 medium-sized carrots | freshly ground pepper |
| salt | a little butter for |
| 1 oz. butter | reheating |

▶ Scrape carrots and slice in very thin slices. Melt butter in a saucepan with a tight cover, add the carrots. Stir slowly until all the carrots are thoroughly coated with the butter. Add 1 teaspoon boiling water, cover saucepan and cook on asbestos mat until carrots are tender. Season to taste with salt and pepper. Set aside.

▶ Next evening, reheat quickly over high flame in a little butter.

# The Guards Trifle

| | |
|---|---|
| 8 eggs | 1 level teaspoon |
| 10½ oz. castor sugar | flour |
| 1½ tablespoons lemon | 12 oz. light cream |
| juice | ½ teaspoon vanilla |
| grated rind of ½ lemon | extract |
| pinch of salt | 8 oz. sherry |
| 4½ oz. flour | 4 tablespoons brandy |
| 3 egg yolks | 1 lb. jar strawberry jam |

To serve:—Icing sugar, whole strawberries and rosettes of whipped cream.

▶ Separate the yolks and whites of 8 eggs. Sift 4½ oz. flour 3 times.

▶ Beat egg yolks until lemon yellow. Gradually beat in 8 oz. sugar, 1½ tablespoons lemon juice and the grated rind of ½ lemon. Beat until thick and smooth.

▶ Add a pinch of salt to the egg whites, beat until stiff. Fold into the egg yolks. Fold in the sifted flour, sifting about an ounce at a time over the surface. Fold in vanilla extract.

▶ Oil a large baking sheet with sides or an oblong baking tin. Cover with greaseproof or bakewell paper. Brush the greaseproof paper with oil. Pour in the batter and bake in a moderately slow oven 325°F, Reg 2–3 about 30 minutes or until tooth-pick stuck into the centre comes out clean. Let cake cool in the pan. Remove from the cake tin by inverting it over a sheet of greaseproof paper. Peel off the bottom paper.

▶ In a bowl, stir 3 egg yolks and 2½ oz. castor sugar until smooth and creamy. Stir in 1 teaspoon flour. Blend well.

▶ Scald 12 oz. single cream. Stir into the egg mixture little by little. Return to stove and cook over a low heat, stirring continuously until it nearly comes to a boil and will coat a spoon; take care not to boil. Remove from heat.

▶ Place a deep round serving dish on the cake. With a sharp pointed knife cut a round from the cake. Wrap in greaseproof paper and set aside.

▶ Break the remaining cake in large pieces. Put them in the bottom of the serving dish. Pour over a mixture of 8 oz. sherry and 4 tablespoons brandy.

▶ Coat the pieces of cake with 1 lb. strawberry jam and pour warm custard all over. Cover dish and chill overnight in the refrigerator.

▶ Next day place the reserved round of cake on top of the trifle. Sprinkle the top with icing sugar and score the top diagonally with heated metal skewers to form a pattern of diamonds. Decorate the edge with whole strawberries and rosettes of whipped cream alternately.

4

MENU

*Eggs Mollet with Prawn Sauce*

*Braised Veal Chops in Aspic*

*Broccoli Salad*

*Chestnut Purée with Hot Chocolate Sauce*

# Eggs Mollet with Prawn Sauce

| | |
|---|---|
| 6 eggs | ½ teaspoon salt |
| 2 oz. butter | ¼ teaspoon pepper |
| 1 oz. flour | 2 tablespoons grated |
| 16 oz. milk | cheddar cheese |
| 2 oz. dry white wine | 1 egg yolk |
| 1½ tablespoons vinegar | 4 oz. double cream |
| 1½ tablespoons single cream | 1 packet frozen prawns |

▶ Put 6 eggs in a saucepan. Pour over boiling water to cover. Add 1½ tablespoons vinegar and cook over low heat for 5 minutes. Drain and run cold water over them for about 5 minutes. Drain again and set aside until required.

▶ Melt over low heat the 2 oz. butter, and blend with 1 oz. of flour over low heat— stir in slowly 16 oz. milk and 2 oz. dry white wine using a wooden spoon. Add ½ teaspoon of salt and the ¼ teaspoon of pepper. Stir constantly until smooth and thickened. Remove from stove and continue to stir from time to time until cool. Film the surface with 1½ tablespoons of cream to prevent a skin forming. Store in refrigerator.

▶ Beat together 1 egg yolk and 4 oz. of double cream. Store in refrigerator.

▶ Next evening, carefully peel eggs and re-heat in top of a double boiler or steamer for about 3 minutes. Re-heat the sauce over a low heat adding slowly the egg and cream mixture, also 2 tablespoons of grated cheddar cheese. Be careful sauce does not boil. Lastly, add the packet of de-frozen prawns having followed the correct directions on the packet for preparation if uncooked. If sauce has thickened too much a little warm milk may be added. Keep warm in double boiler off the heat. To serve, place each egg in a ramekin and pour the sauce over.

## Braised Veal Chops in Aspic

| | |
|---|---|
| 6 veal chops | 1½ pints chicken stock |
| 1½ oz. butter | 2 tablespoons gelatine |
| salt and pepper | |

▶ Ask the butcher to trim neatly 6 veal chops to a uniform size.

▶ Melt 1½ oz. butter in a frying pan and brown the chops on both sides. Pour over them 8 oz. chicken stock—you can use the tinned variety, but not cubes. Cover tightly and simmer on moderate heat for at least 1 hour. Remove chops and pour juice left in the bottom of the pan through a fine sieve into a small bowl. Put in the refrigerator so that the fat will rise to the surface. Carefully skim off this fat and pour the remaining juice over the chops.

▶ Dissolve 2 tablespoons gelatine in 4 oz. chicken stock. Heat the remaining 12 oz. stock, pour into the gelatine mixture. Mix thoroughly and set aside.

▶ Pour some of the stock into a shallow serving dish. Place in refrigerator to set. When set, lay the chops on top. Pour over the rest of the aspic when on the point of setting, and place in refrigerator until next day.

## Broccoli Salad

| | |
|---|---|
| 2 packets frozen broccoli | ¼ pint vinaigrette |

▶ Cook 2 packets frozen broccoli according to the directions on the packet. Drain. Chill. Serve with ¼ pint Vinaigrette poured over it (Menu 59).

## Chestnut Purée

| | |
|---|---|
| 1 large tin chestnut purée, sweetened or unsweetened | 8 oz. double cream |
| | 2 tablespoons rum or brandy |

▶ Empty 1 tin of chestnut purée into a bowl. Stir in 8 oz. double cream. If the purée is the unsweetened variety, add sugar to the cream, taste the purée, and add more sugar if necessary. Stir in 2 tablespoons rum or brandy. Mix well and keep covered in the refrigerator.

▶ To serve, heap in a mound on a serving dish, with a bowl of hot chocolate sauce to pour over.

## Hot Chocolate Sauce

| | |
|---|---|
| 2 oz. tablets bitter chocolate | 2 tablespoons very strong coffee |
| ½ oz. butter | 2 tablespoons golden syrup |
| 7 oz. sugar | |

▶ Melt in a double boiler, over but not in hot water, 2 oz. tablets bitter chocolate. Stir until well blended. Dissolve 7 oz. sugar with 2 tablespoons very strong, boiling coffee. Add to the chocolate. Remove from the double boiler. Stir in 2 tablespoons golden syrup and ½ oz. butter. Over direct heat boil gently for 5 minutes. Do not stir. Put aside. The sauce becomes very thick when cold. Reheat in a double boiler.

# 5

## MENU

*Chicken Liver Pâté*

*Turkish Lamb Stew, Saffron Rice*

*Austrian Marrow*

*A Stranger's Cheese Board*

*Fresh Fruit*

## Chicken Liver Pâté

| | |
|---|---|
| 2 medium-sized onions | 2 tablespoons brandy |
| 2 oz. butter | 4 oz. unsalted butter |
| $\frac{1}{2}$ lb. chicken livers | salt and fresh ground pepper |
| | sliced pumpernickel and butter |

▶ Peel and chop 2 medium-sized onions very finely.

▶ In a pan, melt 2 oz. butter. Add the onions and cook over low heat until the onions are soft and slightly brown. Add $\frac{1}{2}$ lb. chicken livers. Stirring constantly, cook for 10 minutes until the livers are done but not hard. Put in a bowl. Reserve the juices in the pan. With a fork mash the livers.

▶ Stir 2 tablespoons brandy into the juices in the pan. When thoroughly mixed, stir into the liver mixture. Cool.

▶ Cream until very soft 4 oz. unsalted butter. Stir in the liver mixture. Mix well. Season to taste with salt and freshly ground pepper. Pack in a small bowl and store in refrigerator.

▶ Serve in the bowl with slices of buttered pumpernickel or unmould and arrange on a serving dish.

## Turkish Lamb Stew, Saffron Rice

| | |
|---|---|
| 24 large prunes | $\frac{1}{4}$ teaspoon allspice |
| 4 lb. shoulder of lamb | $\frac{1}{4}$ teaspoon cinnamon |
| 3 tablespoons flour | $1\frac{1}{4}$ pints chicken |
| 1 teaspoon salt | bouillon |
| $\frac{1}{2}$ teaspoon pepper | 12 oz. rice |
| 2 oz. butter | $1\frac{3}{4}$ pints water |
| 3 large onions | $\frac{1}{2}$ lemon |
| | 1 teaspoon saffron |

▶ Soak prunes overnight, drain, remove stones and set aside.

▶ Cut 4 lb. lamb into 3-inch cubes, dredge in a mixture of 3 tablespoons flour, 1 teaspoon salt and $\frac{1}{2}$ teaspoon pepper.

▶ Melt 2 oz. butter in an iron sauté pan or saucepan and fry 3 coarsely chopped onions until golden. Raise heat, put in the meat and brown quickly on all sides. Add $\frac{1}{4}$ teaspoon allspice, $\frac{1}{4}$ teaspoon cinnamon and $1\frac{1}{4}$ pints chicken bouillon. Stir, cover and simmer for $1\frac{1}{2}$ hours. Add the prunes and continue simmering for 15 minutes. Correct seasoning if necessary. Uncover, cool, recover and keep cold overnight.

*Saffron Rice*

▶ Cook 12 oz. rice in $1\frac{3}{4}$ pints salted water with 1 teaspoon lemon juice and 1 teaspoon saffron added. Cook until just tender, drain and leave in colander ready to reheat next evening.

▶ Before guests arrive, reheat the lamb in saucepan slowly and the rice over boiling water. Serve in separate hot serving dishes or arrange rice in a ring with the lamb stew in the centre.

## Austrian Marrow

| | |
|---|---|
| 1 medium-sized marrow | ½ small onion |
| 1 heaped teaspoon salt | 2 tablespoons chopped parsley |
| 1 heaped tablespoon chopped dill | 1 oz. flour |
| 2 pinches sweet paprika | 7 oz. hot milk |
| ½ oz. lard | 1 scant tablespoon vinegar |
| ½ oz. butter | 1 carton (5 oz.) sour cream |
| | paprika to garnish |

▶ Peel, quarter, and remove seeds from 1 medium-sized marrow. Slice into thin slices. Put slices on a wooden board. Sprinkle with 1 heaped teaspoon salt. Let stand 1 hour, then squeeze dry in a soft cloth to remove all moisture. Mix with 1 heaped tablespoon chopped dill and 2 pinches sweet paprika.

▶ In a saucepan melt ½ oz. each of butter and lard. Add ½ onion finely chopped and 2 tablespoons chopped parsley. Stir in 1 oz. flour, cook 5 minutes, stirring constantly, do not let it colour. Slowly stir in 7 oz. hot milk. Cook over low heat, stirring continuously until the sauce becomes quite thick. Add the marrow to the sauce, add 1 scant tablespoon vinegar. Mix well. Correct seasoning, adding more salt if necessary. Put in lightly buttered ovenproof dish. Cover and bake in a medium oven 350°F, Reg 4 for 20 minutes. Remove from oven and store in a cool place.

▶ To serve. Stir in a carton of sour cream and reheat in a medium oven 350°F, Reg 4 for 10–15 minutes. Sprinkle with sweet paprika when serving.

## A Stranger's Cheese Board

▶ Serve Brie, Camembert, Roquefort, Bel Paese, Pont l'Evêque cheeses on a cheese board with cheese biscuits and butter.

## Fresh Fruit

▶ Arrange seasonal fruits in a large bowl or basket.

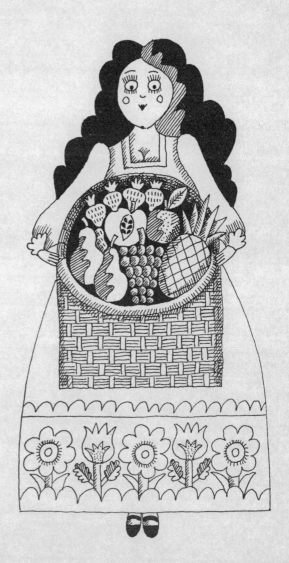

**6**

## MENU

*Curried Eggs*

*Cold Honey Pork*

*White Cabbage Salad*

*Pears in Raspberry Sauce*

## Curried Eggs

| | |
|---|---|
| 8 hard-boiled eggs | $\frac{3}{4}$ pint chicken stock, fresh or cubes |
| 2 oz. butter | |
| 4 medium onions | $1\frac{1}{2}$ tablespoons chutney, finely minced |
| 2 tablespoons curry powder | |
| 1 tablespoon flour | 2 oz. sultanas |
| | $\frac{1}{2}$ tablespoon lemon juice |
| | salt and pepper |
| | croutons |

▶ Melt 2 oz. butter in top of double boiler. Add 4 medium onions finely chopped and 2 tablespoons curry powder. Cook for 10 minutes. Stir in 1 tablespoon flour. Add $\frac{3}{4}$ pint chicken stock, $1\frac{1}{2}$ tablespoons finely minced chutney, 2 oz. sultanas, $\frac{1}{2}$ tablespoon lemon juice, salt and pepper. Simmer for $\frac{1}{2}$ hour.

▶ Add 8 peeled whole hard-boiled eggs. Cover and put aside.

▶ Reheat in a double boiler. Dish on a serving plate and surround with croutons.

## Cold Honey Pork

| | |
|---|---|
| $2\frac{1}{2}$ lb. loin pork | 3 tablespoons prepared Colman's mustard |
| 12 oz. strained honey | |
| | salt and pepper |

▶ Ask the butcher to bone and roll a $2\frac{1}{2}$ lb. loin of pork and have him salt and pepper the inside beforehand, if he will do it.

▶ Mix thoroughly 12 oz. strained honey and 3 tablespoons of prepared Colman's mustard.

▶ Sprinkle the roast with salt and pepper.

▶ With a palette knife coat all of the sides of the pork with the honey and mustard mixture.

▶ Wrap the roast in tin foil. Place on a rack in a baking pan. Place in a pre-heated moderate oven 400°F, Reg 6 and bake for at least two hours. Test with a skewer to be sure that it is done.

▶ For the last 20 minutes of baking unfold the tin foil so the roast can turn to golden brown but do not let it burn. Lower the heat if necessary.

# White Cabbage Salad

| | |
|---|---|
| 1 small head white cabbage | 8 oz. thick cream |
| juice of 1 lemon | $\frac{1}{2}$ teaspoon castor sugar |
| chopped chives and parsley | 1 teaspoon salt |
| $\frac{1}{2}$ lb. seedless white grapes | $\frac{1}{4}$ teaspoon white pepper |
| 3 oz. finely shredded almonds | $\frac{1}{4}$ teaspoon Colman's mustard |
| $\frac{1}{2}$ teaspoon celery seed | 1–2 oz. caraway seed—optional |

▶ Remove the core of a small head of cabbage. Cut it into very thin shreds. Add the juice of 1 lemon, chopped chives and parsley, $\frac{1}{2}$ lb. seedless white grapes, and 3 oz. finely shredded almonds. Mix well. Put in a covered bowl in the refrigerator.

▶ Beat until stiff 8 oz. of thick cream. Fold in $\frac{1}{2}$ teaspoon castor sugar, 1 teaspoon salt, $\frac{1}{4}$ teaspoon white pepper, $\frac{1}{4}$ teaspoon Colman's mustard thinly prepared, $\frac{1}{2}$ teaspoon celery seed, and 1–2 oz. caraway seed.

▶ When ready to serve the salad, pour the dressing over the cabbage. Toss quickly until it is well coated and serve.

# Pears in Raspberry Sauce

| | |
|---|---|
| 6 ripe pears | 14 oz. castor sugar |
| $\frac{3}{4}$ pint white wine | 2 packets frozen raspberries |
| 1 lemon | 3 tablespoons port |
| 8 oz. double cream | |

▶ Bring to a boil in a saucepan, sufficiently large to hold 6 pears upright, $\frac{3}{4}$ pint white wine, 8 oz. water, the juice of $\frac{1}{2}$ lemon, and 10 oz. castor sugar. Continue cooking slowly while preparing fruit.

▶ Peel 6 pears. Leave them whole with stems attached. Place them upright in the boiling syrup and poach until transparent and tender. Drain, arrange in glass serving dish and cool.

▶ Purée 2 packets of frozen raspberries, previously thawed and add the juice of $\frac{1}{2}$ lemon, 2 tablespoons port and 4 oz. castor sugar (more if too sour). Mix well and pour over pears. Chill in refrigerator. Turn pears in syrup occasionally to colour evenly.

▶ Next evening, beat 8 oz. double cream stiffly, fold in 1 tablespoon port, pile into glass bowl and keep chilled until needed.

▶ Serve pears and cream separately.

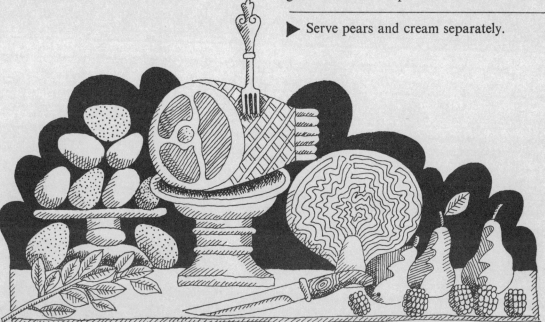

# 7

## MENU

*Cold Asparagus Soup*

*Seafood Risotto*

*Tipsy Fruit Cup*

## Cold Asparagus Soup

| | |
|---|---|
| 1½ lb. green asparagus | 1½ oz. flour |
| 2 pints chicken stock | 12 oz. single cream |
| 3 oz. butter | pepper |

▶ Wash 1½ lb. asparagus, cut off tips 1½ inches from top. Dice the stalks very finely. Pour 2 pints chicken stock into a saucepan.

▶ Bring stock to a boil, add asparagus tips and stalks and cook 5 minutes until tips are just tender. Do not overcook. Remove tips from stock with a perforated spoon. When cool, wrap in foil and refrigerate until serving time.

▶ Leave diced stalks in the same stock and cook covered until very tender, ½ hour or more. Rub the vegetables and stock through a coarse sieve or whirl in liquidizer. Keep warm.

▶ Melt 3 oz. of butter in large saucepan with 1½ oz. flour. Slowly add the puréed vegetables. Cook over low heat 10 minutes stirring constantly. Heat 12 oz. single cream, pour into thickened soup. Mix well, remove from fire, cool and chill in refrigerator.

▶ Serve in chilled cups garnished with reserved asparagus tips.

# Seafood Risotto

| | |
|---|---|
| 1 large tin mussels | 1 teaspoon pepper |
| 8 oz. dry white wine | 1 teaspoon sugar |
| 2 12-oz. packets frozen prawns | 3 oz. butter |
| | $\frac{1}{2}$ oz. flour |
| 3 tablespoons Italian tomato purée | 2 tablespoons dry sherry |
| 1 clove garlic | $1\frac{1}{2}$ lb. long-grained rice |

▶ Drain 1 tin of mussels over large saucepan. Pour in 8 oz. wine. If the prawns are uncooked, bring to a boil and add 2 packets of defrosted prawns and cook rapidly until just pink. Do not overcook as prawns should remain firm.

▶ If prawns are cooked, defrost and drain over another saucepan and put aside. Add to liquid enough water to make 1 pint. Add 3 tablespoons tomato purée, 1 whole clove garlic, 1 teaspoon freshly ground pepper and 1 teaspoon sugar. Bring slowly to a boil. Rub $\frac{1}{2}$ oz. flour into $\frac{1}{2}$ oz. butter, add to the boiling liquid and continue cooking, stirring constantly for 10 minutes. Remove from stove, take out garlic clove and stir in $\frac{1}{2}$ oz. butter and 2 tablespoons sherry. Cool and add $\frac{1}{3}$ of the prawns, each one cut into 2 or 3 pieces. Taste, add salt if necessary and a little more sugar if sauce is too acid. Keep in refrigerator until next afternoon.

▶ Cook the rice in a large pan of boiling salted water, drain when just tender, not mushy.

▶ Toss in 2 oz. butter and cool. Add the reserved mussels and the remaining $\frac{2}{3}$ of the prawns (left whole), to the rice. Mix very gently but thoroughly to distribute sea food intact through the rice. Put mixture into well-buttered casserole or ring mould, cover and refrigerate.

▶ Next evening reheat rice in the casserole or mould placed in a pan of hot water in a slow oven. Reheat the sauce gently over low heat on top of stove.

▶ Serve the rice mounded on a heated serving dish and pass the sauce separately. If ring mould is used, the sauce may be put in the centre.

# Tipsy Fruit Cup

| | |
|---|---|
| 1 small tin sliced pineapple | 2 large oranges |
| 1 small tin white peaches | 3 oz. sugar |
| | 3 tablespoons white wine |
| 1 small tin pears | 4 oz. brandy |
| 1 small tin grapefruit sections | $1\frac{1}{2}$ tablespoons maraschino liqueur |
| 1 small tin cherries | |

▶ Drain carefully and cut into even pieces the 5 tins of fruit. Peel, section and cut in same-size pieces 2 oranges. Add 3 oz. sugar, 3 tablespoons white wine, 4 oz. brandy and $1\frac{1}{2}$ tablespoons maraschino liqueur. Mix gently but well. Put into glass serving dish and keep covered in refrigerator until ready to serve.

8

MENU

*Mock Cheese Soufflé*

*Cold Roast Beef, Horseradish Sauce*

*Stella's Baked Potatoes, Carrot Salad*

*Pineapple Betty*

## Mock Cheese Soufflé

| | |
|---|---|
| 14 thin slices of stale bread | 4 egg yolks |
| 4 oz. butter | 8 oz. double cream |
| ¾ lb. cheddar cheese | 8 oz. milk |
| salt and pepper | pinch nutmeg |

▶ Cut crusts from 14 thin slices of stale bread. Spread on both sides with 4 oz. softened butter. Cut the slices in thirds and line the bottom of a well-buttered mould. Cut ¾ lb. cheddar cheese in thin slices. Place a layer of cheese slices on the bread in the mould. Sprinkle lightly with salt and pepper and pinch of nutmeg. Repeat until the bread is used, alternating the bread and cheese slices for each layer, with a layer of bread last. Sprinkle with salt and pepper each time, and the pinch of nutmeg once.

▶ Beat 4 egg yolks until foamy with the 8 oz. double cream and 8 oz. milk. Mix thoroughly and pour over the bread and cheese. Set aside until next day.

▶ Just before your guests arrive, put in a moderate oven 350°F, Reg 4, in a bain-marie, for 40 to 50 minutes.

## Cold Roast Beef

| | |
|---|---|
| 3 lb. sirloin of beef | mustard—optional |
| 1½ oz. dripping | 2 pieces fat streaky |
| pepper and salt | bacon |
| | horseradish sauce |

▶ Carefully trim the meat, removing all superfluous fat. Wipe well with a damp cloth. If so desired, rub meat with mustard on all sides. If possible use a double roasting tin, the under one large enough to hold a little water.

▶ Place the meat on a low stand in the baking tin to prevent it soaking in the dripping. Pre-heat your oven to 500°F, Reg 9. Place the meal on the stand.

▶ Melt the dripping and pour it at once, very hot, over the roast. Roast for 10 minutes or longer to brown. Then cover the top with the two slices of bacon, turn the heat down to 350°F, Reg 4. Baste at intervals of 10–15 minutes to prevent the roast from drying up. Only sprinkle the meat with pepper and salt when it is nearly ready.

▶ Approximate cooking time is 18–20 minutes per lb., plus 15 minutes for rare, 22–25 for medium. But one cannot lay down a rule, as it depends on form and thickness of the roast. When meat is done, lift it onto a serving dish and let it cool. When cold, wrap it in silver foil and keep in refrigerator. Next evening cut meat into even slices.

▶ Serve with horseradish sauce.

## Stella's Baked Potatoes

| | |
|---|---|
| 6 large even-sized potatoes, the mealy type | butter or Gruyère cheese |

▶ Choose 6 large even-sized mealy-type potatoes. Wash and scrub them. Prick each one with a fork. Pre-heat oven to 425°F, Reg 7. Place potatoes on a rack in the oven. Reduce heat to 400°F, Reg 6. Bake for 1 hour. Turn out the oven if they are to be left any longer. These must be baked the night of the dinner; they cannot be reheated.

▶ To serve. Slash a cross in the top of each potato, and squeeze it from both ends with your hands. Put a lump of butter in the opened potato, or grated Gruyère cheese.

## Carrot Salad

| | |
|---|---|
| 1 lb. carrots | $\frac{1}{8}$ teaspoon salt |
| 1 tablespoon wine or cider vinegar | 1 pinch castor sugar |
| 2 tablespoons olive oil | 3 tablespoons single cream |
| chopped peanuts | |

▶ Wash and peel 1 lb. of carrots. Grate them on a coarse grater. Store in a plastic bag in the refrigerator.

▶ Stir 1 tablespoon vinegar with 2 tablespoons olive oil, $\frac{1}{8}$ teaspoon salt and 1 pinch of castor sugar until thoroughly blended. Set aside.

▶ An hour before serving, blend again the vinegar and oil, add 3 tablespoons single cream and stir until thoroughly mixed. Pour over the carrots, mix well. Let stand in refrigerator until served.

▶ Sprinkle with finely chopped peanuts when serving.

## Pineapple Betty

| | |
|---|---|
| scant 3 oz. melted butter | 3 oz. chopped almonds |
| 6 oz. soft bread-crumbs | grated rind lemon |
| $1\frac{1}{2}$ medium-sized cans diced pineapple | 2 tablespoons lemon juice |
| $1\frac{3}{4}$ oz. sugar | $\frac{1}{4}$ pint pineapple juice |
| | cinnamon to taste |
| | $\frac{1}{4}$–$\frac{1}{2}$ pint double cream for serving |

▶ Mix a scant 3 oz. of melted butter with 6 oz. soft breadcrumbs. Arrange in a buttered baking dish first a layer of crumbs, then a layer of pineapple. Sprinkle the pineapple with some of the sugar, chopped almonds, and cinnamon. Repeat until the fruit and crumbs are used, topping the dish with crumbs.

▶ Combine grated rind 1 lemon, 2 tablespoons lemon juice and $\frac{1}{4}$ pint pineapple juice. Pour over top of dish. Bake in a moderate oven 350°F, Reg 4 for 45 minutes. If crumbs get too brown before the time is up, cover the dish. This can be baked at the same time as the potatoes. Turn out the oven, open the door when the potatoes are finished and leave until dessert time. Serve with cream.

# 9

## MENU

*Turtle Soup with Avocado Slices*

*Hot Steamed Turkey, Cream of Carrot Sauce*

*Mushroom Rice*

*Viennese Cherry Cake*

## Turtle Soup with Avocado Slices

| | |
|---|---|
| 2 tins turtle soup | 2 avocados |

▶ Heat the soup, fill into individual small cups. Peel avocados only ½ hour before serving, remove stones and cut into small pieces. Drop a few into each cup.

## Hot Steamed Turkey

| | |
|---|---|
| 1 small turkey 6–8 lb. | 1 bottle dry white wine |
| 4 carrots | 2–2½ pints chicken |
| 3 sticks of celery | stock made with |
| handful of parsley | cubes |
| 1 tablespoon salt | |
| 20 peppercorns | |

▶ Chop coarsely 4 peeled carrots, 3 sticks of celery and a good handful of parsley. Put them on the bottom of a large pot with 1 tablespoon of salt and 20 peppercorns. Place a 6- to 8-lb. turkey breast-down on a stand that will fit into your pot with the vegetables. Heat 2–2½ pints chicken stock, pour over the bird; then add 1 bottle dry white wine and cook over a low heat for two hours. Test with a skewer for softness; if still hard replace and cook over a still lower heat. It may take another hour depending on the size and age of the bird.

▶ Remove from heat and let it cool in the stock. When cold take the bird out. Wrap it in silver foil and keep in the refrigerator. Strain the stock and put aside, but keep 8 oz. separately for the carrot sauce.

▶ Next day skin and carve the turkey. Cover with the remaining cold stock and reheat over moderate heat. Serve with carrot sauce.

## Cream of Carrot Sauce

| | |
|---|---|
| 4 carrots | ¾ oz. flour |
| 1 medium-sized onion | 8 oz. milk |
| 3 oz. butter | 4 oz. single cream or |
| 2 cloves | more |
| | 8 oz. turkey stock |
| salt and pepper | |

▶ Peel and slice in thin rounds 4 carrots. Peel the onion, cut diagonally in thin slices. In a saucepan melt 1 oz. butter, add the carrots, onions and 2 cloves, mix thoroughly until they are well coated with the butter, cover and put the saucepan on a very low fire for 10 minutes. Do not let them brown.

Add 8 oz. turkey stock and let simmer on a low fire until the carrots are soft. Remove the 2 cloves and blend in a liquidizer.

▶ In another saucepan melt 2 oz. butter, add and blend over low heat for 3 minutes ¾ oz. flour. With a wooden spoon stir in slowly 8 oz. milk, cook, stirring constantly until the sauce is thickened and smooth. Add the blended carrots mixture to the white sauce, salt and pepper to taste and blend again. Put mixture back into the saucepan. Add 4 oz. single cream and reheat. If the sauce is too thick add more cream.

▶ Serve hot with the turkey and mushroom rice.

## Mushroom Rice

| | |
|---|---|
| ¾ lb. rice | 8 sliced mushrooms |
| 1½ oz. butter | ¾ oz. butter |
| 1¼ pints water | ½ teaspoon salt |
| 1 squirt of lemon juice | |
| ¼ onion | |

▶ Melt 1½ oz. butter in a saucepan, add rice and fry until slightly transparent. Stir continuously. Add ½ teaspoon salt and 1¼ pints boiling water. Add ¼ onion. Simmer covered for 15 minutes. Test if rice is done, but still firm. Remove from heat, remove ¼ onion. Loosen rice with a fork and cool. Wash mushrooms, then soak them for 5 minutes in cold water, adding a little lemon juice. Drain and dry them. Peel and cut the heads into thin slices. Do not use the stalks. Melt ¾ oz. butter in a frying pan and sauté the mushrooms for 3 minutes over low heat. Mix into the rice and store mushroom rice in refrigerator.

▶ Next evening loosen the rice again with a fork, reheat covered in oven at 250°F, Reg ½ for half-an-hour. If rice looks dry add a little turkey stock or water.

## Viennese Cherry Cake

| | |
|---|---|
| 4 oz. unsalted butter | 2½ oz. grated chocolate |
| 4 oz. castor sugar | ¾ oz. brown breadcrumbs |
| 2 eggs | 4 oz. grated almonds |
| 2 egg yolks | 2 egg whites |
| | ½ lb. of unpitted cherries |
| | castor sugar to finish |

▶ Beat in your electric mixer 4 oz. unsalted butter until creamy; add 4 oz. castor sugar gradually, beating all the time. When smooth, beat in one at a time the 2 eggs, 2 egg yolks and 2½ oz. grated chocolate.

▶ Beat the whites of 2 eggs until stiff, fold in ¾ oz. breadcrumbs and 4 oz. grated almonds. Mix all ingredients until smooth. Grease lightly a round cake tin, sprinkle with a little flour and shake the tin until it has a very thin coating of flour. Pour in the cake mixture. Stick cherries one beside the other on top of the cake, until it is thickly covered, but do not press them in deeply. Bake 30 to 40 minutes in a pre-heated oven at 275°F, Reg ½. Remove from oven and sprinkle with a little sugar. Let the cake cool on a cake rack.

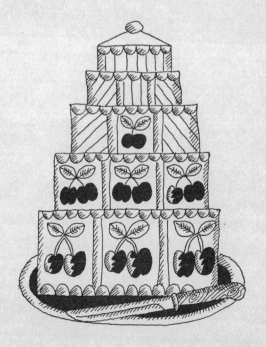

# 10

## MENU

*Avocados with Cottage Cheese*

*Paprika Veal Schnitzel*

*Tagliatelli*

*Pineapple Surprise*

## Avocados with Cottage Cheese

| | |
|---|---|
| 3 avocados | 1 clove garlic |
| juice of 1 lemon | 1 tablespoon chopped |
| 9 heaped tablespoons | chives |
| cottage cheese | $\frac{1}{4}$ teaspoon salt |
| | paprika |

▶ Cut 3 avocados lengthwise and remove their stones. Sprinkle with the juice of 1 lemon. Do this only an hour before dinner otherwise they blacken.

▶ Mix 9 heaped tablespoons cottage cheese with 1 clove garlic chopped and mashed very fine, 1 tablespoon chopped chives and $\frac{1}{4}$ teaspoon salt.

▶ Fill avocado cavities with the cottage cheese mixture. Dust with paprika.

▶ Serve on individual plates.

# Paprika Veal Schnitzel

| | |
|---|---|
| 3 lb. leg of veal, cut into $\frac{1}{4}$-inch slices | 5 tablespoons chicken stock |
| 2 oz. lard | 1 dash of salt |
| 2 oz. bacon | $\frac{1}{2}$ oz. flour |
| 3 tablespoons finely chopped onions | $1\frac{1}{2}$ cartons sour cream ($7\frac{1}{2}$ oz.) |
| 2 level teaspoons sweet Hungarian paprika | 1 teaspoon tomato purée |

▶ Ask your butcher to cut the meat into $\frac{1}{4}$-inch slices and pound them flat. Cut incisions at borders.

▶ Dip them on one side into flour, shake off excess. Now heat the fat, cook schnitzel over medium heat for 3 minutes each side, the flour-covered side first; they ought to be golden yellow. Put the schnitzel aside. Reheat the fat, fry the finely chopped bacon until transparent, add the finely cut onions until they are lightly coloured, about 10 minutes.

▶ In a bowl beat $\frac{1}{2}$ oz. flour into the sour cream with a wire whisk. Remove the pan from the heat, stir in the paprika, continue stirring until the onions are well coated.

▶ Return to medium heat, add the 5 tablespoons chicken stock. Bring to a boil, stirring in the brown bits sticking to the pan. Add the sour cream mixture, simmer for 2 minutes.

▶ Keep schnitzel and sauce in bowls, both covered lightly in tinfoil in the refrigerator until next day.

▶ Towards the evening add 1 teaspoon tomato purée to the sauce, taste for seasoning, pour over the schnitzel and cook them 30 minutes over very low heat. Then keep them warm until ready to serve.

# Tagliatelli

| | |
|---|---|
| 2 packets tagliatelli | 2 oz. butter |

▶ Cook 2 packets tagliatelli according to instructions written on the packet. When cooked toss into a colander, pour boiling water over. Shake well. Put aside.

▶ To serve, reheat in a steamer. It will only take a few minutes. Add 2 oz. butter broken into small lumps and mix until butter is melted.

# Pineapple Surprise

| | |
|---|---|
| 1 fresh pineapple | 1 handful red-currants |
| 2 peaches | 1 tablespoon castor sugar |
| 1 orange | 2 tablespoons kirsch or vodka |

▶ Cut top off the pineapple. Scoop out the flesh with a curved knife, remove the eyes and cut into cubes.

▶ In a bowl prepare the following: peel 2 peaches and cut into slices, 1 handful of red-currants. (If not in season use tinned stoned morello cherries.) Add orange peeled and cut in sections. Add the pineapple cubes. Sprinkle with a tablespoon of castor sugar and pour over the 2 tablespoons of kirsch or vodka.

▶ Fill the pineapple with this mixture, put its top on and keep in the refrigerator until served.

# 11

## MENU

*Crab Soup*

*Ruth's Lamb in Aspic*

*Russian Beetroot Salad*

*Raspberry Pudding, Custard Sauce*

## Crab Soup

| | |
|---|---|
| 2 tins crabmeat | 12 oz. single cream or |
| 2 oz. butter | more |
| 1¼ pints milk | 2 egg yolks |
| paprika | 2 tablespoons sherry |
| salt and pepper | |

▶ Flake and remove membranes from 2 tins crabmeat. Reserve all of the liquid in the tin.

▶ Melt 2 oz. butter in the top of a double boiler. Add the flaked crabmeat and any of the liquid from the tin. Heat through. Add 1¼ pints heated milk.

▶ Beat 2 egg yolks slightly. Add 12 oz. single cream. Mix thoroughly. Add to the crabmeat mixture and, stirring constantly, cook until slightly thickened. Season to taste with salt and pepper. Add 2 tablespoons sherry. Put aside to cool, stirring occasionally. When cool pour over a thin layer of cream and put in the refrigerator.

▶ To serve. Reheat in a double boiler, if too thick add a bit of cream. Serve in cups with a dash of paprika on top.

## Ruth's Lamb in Aspic

| | |
|---|---|
| 3 lb. lamb, boned shoulder or leg | 2 tins bouillon |
| 2 oz. butter | 1½ tablespoons gelatine |
| 3 large onions | 1 tablespoon sherry |
| 1 large dill gherkin | |
| slices of stuffed olives | thin slices radishes |
| a few capers | |
| 4 tomatoes | 1 bunch watercress |
| 4 hard-boiled eggs | 1½ tablespoons vinegar |
| 1 small tin stuffed anchovies | 4 tablespoons olive oil a little mayonnaise |
| salt and pepper | (Menu 48) |

▶ Melt 2 oz. butter in a frying pan. Sauté lightly on both sides 3 lb. lamb, all fat removed, cut into very thin slices. Add 3 large onions chopped fine. Cook 5 minutes. Add 4 oz. bouillon and cook 5 minutes longer. Remove slices of lamb. Cut into small pieces. Add onions and 1 large dill gherkin, all of it chopped finely. Mix well.

▶ Heat the rest of the 2 tins of bouillon. Add 1½ tablespoons gelatine dissolved in a little cold water and 1 tablespoon sherry. Pour a small amount of the bouillon into a large ring mould. Place in refrigerator until it starts to set. Decorate with slices of stuffed olives, radishes, and a few capers. Again add a thin layer of bouillon and put back into the refrigerator. After the ring has well set, put the lamb mixture into the jelly coated ring. Cover with the remaining liquid jelly mixture and return to refrigerator.

▶ To serve, dip mould in hot water for a few moments and turn out on serving plate. Make a vinaigrette with 1½ tablespoons vinegar, 4 tablespoons olive oil, salt and pepper. Toss over watercress, fill centre of ring with it. Surround with sliced tomatoes topped with sliced eggs and a little mayonnaise. Decorate with stuffed anchovies.

# Russian Beetroot Salad

4 large beetroots
1½–1¾ pints hot wine vinegar—if your vinegar
   tastes very sour use 1 pint vinegar and
   ½–¾ pint hot water
salt and pepper
2½ tablespoons horseradish or English
   horseradish sauce, not horseradish cream

▶ Cut the 4 cooked beetroots into slices,
but not too thinly. Place in a salad bowl,
preferably wooden, and mix the horseradish
into the cut beetroot.

▶ Pour enough hot vinegar over them to
cover them completely.

▶ This salad must be prepared at least
24 hours before serving.

# Raspberry Pudding

2 12-oz. boxes frozen    6 tablespoons kirsch
  raspberries         6 tablespoons water
24 sponge fingers
3½ oz. sugar

▶ Take a medium mould. Mix
6 tablespoons kirsch with 6 tablespoons
water, and lightly moisten 8 of the sponge
fingers and pack them tightly into the
bottom of your mould.

▶ Add 1 box of raspberries mixed with
1¾ oz. sugar if it is needed.

▶ Moisten 8 sponge fingers with the kirsch
and place on the raspberries.

▶ Add the second box of raspberries,
sugared if needed.

▶ Moisten the remaining 8 sponge fingers
with the kirsch and place on the
raspberries.

▶ Finally cover with a flat plate which
fits inside the mould. Weight, and place
in the refrigerator until the next day.
Unmould, serve with the custard sauce
poured over it.

# Custard Sauce

3 egg yolks        12 oz. milk
3 oz. sugar        1 piece vanilla bean
1 scant teaspoon plain    or few drops
  flour              vanilla essence

▶ Beat 3 egg yolks with a wooden spoon.
Add sugar and continue beating until
smooth and creamy. Add 1 scant teaspoon
flour.

▶ Scald 12 oz. of milk and a piece of
vanilla bean or essence. Pour slowly over
the egg mixture, mixing well. Return to
saucepan and cook over low heat, stirring
constantly until it coats the wooden spoon.
Do not allow to boil. Cool, stirring
vigorously at first and then from time to
time to prevent a crust forming. Put in a
covered bowl in refrigerator until used.

▶ If it is too thick at serving time, add a
bit of cream.

# 12

## MENU

*Quiche Lorraine*

*Normandy Pheasant,*

*Steamed Brussels Sprouts*

*Charlotte Française*

## Quiche Lorraine

| Crust | Filling |
|-------|---------|
| 10 oz. flour | ¼ lb. sliced bacon |
| 7 oz. butter | 4 eggs |
| 2 egg yolks | 8 oz. single cream |
| 2½ tablespoons single cream | ⅛ teaspoon salt |
| | ⅛ teaspoon fresh ground pepper |
| | 2 oz. diced gruyère cheese |

▶ Put 10 oz. flour in a bowl and with a pastry cutter or 2 knives cut 7 oz. butter into it. Add 2 egg yolks and 2½ tablespoons single cream. With your hand, knead the dough lightly to make a soft dough that barely holds together. Put in a plastic bag or a damp cloth and refrigerate for 2 hours.

▶ Roll out the dough on a lightly floured board to ⅛ inch thick. Line a 9-inch pie tin. Trim off the edges. Brush it with the slightly beaten white of an egg. Prick it well with a fork. Wrap in silver foil and store until next day in refrigerator.

▶ Slice in 1-inch lengths ¼ lb. sliced bacon. Cook in a heavy saucepan, until the fat is almost rendered out but the bacon is not crisp. Drain on absorbent paper. Store in a bowl. Do not put in refrigerator.

▶ Beat 4 eggs lightly with a wire whisk. Beat in 8 oz. single cream, ⅛ teaspoon salt and ⅛ teaspoon freshly ground pepper. Store in the refrigerator.

▶ Dice 2 oz. gruyère cheese. Store in the refrigerator.

▶ To serve, sprinkle the bacon and the diced gruyère cheese in the bottom of the unbaked pie shell. Beat the egg mixture again. Pour over the bacon and cheese. Bake in a moderate oven, 350°F, Reg 4 for 40 minutes. Turn off the oven and keep it warm there until served.

## Normandy Pheasant

| | |
|---|---|
| 2 small pheasants | 4 oz. double cream |
| 6 sour cooking apples | 2 tablespoons calvados or brandy |
| 5 tablespoons butter | salt and pepper |

▶ Ask your butcher to clean and truss 2 small pheasants.

▶ Melt 2½ tablespoons butter in a saucepan. Over slow heat, so that the butter does not burn and become black, brown the pheasants slowly on all sides.

▶ Peel, core and cut in coarse dice 6 cooking apples. Melt 2½ tablespoons butter. Add the apples and cook slowly over low heat until partially done. Do not brown.

▶ Cover with some of the apples the bottom of an ovenproof casserole large enough to hold the 2 birds. Place the 2 birds on this bed. Surround them with the rest of the apples. Season with salt and pepper and cover. Cook 30 minutes in a moderate oven, 350°F, Reg 4. Remove from oven. When cool store in the refrigerator.

▶ To serve, reheat in a moderate oven. Just before serving stir in 4 oz. double cream and 2 tablespoons calvados. Brandy can be substituted for the calvados.

# Steamed Brussels Sprouts

a little lemon juice    salt
2 lb. Brussels sprouts    pepper
scant ¼ oz. butter

▶ Trim the sprouts neatly, removing discoloured leaves and cutting off unnecessary length of stalks.

▶ Wash well, add a little lemon juice to cold water and soak the sprouts for ½ hour. Rinse and drain. Then cook them in a steamer over boiling water for 30 to 40 minutes, when they can be easily pierced with a fork.

▶ Store in the refrigerator.

▶ In the evening melt a scant ¼ oz. butter in a frying pan, sprinkle the sprouts with salt and pepper, toss them in the butter for a few minutes.

▶ Keep warm until serving time.

# Charlotte Française

8 oz. castor sugar    8 oz. unsalted butter
4 egg yolks    7 oz. ground almonds
12 oz. milk    ½ teaspoon almond
3 oz. bitter chocolate     extract
1 teaspoon flour    2½ tablespoons Grand
     Marnier
   24 sponge fingers
   8 oz. double cream

▶ Beat 4 egg yolks. Gradually add 8 oz. castor sugar. Beat until light and creamy. Beat in 1 teaspoon flour.

▶ Scald 12 oz. milk, add 3 oz. grated bitter chocolate. Stir until chocolate is melted. Add the egg mixture little by little. Cook slowly over low heat until it thickens, stirring constantly. Do not let it boil. Cool, stirring vigorously at first and then from time to time to prevent a crust forming.

▶ Cream 8 oz. unsalted butter and 7 oz. ground almonds. When creamy and well mixed, beat in the custard. Beat in 2½ tablespoons Grand Marnier, ½ teaspoon almond extract.

▶ Line a deep mould with sponge fingers, fitting them in the bottom so they radiate from the centre and are parallel on the sides. Fill the mould with the custard alternating with layers of sponge fingers, the last layer being sponge fingers. Cover with greaseproof paper. Chill in refrigerator overnight.

▶ Unmould and serve with a bowl of lightly whipped cream.

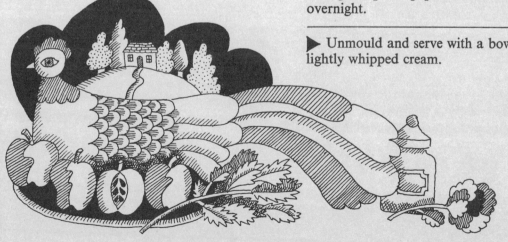

# 13

## MENU

*Gull or Quail Eggs*

*Swedish Fish Pudding, Green Salad*

*Chocolate Mousse Royale*

## Gull or Quail Eggs

| | |
|---|---|
| 12 gull eggs or | 1 bunch watercress |
| 18 quail eggs | 1 bunch red radishes |
| White bread, black Swedish bread, butter | |

▶ If the eggs have been bought uncooked, plunge them into cold water. Should any float, discard as not fresh. Put the eggs into a saucepan of cold water, bring to the boil and cook for 8–9 minutes. Run cold water over them. Drain. Store in refrigerator until used.

▶ Wash and clean the radishes and remove leaves. Place eggs and radishes on a bed of watercress.

▶ Butter thin slices of white bread and black Swedish bread. Stick them together and cut into 1½-inch strips to serve with the eggs.

## Swedish Fish Pudding

| | |
|---|---|
| 1¼ lb. fresh salmon | 8 oz. double cream |
| ¾ lb. firm white fish (sole, cod, hake) | 1 scant teaspoon salt |
| 4 eggs | ⅛ teaspoon cayenne pepper |
| 8 oz. single cream | ¼ teaspoon nutmeg |

▶ Ask the fishmonger to bone and skin 1¼ lb. fresh salmon and ¾ lb. any firm white fish such as sole, cod, hake.

▶ Cut the fish in pieces and beat to a pulp in a wooden bowl using a potato masher or mallet. Remove any tiny membranes as they appear.

▶ Beat the yolks of 4 eggs. Add to the beaten fish and stir until thoroughly mixed. Stir in 8 oz. single cream. Mix well again. Whip 8 oz. double cream, fold into the fish mixture. Store in the refrigerator.

▶ In the evening, beat the whites of 4 eggs until stiff and fold into the fish mixture. Pour into a greased mould. Put mould into a pan of hot water and bake in a moderate pre-heated oven 350°F, Reg 4 for 40 to 50 minutes.

▶ Unmould and serve with Fish Pudding Sauce and a green salad (Menu 1).

# Fish Pudding Sauce

2 egg yolks
1 teaspoon Dijon
  mustard
8 oz. olive oil
2 tablespoons lemon
  juice
1 tablespoon
  Worcester sauce
4 oz. ketchup
⅛ teaspoon white pepper

2 tablespoons butter
1 tablespoon flour
8 oz. single cream
1½ teaspoons caper
  juice
1 packet frozen
  asparagus tips
meat of 1 lobster
4 oz. sherry

▶ Mix 2 egg yolks and 1 teaspoon Dijon
mustard in a bowl with a wooden spoon.
Pour in drop by drop at first and then in
larger quantities 8 oz. oil, stirring constantly
until it thickens, or blend in a liquidizer.
Stir in 2 tablespoons lemon juice,
1 tablespoon Worcester sauce, 4 oz.
ketchup and ⅛ teaspoon white pepper.

▶ Melt 2 tablespoons butter in a saucepan,
blend in 1 tablespoon flour, cook on low
heat for a few minutes; do not let it brown.
Add 8 oz. single cream and 2 teaspoons
caper juice and cook until it thickens.
Set aside to cool.

▶ When cool stir in the egg sauce, blend
thoroughly and store in the refrigerator
overnight.

▶ Cook 1 packet frozen asparagus tips
according to instructions on the packet.

▶ To serve, add the meat of 1 lobster cut
into pieces, the asparagus tips cut into
short lengths, and 4 oz. sherry. Heat in the
top of a double boiler over hot, not boiling
water. The sauce should be just warm as a
hollandaise; if allowed to get too hot it will
separate.

# Chocolate Mousse Royale

7 oz. of very good bitter chocolate (Belgian, if
  possible!)
2 teaspoons of strongly made black coffee
3½ oz. castor sugar
½ teaspoon of rum
4 egg whites
8 oz. double cream

▶ Melt the chocolate in a double boiler,
add the coffee and stir slowly until smooth.
Add sugar and rum, continue stirring
slowly. Allow to cool.

▶ With a wire whisk beat the egg whites
until stiff and fold into the mixture; stir
gently until the colour is even.

▶ Whip cream until very stiff and fold
into the mixture, stirring slowly until
evenly coloured. Allow to cool.

▶ Serve in individual bowls if possible.

# 14

## MENU

*Tomatoes Filled with Tunny Fish*

*Spiced Beef, Vermicelli*

*Melon Suprême*

## Tomatoes Filled with Tunny Fish

| | |
|---|---|
| 13 small round tomatoes | a few leaves of tarragon |
| 1 large onion | 1 large tin tunny fish |
| 1 teaspoon capers | 4 tablespoons mayonnaise (Menu 48) |
| 1 handful chervil or parsley | salt and pepper |

▶ Chop 1 onion finely; boil, in a small quantity of water, for about 5 minutes. Drain.

▶ Take 1 tomato, peel, remove seeds, press out liquid and then chop together with the capers, chervil and tarragon leaves. Add the tin of tunny fish, having drained and flaked it first. Now bind the mixture with 4 tablespoons of well-seasoned mayonnaise. Put in a bowl, cover and chill overnight in refrigerator.

▶ Cut 12 tomatoes in half, remove seeds and liquid and sprinkle interiors with salt and pepper. Place cut-side down on absorbent paper and keep cold until time to fill.

▶ To serve, fill each tomato half with tunny filling and place on bed of lettuce leaves. A round serving dish with the tomatoes placed in a circle looks most attractive.

# Spiced Beef

| | |
|---|---|
| 2 lb. heel or first cut of top rump | $\frac{1}{2}$ teaspoon ground ginger |
| 1$\frac{1}{2}$ tablespoons lard | 1 teaspoon salt |
| 4 onions | $\frac{1}{2}$ teaspoon pepper |
| 4 carrots | pinch of nutmeg |
| $\frac{1}{4}$ lb. lean bacon | 3 oz. seedless raisins |
| $\frac{1}{2}$ calves foot | 2$\frac{1}{2}$ oz. unsalted almonds |
| 2 small bottles lager beer | $\frac{1}{4}$ lb. ginger biscuits |

▶ Thoroughly dry the beef; melt the lard in a heavy casserole and lightly brown the meat on all sides, being careful that the fat does not burn and blacken the meat. When light brown, remove.

▶ Cut bacon into small pieces, peel and slice finely the onions and carrots and slightly brown in the fat in which the meat was cooked.

▶ Place $\frac{1}{2}$ calves foot and piece of beef into casserole and pour over 2 bottles of lager. Now add salt, pepper, ginger and nutmeg. Cover and cook slowly on a low heat for at least three hours. From time to time test with a skewer—when beef is cooked remove.

▶ Discard calves foot and pass sauce through a sieve. Add to liquid $\frac{1}{4}$ lb. of ginger biscuits broken into small pieces, and cook slowly over low heat until biscuits are dissolved. Add raisins and unsalted almonds, stirring slowly.

▶ Pour sauce over beef, cover, and set aside in cool place until next day. Re-heat over low heat. Serve meat sliced, surrounded with fried vermicelli.

# Vermicelli

| | |
|---|---|
| $\frac{1}{4}$ lb. vermicelli | 1 pint tinned bouillon |
| 5 tablespoons olive oil | salt and pepper |

▶ Mix in a saucepan the vermicelli and olive oil and cook over a low heat until the vermicelli is lightly browned. Stir continually to ensure vermicelli does not burn. Cover and set aside.

▶ Next evening, heat to boiling point the 1 pint of bouillon and pour over vermicelli. Cover saucepan and cook over low heat for about 5 minutes until liquid is fully absorbed. Season to taste with salt and pepper.

# Melon Suprême

| | |
|---|---|
| 3 small melons | 4 oz. walnuts |
| 1 small pineapple | 8 oz. double cream |
| 7 oz. castor sugar | |

▶ Cut 3 small melons in half. Remove flesh carefully, cut in cubes and reserve empty shells.

▶ Pare pineapple, taking care to remove eyes, cut in quarters lengthwise, remove hard core from each quarter, cut in strips lengthwise, and slice strips crosswise into cubes.

▶ Combine the 2 fruits with 5 oz. of sugar. Chill in a bowl or divide in melon shells if refrigerator space available.

▶ Chop walnuts very fine and reserve.

▶ Next day whip 8 oz. double cream stiff, fold in 2 oz. castor sugar, and keep cold until serving time.

▶ To each fruit-filled melon add 2 generous tablespoons of whipped cream, and dust with prepared chopped walnuts.

# 15

## Venetian Risotto

| | |
|---|---|
| 12 oz. long-grained rice | 4 tablespoons Italian tomato purée |
| 7 oz. butter | 12 oz. beef stock, fresh or cubes |
| $\frac{1}{3}$ lb. mushrooms | 4 oz. dry white wine |
| 2 duck livers | 2 sprigs parsley |
| 6 chicken livers | 1 sprig thyme |
| 1 large onion | 1 bay leaf |
| 1 clove garlic | 1 teaspoon sweet basil leaves |
| | 2 oz. grated parmesan cheese |

▶ Boil 12 oz. rice in a large pan of boiling, salted water until just tender but still firm. Turn into colander, rinse under running cold water and set aside.

▶ Clean, slice and fry $\frac{1}{3}$ lb. mushrooms in 2 oz. hot butter in a frying pan until lightly browned. Remove with a perforated spoon and place in a small bowl.

▶ Slice the 2 duck livers and 6 chicken livers. Add 2 oz. butter to frying pan, add livers and brown rapidly over high heat for 2 or 3 minutes, turning constantly. Remove to small plate and set aside.

▶ Add 1 oz. butter to pan and fry 1 onion and 1 clove garlic until lightly brown. Pour the contents of the pan into a saucepan, add 4 tablespoons tomato purée, 12 oz. beef stock, 4 oz. wine, 2 sprigs parsley, 1 sprig thyme, 1 bay leaf and 1 teaspoon basil. Mix well, bring to a boil, stir in the reserved mushrooms, reduce heat and simmer, covered, for 1 hour. Remove from stove, cool, and add cooked chicken and duck livers. Correct seasoning and mix gently with 2 forks into cold rice.

▶ Turn the mixture into a well-buttered ovenproof serving dish. Spread the top with 2 oz. grated parmesan and dot with the remaining butter. Cover and chill overnight.

▶ Next evening, place the dish in a pan of hot water and reheat uncovered in moderate oven 350°F, Reg 4 until bubbling and top is brown and crusty. If necessary, place under grill for a minute or two before serving.

## Cold Roast Duckling, Cumberland Sauce

| | |
|---|---|
| 2 plump ducklings | salt and pepper |
| 1 clove garlic | 1 bottle Cumberland |
| 4 celery sticks | sauce (or see Menu |
| 2 carrots | 50 for recipe) |
| 2 onions | |

▶ Have ducklings prepared for roasting but untrussed. Rub inside and out with 1 clove garlic cut in half, salt and pepper. Place 2 stalks of celery, 1 carrot peeled and cut lengthwise and 1 onion cut in two in the cavity of each bird and truss. Reserve livers for Venetian Risotto.

▶ Pre-heat oven to hot, 425°F, Reg 7. Place the ducklings on a rack over dripping pan, reduce heat to moderate, 350°F, Reg 4, and roast 20 minutes per lb. or until tender. Cool, wrap loosely in aluminium foil and chill overnight.

▶ Next evening remove the vegetables, carve and arrange pieces on a chilled serving dish. Serve with Cumberland sauce and Watercress and Orange Salad.

## Watercress and Orange Salad

| | |
|---|---|
| 1 bunch of watercress | 1 tablespoon wine |
| 4 large oranges | vinegar |
| 4 tablespoons of olive | salt and pepper |
| oil | |

▶ Wash the watercress and drain well. Dry in a towel or in a wire salad basket.

▶ Using a sharp serrated knife, cut the orange skins off very carefully so as to leave no traces of white pith. Slice each orange into thin round slices, removing the pips. Leave covered in a cool place.

▶ Make a salad dressing with the 4 tablespoons of olive oil, the tablespoon of wine vinegar and the salt and pepper by shaking together all these ingredients in a screw-top jar.

▶ Shortly before you are ready to serve, reform the watercress into a bunch and twist off the long stalks so as to leave the sprigs. Arrange some of the watercress round the sides of a bowl or serving plate with the orange slices in the centre. Scatter the remaining watercress over the oranges.

▶ Sprinkle the dressing over both oranges and watercress and serve at once.

## Caramel Custard

| | |
|---|---|
| 6 oz. condensed milk | 12 oz. castor sugar |
| 12 oz. water | 1 oz. butter |
| 1 teaspoon vanilla | 6 eggs |
| extract | |

▶ Scald 6 oz. condensed milk with 12 oz. water and 1 teaspoon vanilla extract.

▶ Caramelize 4 oz. sugar, moistened with a few drops of water in a saucepan. When brown, remove from heat, stir in 1 oz. butter. Take care as it may splutter. Remelt, if necessary, and add to the hot milk.

▶ Beat 2 whole eggs and 6 yolks with 4 oz. sugar until smooth and creamy and pour in the caramel milk.

▶ Caramelize the remaining 4 oz. sugar in a straight-sided aluminium mould. When brown, tilt and turn the mould in order to coat the side walls with caramel and cool.

▶ Pour the custard mixture into the mould, set in a pan of hot water in a moderate oven 350°F, Reg 4 and bake 45 minutes until firm and knife inserted into centre comes out clean.

▶ Cool and chill overnight. To unmould, dip pan into boiling water for a few seconds and invert into shallow serving dish. Do not use a flat plate as there will be a considerable quantity of caramel sauce. Replace in refrigerator until serving time.

# 16

## MENU

*Crab Mousse*

*Veal Pepperonata*

*Celeriac Salad*

*Lisl's Chocolate Cake*

## Crab Mousse

| | |
|---|---|
| 12 oz. fresh flaked crabmeat | 1 tablespoon ketchup |
| 1 tablespoon gelatine | $\frac{1}{2}$–1 tablespoon lemon juice |
| 3 tablespoons cold water | 4 oz. mayonnaise (Menu 48) |
| $\frac{1}{2}$ tablespoon chopped parsley | 8 oz. double cream |
| $\frac{1}{2}$ tablespoon chopped chives | bunch of watercress |

▶ Bone the crabmeat, if necessary.

▶ Soak the tablespoon of gelatine in 3 tablespoons of cold water. Dissolve it over hot water.

▶ Add the gelatine to 4 oz. mayonnaise, mix well. Add the parsley, chives, ketchup and lemon juice and mix well.

▶ Fold into the mayonnaise 12 oz. flaked fresh crab and 8 oz. double cream, whipped.

▶ Place in refrigerator overnight.

▶ Unmould on a bed of watercress.

## Veal Pepperonata

| | |
|---|---|
| 6 veal escalopes (let the butcher cut them into $\frac{1}{3}$-inch-thick slices) | |
| 2 tablespoons oil | 4 small green peppers |
| 2 tablespoons butter | a handful of chopped parsley |
| 4 large tomatoes | |
| 1 chopped tinned red pepper | 2 courgettes (optional) |
| salt and pepper | tablespoon each of butter and oil for frying vegetables |

▶ Sauté the 6 veal escalopes for 10 minutes in 1 tablespoon each of butter and oil on a low heat. Turn once and sauté the other side for a further 10 minutes and remove them.

▶ Pour hot water over the 4 tomatoes, leave 8–12 seconds before draining, then peel and quarter them. Pour boiling water over the 4 green peppers, remove membranes and seeds and cut them lengthwise into slices. Wash and cut the 2 courgettes lengthwise.

▶ Fry all the vegetables in 1 tablespoon oil and 1 tablespoon butter, adding salt and pepper to taste, for half an hour. Then add the 6 veal escalopes, making sure that the veal is covered by vegetables, and cook until tender.

▶ Keep in a cool place and reheat next day on top of the stove.

## Celeriac Salad

| 3 roots of celeriac | 1 bunch of red radishes |
|---|---|

*Dressing*
8 oz. olive oil
3 tablespoons lemon
   juice
1 teaspoon salt
½ teaspoon pepper
2 tablespoons white
   wine

▶ Scrub 3 celeriac roots, peel and cut in thin slices. Cook in salted boiling water for twenty minutes, drain and dry thoroughly. Cut the leaves and roots off the bunch of radishes, wash and dry them.

▶ Mix 8 oz. olive oil with 3 tablespoons of lemon juice, adding the 2 tablespoons of white wine, salt and pepper. Using a wire whisk blend the mixture well.

▶ Heap the celeriac in the centre of a salad bowl, pour the dressing over and surround with the radishes.

## Lisl's Chocolate Cake

| *Cake* | *Icing* |
|---|---|
| 6 eggs | 8 oz. granulated sugar |
| 8 oz. unsalted butter | 4 oz. strong coffee |
| 8 oz. castor sugar | 7 oz. bitter chocolate |
| 5 oz. finely ground | ½ oz. butter |
|    almonds | ½ tablespoon rum |
| 8 oz. bitter chocolate | 4 oz. apricot jam |

▶ Separate the yolks and whites of 6 eggs.

▶ Cream 8 oz. butter. Add gradually 8 oz. castor sugar, cream until smooth and light. Stir in the beaten egg yolks, mix thoroughly. Stir in 5 oz. finely ground almonds.

▶ Melt 8 oz. of bitter chocolate in a double boiler. Cool slightly, add to the creamed mixture and stir until well blended.

▶ Beat the egg whites until stiff, fold into the chocolate mixture. Pour into a lightly greased and floured 9-inch round cake tin. Bake in a pre-heated oven 350°F, Reg 4 until a tooth-pick stuck into the centre comes out clean, approximately 1 hour.

▶ Cool. Remove from pan.

*Icing*

▶ Cook 8 oz. sugar and 4 oz. strong coffee until it is syrupy and will spin a thread, 5 to 10 minutes.

▶ Melt 7 oz. bitter chocolate in the top of a double boiler. Remove from the double boiler and stir in ½ oz. butter. Gradually add the coffee syrup, stirring continuously, until it is smooth and will coat a spoon. Stir in ½ tablespoon rum.

▶ With a palette knife, spread the apricot jam on top of the cake, then the chocolate icing.

# 17

*Onion Tart*

*Boiled Tongue*

*Purée of Dried Peas*

*Pots au Chocolat*

## Onion Tart

| Crust | Filling |
|---|---|
| 4 oz. lard | 8 large onions |
| 2 oz. butter | 1½ oz. butter |
| 8 oz. plain flour | 4 eggs |
| pinch salt | 8 oz. double cream |
| | salt, pepper and nutmeg |

▶ Cut 4 oz. lard and 2 oz. butter into 8 oz. flour sifted with a pinch of salt. Add just enough ice water to hold together, form lightly into a ball and chill for at least 1 hour. Oil an 8-inch tart tin. Roll out the pastry as thin as possible. Line the tin with your pastry. Wrap in foil and keep in refrigerator until next day.

▶ Slice 8 large white onions lengthwise, not in rounds. Melt 1½ oz. butter, stir in the sliced onions, mix well. Cover and cook over a very slow heat for ½ hour, stirring occasionally to prevent browning. Remove from stove. Season with salt and pepper and a pinch of nutmeg.

▶ Beat 4 eggs, add 8 oz. of double cream, mix well. Stir in onion mixture. Cover and put in refrigerator until next day.

▶ To serve, fill the tart with the onion mixture and bake in moderate oven 350°F, Reg 4 for 30 minutes. Serve hot or warm.

## Boiled Tongue

| | |
|---|---|
| 1 small fresh ox tongue | 8 peppercorns |
| a few bones for the stock | ¾ oz. butter |
| 3 beef stock cubes | ¾ oz. flour |
| 3 onions | 1 teaspoon mustard |
| 3 carrots | 3 small dill gherkins |
| 4 sticks of celery with leaves | 1 tablespoon capers |
| 8 sprigs parsley | 4 oz. single cream |
| | salt and pepper |

▶ Wash a fresh beef tongue. Place in large pan with bones. Add water just to cover. Bring to boil. Skim, when the scum comes to the top. Add 3 beef stock cubes, 3 onions, 3 carrots, 4 celery stalks, 8 sprigs parsley and 8 peppercorns. Reduce heat and simmer until tender, about 3 hours. Let tongue remain in stock until cool enough to handle. Peel off outer skin and cut out membranous portions of roots. Strain stock and return tongue to the pan with the stock.

▶ Melt ¾ oz. butter. Add ¾ oz. of flour and blend for 5 minutes over low heat. Add 8 oz. stock from the tongue and stirring constantly cook for 10 minutes. Add 1 teaspoon mustard, 3 small gherkins, sliced thin and 1 tablespoon capers. Salt and pepper to taste. Stir in 4 oz. single cream and simmer for five minutes. Cool and keep in refrigerator.

▶ To serve, slice tongue into ¼-inch thick slices, and reheat in the cold stock over moderate heat. Reheat the sauce in a double boiler, adding a little of the stock or cream if it is too thick. Dish on a serving plate surrounded by purée of dried peas, the sauce served separately.

## Purée of Dried Peas

12 oz. dried peas
water to cover
3 slices of bacon
2 small onions
1 teaspoon salt
pinch of pepper
hot milk

▶ Wash the 12 oz. dried peas well, cover them with water and let them soak for twelve hours.

▶ Chop the three slices of bacon into small pieces and fry them until they are crisp. Remove the bacon and fry the finely chopped onions in the bacon fat.

▶ Drain the peas and put them in a stewing pan. Add 1 teaspoon of salt and cover with boiling water. Cook them gently until they are quite soft. This will take 45 to 60 minutes. Stir frequently, adding more boiling water if necessary.

▶ Rub the peas through a sieve and stir in the onions and the bacon. Put in refrigerator until next day.

▶ Reheat on top of the stove on an asbestos mat over low heat. Add a little hot milk and a pinch of pepper.

## Pots au Chocolat

| | |
|---|---|
| 1 lb. bar sweet plain chocolate | 4 eggs |
| 6 oz. milk | 16 oz. double cream |

▶ In a saucepan break 1 lb. sweet plain chocolate into small pieces. Add 6 oz. milk. Put on a moderate heat. Stir with a wooden spoon until mixture is absolutely smooth. Stir in the beaten yolks of 4 eggs and cook for 10 minutes stirring constantly. Remove from stove and cool.

▶ Beat 3 egg whites until stiff. Stir into the chocolate mixture. Stir in 16 oz. double cream. Blend well. Pour mixture into small pots and put in the refrigerator overnight.

# 18

## MENU

*Leeks Vinaigrette*

*Greek Lamb Stew*

*Purée of French Green Beans*

*Viennese Sacher Cheese*

## Leeks Vinaigrette

| | |
|---|---|
| 18 to 24 leeks | 3 tablespoons tarragon |
| 1 teaspoon salt | vinegar |
| 2 tablespoons | 9 tablespoons olive oil |
| chopped chives | 1 egg |
| paprika | $\frac{1}{2}$ teaspoon dry |
| | mustard |
| | $\frac{1}{4}$ teaspoon pepper |
| | scant tablespoon |
| | single cream |

▶ Wash leeks carefully (3 to 4 per person depending on size) and trim to equal lengths using white portion only.

▶ Using enough boiling water to cover, add $\frac{1}{2}$ teaspoon salt and cook for 15 to 20 minutes or until tender. Drain and place on kitchen paper or a folded napkin to dry. Arrange in glass serving dish and set aside until next evening.

### Vinaigrette Dressing

▶ Hard boil 1 egg, cool rapidly under cool water, peel and chop finely.

▶ Chop $1\frac{1}{2}$ tablespoons chives or, if not available, 1 tablespoon each chopped parsley and onion.

▶ Put $\frac{1}{2}$ teaspoon salt, $\frac{1}{2}$ teaspoon dry mustard, $\frac{1}{4}$ teaspoon pepper in a small bowl and mix in 3 tablespoons tarragon vinegar. Slowly beat in 9 tablespoons olive oil, 1 scant tablespoon cream and fold in chopped egg and chives, set aside.

▶ Next evening pour the sauce over the leeks, dust with paprika and chill until served.

# Greek Lamb Stew

| | |
|---|---|
| 2½-lb. leg or shoulder of lamb | 8 tablespoons hot water |
| 2 finely chopped onions | 1 pinch sugar |
| 4 tablespoons Italian tomato purée | pepper |

▶ Ask the butcher to remove the bone and trim off the fat of a 2½-lb. leg of lamb. Keep the fat.

▶ Render the fat slowly until you have at least 1½ tablespoons. Discard the remaining cracklings.

▶ Cut the lamb into 1-inch cubes. Dry with absorbent paper or a towel. Heat 1½ tablespoons of rendered lamb fat in a flameproof dish. Sauté the lamb cubes until light brown.

▶ Place dish on an asbestos mat over a very low heat, add finely chopped onions and cook for 15 minutes stirring occasionally.

▶ Dilute 4 tablespoons Italian tomato purée with 8 tablespoons hot water. Add 1 pinch of sugar. Pour over the meat. Season with salt and pepper. Mix well and continue cooking until the meat is tender. If the meat seems too dry add a little hot water. Cool and put covered in the refrigerator.

▶ To serve, reheat uncovered on a very low heat.

# Purée of French Green Beans

| | |
|---|---|
| 2 lb. French green beans | 1 oz. butter |
| 1 small clove of garlic, peeled | 4 tablespoons double cream |
| salt and freshly ground pepper | |

▶ Wash the beans thoroughly, trim and cut into medium-sized pieces. Place in boiling water, add the garlic, and cook until the beans are very soft. Drain but keep some of the liquid for future use.

▶ Blend the beans in a liquidizer with a ¼-pint of the liquid.

▶ Melt butter in a saucepan and add the blended bean mixture, cook over a low heat for a few minutes adding salt and pepper to taste.

▶ Cool and store in refrigerator.

▶ Next evening, stir cream into the purée and reheat for a few minutes in a double boiler.

# Viennese Sacher Cheese

| | |
|---|---|
| ½ lb. cottage cheese | ½ teaspoon olive oil |
| 2 hard-boiled egg yolks | ½ teaspoon mustard |
| ½ tablespoon anchovy paste | ½ teaspoon grated onion |
| 1 oz. butter | 1 dash paprika |
| thin slices of gherkin | sprig of parsley |

▶ Blend ½ lb. cottage cheese, the yolks of 2 hard-boiled eggs, ½ tablespoon anchovy paste, 1 oz. butter, ½ teaspoon olive oil, ½ teaspoon mustard, ½ teaspoon grated onion and 1 dash of paprika in a liquidizer. Heap the mixture in the shape of a pineapple onto a plate, stick a sprig of parsley on top. Dust with paprika and surround with thin slices of gherkin.

## 19

MENU

*Devilled Eggs*

*Ham Chablis*

*Boiled Rice, Italian Spinach*

*Clarita's Chocolate Cake*

## Devilled Eggs

| | |
|---|---|
| 8 eggs | $\frac{1}{2}$ teaspoon dry |
| 2 tablespoons double | mustard |
| cream | 1 dash Worcester sauce |
| salt and pepper | bunch of watercress |

▶ Hard boil and cool 8 eggs. Remove from shell and cut them in halves lengthwise. Remove the yolks carefully so as not to damage the whites. Mash the yolks and moisten them with 2 tablespoons double cream that has been mixed with $\frac{1}{2}$ teaspoon mustard and a dash of Worcester sauce.

▶ Fill the whites with the yolk mixture, put covered in the refrigerator until served.

▶ To serve, arrange on a bed of watercress on a serving dish.

## Ham Chablis

| | |
|---|---|
| 8 oz. dry white wine | 3 tablespoons tomato |
| 4 shallots or small | purée |
| onions | 8 oz. double cream |
| 2 tablespoons | 1 oz. butter |
| tarragon | 1 pinch sugar |
| 8 oz. stock, fresh or | 12 thin slices boiled |
| cubes | ham |

▶ Boil 8 oz. dry white wine with 4 chopped shallots and 2 tablespoons chopped tarragon until reduced to 4 oz.

▶ Add 8 oz. stock, tinned or made with bouillon cubes, 3 tablespoons tomato purée and 1 pinch sugar and simmer over a very low heat for $\frac{1}{2}$ hour.

▶ Add 8 oz. double cream and continue cooking very slowly for 10 minutes.

▶ Press through a fine sieve and put aside to cool. Store in the refrigerator covered until ready to use.

▶ To serve, reheat in a double boiler over hot but not boiling water. Put in 1 oz. butter to thicken the sauce slightly. Pour the sauce over 12 thin slices of boiled ham and heat over a very low heat until the ham is hot.

## Boiled Rice

12 oz. long-grained rice
1 teaspoon salt
the juice of ½ lemon
butter for finishing

▶ In a large saucepan bring plenty of water to the boil with 1 teaspoon salt. Pour in the rice and stir for a minute. The rice will take about 20 minutes to cook.

▶ When done, toss the rice into a colander, drain and run cold water over it. Let it drain and keep it in the refrigerator in a buttered ovenproof dish.

▶ Next evening, sprinkle the rice with lemon juice, add little pieces of fresh butter on the top and reheat, covered, in a moderate oven, 350°F, Reg 4, stirring occasionally.

## Italian Spinach

| 3 packets frozen leaf spinach | scant 3 oz. parmesan cheese |
|---|---|
| 2 oz. butter | salt and pepper |

▶ Cook the spinach according to the instructions on the packet. Drain and run cold water over it for a few minutes. With your hands squeeze the spinach until all the moisture is gone. Chop the spinach with a big knife on a chopping board. Keep covered in the refrigerator until next day.

▶ To serve, melt 2 oz. butter in a heavy-bottomed enamelled saucepan. Stir in the spinach and continue cooking for 2 or 3 minutes until all the moisture has boiled off. Season to taste with salt and pepper. Put in a serving dish and sprinkle with a scant 3 oz. of parmesan cheese.

## Clarita's Chocolate Cake

½ lb. very good bitter chocolate (preferably Belgian)
½ lb. butter
½ lb. castor sugar
4 eggs
scant 1 teaspoon flour
4 oz. very strong black coffee
¼ pint whipped double cream

▶ Break chocolate and melt in a saucepan over a very low heat with the butter until smooth. Be careful not to allow the mixture to boil. When chocolate and butter are completely melted add sugar and strong black coffee. Continue stirring until mixture is smooth and creamy.

▶ Mix flour in a little water, add 4 eggs and beat as for an omelette. When thoroughly beaten pour into the chocolate mixture and stir all together slowly.

▶ Line an ovenproof dish with tinfoil extending over the edges. Pour in mixture. Place dish in a bain-marie on top of the stove and cook for ¾ of an hour. Remove dish from bain-marie and place in a hot oven 425°F, Reg 7 for about 10 minutes. Allow to cool overnight.

▶ The next morning, unmould and store in refrigerator. (If any difficulty with unmoulding, dip dish into hot water for a few seconds.)

▶ Decorate with whipped cream before serving.

## Asparagus Vinaigrette

| | |
|---|---|
| 2 lb. green asparagus | 4 oz. boiling water |

▶ Wash 2 lb. green asparagus. Cut off the lower part of stalks. Tie the stalks in bunches with white string. Place them upright in the bottom part of a double boiler, the lower ends in 4 oz. boiling water.

▶ Cover with the top part of the double boiler and cook 10 minutes or until tender. The steam will cook the asparagus tips.

▶ Drain and wrap in a clean towel. Place in refrigerator until served. Serve with a vinaigrette sauce (Menu 18).

## Lobster Clarence

| | |
|---|---|
| 1 cooked lobster | $\frac{1}{2}$ oz. butter |
| 6 cooked large prawns | 1 teaspoon curry powder |
| 8 oz. water | |
| 1 onion | $\frac{1}{2}$ oz. plain flour |
| 1 bay leaf | 8 oz. single cream or more |
| 1 pinch thyme | |
| 6 sprigs parsley | |

▶ Remove the meat from a lobster (cooked) and 6 cooked prawns. Save the shells.

▶ Put lobster and prawn shells in a saucepan with 8 oz. water, 1 sliced onion, 1 bay leaf, 1 pinch thyme, and 6 sprigs of parsley. Cook over medium heat until the liquid is reduced to 4 oz.

▶ Melt $\frac{1}{2}$ oz. butter in a saucepan, add 1 teaspoon of curry powder, blend well. Add $\frac{1}{2}$ oz. flour and stir until mixture begins to foam. Add the 4 oz. of the liquid and 8 oz. of cream, cook over a low fire stirring all the time until it thickens. Cool, add lobster and prawns cut into regular-sized pieces. Pour into a large dish, cover with a thin layer of cream, cover with tin-foil and put into the refrigerator until ready to serve.

▶ Reheat the sauce in a bain-marie, adding more cream if it is too thick. Continue cooking until the mixture is heated thoroughly. Serve in the ring mould of rice.

## Ring Mould of Rice

| | |
|---|---|
| 1 lb. patna rice | 3 pints boiling water |
| 2 teaspoons salt | $\frac{1}{2}$ lemon |
| | butter for finishing |

▶ Boil 3 pints of water and 2 teaspoons salt in a large pot; add 1 lb. of rice, stir with a wooden spoon and continue cooking uncovered for 10 to 15 minutes or until just tender. Strain and rinse in cold water. Grease a ring mould. Fill the mould. Place in the refrigerator.

▶ To serve, sprinkle the rice with the juice of $\frac{1}{2}$ lemon, and a few bits of butter. Place in a slow oven 310°F, Reg 2 until thoroughly heated. Turn the mould on to a serving plate and fill the centre with the lobster mixture.

## Red-currant Tart

| | |
|---|---|
| 8 oz. plain flour | 3 tablespoons double cream |
| 5 oz. butter | 10 oz. fresh red- |
| 2 egg yolks | currants |
| 6 egg whites | 10 oz. castor sugar |

▶ Put 8 oz. plain flour on a board, and with a pastry cutter cut 5 oz. butter into the flour. Add 2 egg yolks and 3 tablespoons cream; with hand, work into a soft dough that barely holds together. Form into a ball, wrap in foil and put in the refrigerator until chilled.

▶ Pat out the dough about $\frac{1}{4}$ inch thick in a greased and floured baking tin with removable base. Prick the surface with a fork to keep bubbles from rising. Bake blind in a 300°F, Reg 2 oven for 20 to 30 minutes. Test with a skewer. Take out of oven and cool.

▶ Mix thoroughly 10 oz. fresh red-currants and 10 oz. sugar. Spread this mixture over the crust.

▶ Beat 6 egg whites until stiff. With a palette knife, spread the beaten egg whites over the tart. Put in a moderate oven 350F°, Reg 4 and bake until slightly brown on top.

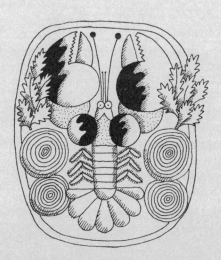

# 21

## MENU

*Acapulco Cocktail*

*Chili con Carne*

*Corn Meal Soufflé Ring*

*Macaroon Peaches*

## Acapulco Cocktail

| | |
|---|---|
| 1 lb. halibut | 4 shallots or ½ onion |
| 6 oz. lemon juice | 2 tablespoons capers |
| 1 teaspoon salt | 5 tablespoons olive oil |
| fresh ground pepper | 2 tablespoons white |
| 2 teaspoons oregano | wine vinegar |
| 1 green pepper | 1 avocado |
| 3 small tomatoes | |

▶ Remove the skin and bones from 1 lb. of fresh halibut and cut into very small pieces. Place in a glass or china dish. Pour over 6 oz. lemon juice mixed with 1 teaspoon salt. Sprinkle with fresh ground pepper and oregano. Put a cover on the bowl and allow to marinate in refrigerator overnight. The fish in this recipe is uncooked.

▶ The next day, remove the seeds from 1 green pepper and chop coarsely. Add 3 small tomatoes cut up after having removed the skin and seeds. Now cut into small rounds 4 shallots (if not available, use ½ medium onion). Mix with the fish. Add the capers.

▶ In a bottle shake together until thoroughly mixed 5 tablespoons olive oil and 2 tablespoons white wine vinegar. Pour over the fish mixture.

▶ Just before serving, peel and cut 1 avocado into pieces and mix lightly with the fish.

▶ Serve very cold in shells or wine glasses.

## Chili con Carne

| | |
|---|---|
| 14 oz. red beans | 2 lb. minced beef |
| 2½ pints warm water | 1½ tablespoons flour |
| 2 strips salt pork | 3 tablespoons chilli |
| 1 teaspoon salt | powder or less |
| ⅛ pint olive oil | 1 teaspoon oregano |
| 4 onions | 16 oz. tinned tomatoes |
| 2 cloves garlic | 1 tablespoon golden |
| | syrup |
| | 1 tablespoon lemon |
| | juice |
| salt and pepper to taste | |

▶ Soak 14 oz. red beans overnight covered in water. Drain. Add 2½ pints warm water, 2 strips salt pork and 1 teaspoon salt. Cook slowly for at least 2 hours until done.

▶ Heat ⅛ pint olive oil. Add 4 chopped onions, 2 cloves crushed garlic. Cook until transparent. Stir in 2 lb. minced beef. Cook until meat is browned. Add 1½ tablespoons flour and 3 tablespoons chilli powder, 1 teaspoon oregano. Mix well. Stir in 16 oz. tinned tomatoes, 1 tablespoon golden syrup and 1 tablespoon lemon juice. Simmer over moderate heat for ½ hour, stirring occasionally.

▶ Combine the meat and the beans, salt and pepper to taste. Add more chilli powder if you prefer a hotter chilli. Put aside to cool.

▶ Reheat next day over low heat. Serve in the centre of a corn meal soufflé ring.

# Corn Meal Soufflé Ring

| | |
|---|---|
| 1¼ pints milk | 3 eggs |
| 6 oz. corn meal | 1 teaspoon salt |
| 1 oz. butter | 1 teaspoon pepper |

▶ Put 1¼ pints milk, 6 oz. corn meal, 1 teaspoon salt and 1 teaspoon pepper in the top of a double boiler and cook over boiling water until thick, stirring occasionally.

▶ Separate the yolks and white of 3 eggs. Beat the yolks slightly, add to the corn meal, mix well and add 1 oz. butter.

▶ Beat the whites of the eggs until stiff and fold them into the corn meal mixture. Pour into a well-greased, floured ring mould. The ring may now be placed in the refrigerator until ready for use.

▶ To use, place the ring in a pan of hot water. Place pan in a moderate oven 350°F, Reg 4 and bake for 25 minutes, until set. Remove from oven and let stand 5 minutes before unmoulding onto a serving dish. Fill the centre with Chili con Carne, keeping it hot and covered with tin-foil until served.

# Macaroon Peaches

| | |
|---|---|
| 8 tinned peach halves | 1 oz. sugar |
| 3 eggs | ½ lb. macaroons |
| juice from peaches | ¼–½ pint whipped cream for serving |

▶ Drain peaches and place in an ovenproof dish. Store in a cool place until required.

▶ Separate the eggs, beat the yolks and add the sugar. Continue beating until smooth, crumble the macaroons and fold into the mixture. When thoroughly mixed store in refrigerator.

▶ Next evening, beat the egg whites until stiff and fold into the mixture. Fill the peach halves with the mixture. Pour the juice into the dish and bake in a moderate oven 350°F, Reg 4 until the peaches are lightly browned.

▶ Serve with whipped cream.

# 22

## Devilled Crab

| | |
|---|---|
| 12 oz. tinned or cooked crabmeat | 1 small onion, grated |
| 1 oz. butter | $\frac{1}{8}$ teaspoon salt |
| $\frac{1}{2}$ oz. cracker crumbs (dried breadcrumbs can be substituted) | 1 teaspoon prepared mustard |
| | $\frac{1}{4}$ teaspoon curry powder |
| 8 oz. double cream | $\frac{1}{2}$ teaspoon Worcester sauce |
| 2 eggs | |

▶ Flake and remove membranes from 12 oz. tinned or cooked crabmeat. Melt in a saucepan 1 oz. butter. Add $\frac{1}{2}$ oz. cracker crumbs, 8 oz. double cream and 2 tablespoons grated onion. Cook until thick. Remove from heat. Beat, then add 2 eggs, $\frac{1}{8}$ teaspoon salt, 1 teaspoon prepared mustard, $\frac{1}{4}$ teaspoon curry powder and $\frac{1}{2}$ teaspoon of Worcester sauce to the cream mixture. Add crabmeat and arrange in shells or ramekins. Put in the refrigerator until needed, covered lightly in tin-foil.

▶ To serve, brush the tops with melted butter and brown them in the oven at 400°F, Reg 6, or under a grill.

## Chicken Chaud Froid

| | |
|---|---|
| 1 large roasting chicken | 6 peppercorns |
| 2 small slices salt pork | salt to taste |
| 1 onion | small tin pâté de foie gras |
| 2 cloves | |
| 3 leeks | 2 rounded teaspoons gelatine |
| 3 carrots | |
| 2 sticks of celery | 1 oz. butter |
| 4 sprigs of parsley | $\frac{1}{2}$ oz. flour |
| | 4 oz. double cream |
| | 2 egg yolks |
| | 3 tablespoons chopped fresh tarragon |
| | parsley and truffles (optional) to garnish |

▶ Put the chicken, breast down, into a large saucepan. Blanch 2 small slices salt pork in boiling water for 5 minutes. Stick cloves in the onion.

▶ Put into the pan with the chicken, the salt pork, the onion, 3 leeks, 3 carrots, 2 celery sticks, 4 sprigs of parsley and 6 peppercorns. Add just enough hot water barely to cover the chicken, not more than 3 pints, cook uncovered, on a high heat until the scum comes to the surface and the water to boiling point. Skim the stock carefully, reduce the heat and let the chicken simmer gently until tender, adding salt to taste when half done.

▶Remove the chicken. Strain the stock and put aside. When the chicken is cool, skin it and take off all the meat by hand, keeping the strips as long and as nearly equal in size as possible.

▶ Arrange the strips in a compact layer in the bottom of a rather deep serving dish and spread with a thin layer of foie gras. (Chicken liver pâté can be substituted.) Put the bones back into the chicken stock, cook uncovered until reduced to $1\frac{1}{2}$ pints.

▶ Strain, add 2 rounded teaspoons gelatine dissolved in 2 tablespoons cold water, and when cooled, remove the fat. Strain again through a dampened cheesecloth or scalded clean tea towel and chill. When nearly jellied, pour $\frac{1}{2}$ pint over the chicken and foie gras and put serving dish into the refrigerator to set the jelly.

▶ Melt 1 oz. butter, blend in $\frac{1}{2}$ oz. flour, add the remaining 1 pint stock and 4 oz. double cream and cook, stirring constantly, until thickened. Beat and add 2 egg yolks and continue cooking 5 minutes. Remove from heat. Put pan in a dish of cold water and continue stirring until the sauce is cool to avoid lumps and scum.

▶ When cool, fold in 3 tablespoons finely chopped tarragon. Spread in a layer over the ingredients on the serving dish and re-chill. Decorate with parsley and truffles, if desired, and keep in refrigerator until ready to serve.

## Celery and Tomato Salad

| | |
|---|---|
| 6 tomatoes | pepper and salt |
| 8 celery stalks | 4 tablespoons mustard |
| 3 tablespoons oil | 3 tablespoons tarragon vinegar |

▶ Wash tomatoes, take out the pips, quarter them and drain. Wash the celery stalks, cut off the bottom part, and chop up.

▶ Mix the oil, salt, pepper, and mustard in a small bowl. Add vinegar and whisk. Heap celery in the middle of the salad bowl, surround with tomatoes, then pour the vinaigrette on top.

## Black-currant Ice

| | |
|---|---|
| 6 oz. sugar | $\frac{1}{2}$ lb. black-currants |
| 12 oz. water | $1\frac{1}{2}$ tablespoons lemon juice |
| 1 1-inch piece cinnamon stick | $\frac{1}{2}$ teaspoon grated orange rind |

▶ Make a syrup by mixing 6 oz. sugar, 12 oz. water, a 1 inch piece of cinnamon stick and bring to a boil. Boil 5 minutes. Remove from heat. Discard cinnamon stick. Cool. Stir $\frac{1}{2}$ lb. black-currants, $1\frac{1}{2}$ tablespoons lemon juice and $\frac{1}{2}$ teaspoon grated orange rind into the cooled syrup.

▶ Pour mixture into a refrigerator tray and freeze until mushy in the freezing compartment of your refrigerator. Pour ice into a chilled bowl. Beat with a rotary beater until all the ice particles are dissolved. Return to refrigerator tray and freeze.

# 23

## MENU

*Clarita's Anchovy Eggs*

*Muscovite Selianka*

*Marinated Mushrooms and
Salted Cucumbers*

*An Englishman's Cheese Board*

*Fresh Fruit*

## Clarita's Anchovy Eggs

| | |
|---|---|
| 10 eggs | 4 oz. double cream, |
| 1 tablespoon vinegar | approximately |
| 8 anchovy fillets | freshly ground pepper |
| ½ tablespoon | 12 lettuce leaves |
| Worcester sauce | chopped parsley |
| | 2 packets sliced |
| | pumpernickel |

▶ Hard boil 10 eggs in boiling water with
the vinegar for 12 minutes. Cool rapidly
and chop coarsely. Chop 8 anchovy fillets
very fine, mix with eggs, add ½ tablespoon
Worcester sauce, a little freshly ground
pepper and enough double cream to bind.
Chill mixture overnight.

▶ Serve on lettuce leaves, sprinkled with
finely chopped parsley, with sliced
and buttered pumpernickel.

## Muscovite Selianka

| | |
|---|---|
| 6 thick slices bacon | 2 tins sauerkraut |
| 2 oz. lard | 1 pint dry white wine |
| 1 large onion | 1 pint chicken stock, |
| 1 large cooking apple | fresh or cubes |
| 1 teaspoon caraway | 6 thick smoked pork |
| seed | cutlets or fresh |
| 1 teaspoon black | cutlets |
| peppercorns | 18 small new potatoes |

▶ If smoked cutlets are not available
fresh ones can be used; in which case fry
them lightly in a little lard on both sides,
dusting them with salt and paprika, before
combining with the sauerkraut.

▶ Cut 6 thick slices bacon into 1-inch
pieces and fry in 2 oz. lard. Peel and chop
1 large onion and 1 large apple coarsely,
put into pan with onions and fry for 2 or 3
minutes. Add 1 teaspoon each of caraway
seed and peppercorns and the contents of
2 tins of sauerkraut well drained. Mix and
pour in 1 pint dry white wine and 1 pint
chicken stock . Mix well again and
bring to a boil. Place on asbestos mat over
low heat and in a good-sized ovenproof
serving casserole. Put in first ⅓ of the
sauerkraut, then 3 smoked cutlets, then
another ⅓ sauerkraut, 3 more cutlets and
the remaining ⅓ of the sauerkraut to
finish. Pour liquid remaining in saucepan
over all and simmer very slowly 1 to 2
hours until cutlets are tender. Add a little
more wine from time to time if liquid
evaporates too rapidly, taking care when
stirring not to disturb the layers of
sauerkraut and meat.

▶ Cool and chill. Peel 18 small new
potatoes and leave them in cold water
overnight.

▶ 1 hour before arrival of guests steam
over boiling water until tender. Drain in
colander and keep warm over hot water.
Reheat casserole in slow oven 310°F, Reg 2
or on an asbestos mat on low heat;
when warm add freshly cooked warm
potatoes and continue heating slowly,
adding a little more wine if too dry.

▶ Serve very hot in same casserole, with marinated mushrooms and salted cucumbers.

## Marinated Mushrooms and Salted Cucumbers

| | |
|---|---|
| 1 lb. mushrooms | scant tablespoon of salt |
| 2 cucumbers | 2 tablespoons of olive oil |
| | $\frac{3}{4}$ pint vinaigrette dressing (Menu 18) |

▶ Wash the 1 lb. of mushrooms and remove any parts of the stalks that are not fresh. Leave button mushrooms whole, but larger ones should be cut into quarters. The cultivated mushrooms which are bought nowadays do not need to be peeled.

▶ Heat the 2 tablespoons of olive oil in a sauté or frying pan and fry the mushrooms for 1–2 minutes only or until they become shiny and change colour slightly. Turn at once into a bowl and cover with $\frac{1}{2}$ pint of vinaigrette dressing. Refrigerate, covered, until required.

▶ Peel the cucumbers and cut into pieces about 1 inch long. Cut each piece lengthways into 4. Sprinkle all the slices with the salt, cover and put in a cool place.

▶ Before serving, squeeze the cucumbers between 2 plates or with your hands so as to extract all the liquid. A considerable amount should come out, so continue until the cucumbers are as dry as possible. Serve on a flat dish and spoon the remaining $\frac{1}{4}$ pint of vinaigrette dressing over the cucumbers.

▶ Arrange the marinated mushrooms in another salad bowl or dish.

## An Englishman's Cheese Board

▶ Serve assortment of English cheeses such as Caerphilly, Wensleydale, Stilton, Double Gloucester and Cheddar, on a cheese board or large flat plate together with cheese biscuits and butter.

## Fresh Fruit

▶ Arrange seasonal fruits in large bowl or basket. A smaller bowl of nuts and dried fruits may be served at the same time.

# 24

*Greek Onions*

*The Emperor's Meat Loaf*

*Creamed Spinach with Croutons*

*Swiss Rice*

## Greek Onions

| | |
|---|---|
| 1½ lb. small onions | 6 oz. sugar |
| 2½ oz. sultanas | ¼ pint olive oil |
| ½ teaspoon peppercorns | ½ pint dry white wine |
| 1½ tablespoons tomato purée | ½ teaspoon salt |

▶ Use small onions of approximately the same size, white ones if available.

▶ Blanch in boiling water and then peel the onions and put them in a saucepan with all the other ingredients. Add sufficient water to cover completely. Bring rapidly to a boil, reduce heat and simmer uncovered until oil rises to the surface and the onions are tender.

▶ Serve cold.

## The Emperor's Meat Loaf

| | |
|---|---|
| 1½ lb. lean veal | 1 clove garlic |
| 1½ lb. lean pork | ½ teaspoon salt |
| ¼ lb. mushrooms | ¼ teaspoon pepper |
| ½ lb. fresh breadcrumbs | 2 eggs |
| ¼ pint dry white wine | 8 oz. chicken stock |
| 2 cartons sour cream (10 oz.) | |

▶ Put the 1½ lb. veal and 1½ lb. pork twice through fine blade of the mincing machine.

▶ Wash, dry and chop ¼ lb. mushrooms very fine. Add them to meat. If tinned mushrooms are used, drain carefully before chopping.

▶ Soak ½ lb. breadcrumbs in ¼ pint white wine and squeeze to remove all excess moisture. Add to meat and mushrooms with 1 clove of crushed garlic, ½ teaspoon salt, ¼ teaspoon freshly ground pepper, 2 eggs and 2 tablespoons sour cream.

▶ Knead all these ingredients together thoroughly, place the mass on a floured board and form into an oblong loaf.

▶ Put 4 tablespoons of sour cream on the bottom of a shallow pan, spacious enough to permit basting easily, and place loaf on cream. Spread 2 tablespoons sour cream on top and sides of loaf, score surface with prongs of a fork and bake in pre-heated moderate oven, 350°F, Reg 4, basting frequently, until juice is perfectly clear when loaf is pierced with a skewer, about 1½ hours. The cooking time depends on the size and shape of the receptacle chosen.

▶ Remove loaf carefully from pan to a large sheet of heavy foil and add 8 oz. stock to remaining juices in pan. Scrape the sides and bottom, bring to a quick boil and store the sauce in the pan in a cold place overnight. When loaf is cool, wrap the foil around it and refrigerate.

▶ Next day remove meat from refrigerator several hours before needed. Replace it in the pan with the sauce, spread with the remaining sour cream, cover lightly with the foil and reheat in a moderate oven for about 25 minutes at 310°F, Reg 4.

▶ Serve on a heated dish covered with the pan gravy.

# Creamed Spinach with Croutons

| | |
|---|---|
| 3 lb. fresh spinach, or frozen leaf spinach | 12 oz. single cream |
| 5 oz. butter | salt |
| 1½ oz. flour | pepper |
| | 6 thin slices bread |

▶ Remove stalks and wash 3 lb. of spinach 3 times in cold water or use 2–3 packets of frozen leaf spinach.

▶ Cook rapidly in 8 oz. boiling salted water until tender. Frozen spinach should be cooked with a little butter only, and no water. If spinach is young and fresh this will take only a few minutes. If not, about 10 minutes.

▶ Remove from fire and drain over saucepan. There will be at least ¾ pint of liquid as spinach contains a high percentage of water. Reserve, pass leaves under cold water, drain well, pressing to remove any excess water, and chop finely or whirl in liquidizer until smooth.

▶ Reheat ¾ pint of spinach liquid and 8 oz. single cream to boiling point.

▶ Melt 1½ oz. butter in a saucepan, put in 1½ oz. flour and stir until flour is slightly brown. Add hot liquid gradually, stirring constantly, and continue cooking over medium heat until sauce is thickened. Taste, add freshly ground pepper and salt if necessary, and cool.

▶ Cool the sauce, fold in the chopped spinach, cover the surface with butter paper or foil, and store in cold place until next day.

▶ Prepare croutons to reheat in oven for last 5 minutes of rewarming meat. Remove crusts from 6 slices bread, cut them in half diagonally and fry until golden brown on both sides in 3½ oz. butter. Place on tin ready to rewarm.

▶ Reheat spinach next day in double boiler with 4 oz. cream over boiling water. Stir occasionally to prevent sticking. The purée should not be too liquid, but, if too dry, add a small quantity of heated cream.

▶ Serve mounded in a heated dish. Garnish with crouton triangles.

# Swiss Rice

| | |
|---|---|
| 1½ pints milk | 1 small tin pears |
| 9½ oz. rice | 1 small tin cherries |
| small piece vanilla bean | 4 oz. double cream |
| 3 oz. granulated sugar | 1 small bottle raspberry syrup |
| 2 tablespoons water | 5 dried apricots |

▶ Scald 1½ pints milk in a double boiler, add 9½ oz. rice and small piece of vanilla bean. Cook until milk is absorbed and the rice is tender.

▶ Boil 3 oz. sugar and 2 tablespoons water to thread stage. Test by plunging a spoon straight down into the liquid which will spin a thin thread, not a drop, from the tip of the spoon when it is lifted out of the pan. Mix the sugar syrup into the hot rice and cool.

▶ Whip 4 oz. cream stiff and fold into the cold rice.

▶ Drain the tinned fruits well, add the 5 dried apricots soaked in warm water, drained, cut in thin slivers. Halve the cherries and slice the pears. Fold the combined fruits into the rice cream— about ¼ lb. of each. Chill overnight.

▶ Serve in chilled cups or shallow stem glasses with raspberry syrup poured over.

# 25

## Celeriac in Sauce Remoulade

| | |
|---|---|
| 3 medium-sized celeriac | 4 oz. olive oil |
| 2 teaspoons salt | 2 oz. tarragon vinegar |
| 2 tablespoons lemon juice | 2 tablespoons chopped parsley |
| 3 tablespoons Dijon French mustard | salt and pepper |
| 3 tablespoons hot water | 3 hard-boiled eggs |
| | chopped chives |

▶ Pare off the fibrous outside of 3 medium-sized celeriac. Cut in thin slices and then crosswise in very thin strips. Toss in a bowl with 2 teaspoons salt and 2 tablespoons lemon juice. Let stand at least $\frac{1}{2}$ hour. Rinse in cold water, drain and dry with a towel.

*Sauce Remoulade*

▶ Put 3 tablespoons Dijon mustard in a bowl. Beat in drop by drop 3 tablespoons hot water, then again drop by drop 4 oz. olive oil, and finally 2 oz. tarragon vinegar. Salt and pepper to taste. Stir in 2 tablespoons chopped parsley. Add the celeriac and chill in the refrigerator overnight.

▶ To serve, put in a bowl, sprinkle with chopped chives and arrange quartered hard-boiled eggs around the edge.

## Pork Chops in Cider

| | |
|---|---|
| 6 loin pork chops | 1 tablespoon rosemary |
| ½ oz. bacon fat | 1 clove garlic |
| ½ oz. plain flour | 2 tablespoons capers |
| 8 oz. cider | salt and pepper |

▶ Cut away any fat from the edges of 6 lean loin pork chops. Brown in ½ oz. bacon fat in a frying pan, lightly on both sides. Remove the chops to a warm dish.

▶ Add ½ oz. flour to the fat, stir well until blended and brown. Pour in 8 oz. cider, season to taste with salt and pepper and cook until thickened. Chop 1 clove garlic finely and add to the sauce as well as 1 tablespoon rosemary.

▶ Return the chops to the sauce in the pan, cover tightly and cook in a moderate oven, 310°F, Reg 4, or over a slow heat for 20 minutes. If the sauce becomes too thick add a little extra cider (water down if the cider is very strong). Stir in 2 tablespoons of capers.

▶ Reheat next day in a slow oven, 310°F, Reg 2, or on an asbestos mat over a very low heat.

## Steamed Turnips

| | |
|---|---|
| 12 round white turnips | salt and pepper |
| juice of 1 lemon | melted butter |

▶ Scrub 12 small round white turnips (if they are young it is not necessary to peel them), grate them in strips. Sprinkle them with juice of 1 lemon. Mix well. Store in a plastic bag in refrigerator.

▶ To serve, sprinkle them with salt and pepper. Put them in a steamer over boiling water and cook over low heat until tender—half an hour to an hour will be enough. Keep them hot, and serve with melted butter poured over them.

## Floating Island

| | |
|---|---|
| 8 eggs | 1 heaped teaspoon |
| 2 pints milk | plain flour |
| 8 oz. castor sugar | piece vanilla bean |
| | grated chocolate |

▶ Separate the yolks and the whites of 8 eggs. Beat the whites until stiff; as they start to stiffen add 4 oz. castor sugar little by little. Scald 2 pints milk with a large piece of vanilla bean. Away from fire, drop large spoonfuls of egg-white mixture, no more than 4 at a time, on to the hot milk. Cook 2 minutes on each side over a very low heat. Remove with a skimmer or kitchen slice, place on a towel to drain. Repeat until all the egg whites are used.

▶ Beat egg yolks, add 4 oz. castor sugar and beat until smooth and creamy. Add a heaped teaspoon of flour and beat again. Stirring constantly, pour the hot milk, in which you have poached the whites, over the egg-yolk mixture. Do not let it boil. Strain through a fine sieve into a serving bowl. Float the egg white on top, sprinkle with grated chocolate. Chill in refrigerator until serving time.

# 26

## MENU

*Jellied Eels, Midget Gherkins*

*Magyar Chicken,  Rice or Noodles*

*Coffee Ice Cream*

## Jellied Eels, Midget Gherkins

| | |
|---|---|
| 2 cartons jellied eels | 1 jar of very small dill gherkins |

▶ Open the 2 cartons of jellied eels (Norwegian fillets if obtainable), arrange in the centre of a gaily coloured serving dish and surround with the gherkins.

## Magyar Chicken

| | |
|---|---|
| 1 large or 2 small chickens | 1 oz. plain flour |
| 2 oz. lard | $1\frac{1}{4}$–$1\frac{1}{2}$ pints chicken stock |
| 2 oz. butter | 2 medium onions |
| 1 carton sour cream (or 4 oz. double cream plus $\frac{1}{2}$ teaspoon lemon juice) | 2 tablespoons paprika |
| | 1 teaspoon tomato purée |
| | salt to taste |

▶ Skin the chicken(s), cut into pieces and thoroughly dry.

▶ Melt the lard and butter in a frying pan and brown the chicken pieces quickly on all sides. Remove to an ovenproof casserole.

▶ Peel and slice finely the onions. Pour off half the fat in which the chicken has been browned and lightly fry the onion in the remaining fat until golden. Take the pan off the heat and stir in 2 tablespoons of paprika and the tomato purée. Return the pan to the heat and slowly stir in the flour; when thoroughly mixed add the chicken stock slowly and bring to the boil. If the sauce seems too thick add a little more stock.

▶ Pour sauce over the chicken and bring again to the boil, turn the heat very low, cover the casserole tightly and allow to simmer for 25–35 minutes or until chicken is tender. Remove the chicken, taste the sauce and if it seems too bland add salt and a little more paprika. Strain sauce and pour over chicken pieces. Set aside to cool and then store in refrigerator.

---

▶ Next evening mix in the sour cream or cream/lemon mix. Heat slowly on a low flame, using an asbestos mat, for approx. 1 hour. Serve with Rice (Menu 1) or noodles.

## Coffee Ice Cream

---

| | |
|---|---|
| 5 oz. castor sugar | 2 eggs |
| 1 tablespoon cornflour | 1 teaspoon vanilla |
| 8 oz. milk | $\frac{1}{8}$ teaspoon salt |
| 4 oz. very strong black coffee | 8 oz. double cream |

---

▶ Combine 5 oz. castor sugar and 1 tablespoon cornflour in the top of a double boiler. Gradually stir in 8 oz. milk and 4 oz. very strong black coffee. When well mixed, cook over boiling water until mixture thickens. Cover and cook 10 minutes.

---

▶ Beat 2 egg yolks. Stir in a little of the hot mixture and then add to the rest of the hot mixture. Cook over hot, not boiling, water, stirring constantly for 3 minutes. Cool. Add 1 teaspoon vanilla and $\frac{1}{8}$ teaspoon salt.

---

▶ Beat 2 egg whites until stiff. Fold into the cooled custard. Pour into a refrigerator tray and freeze until firm throughout.

---

▶ Remove to a chilled bowl. Beat with a rotary beater. Whip 8 oz. double cream. Fold into the beaten custard. Return to tray and freeze.

# 27

## Oeufs Martiniquaises

| | |
|---|---|
| 2 large green peppers | 8 oz. salad oil |
| 5 hard-boiled eggs | 1 teaspoon curry |
| 1 breakfast cup | powder |
| chopped tinned | 6 eggs |
| pimentoes | 3 tablespoons gelatine |
| 1 egg | 12 oz. tinned beef |
| $\frac{1}{8}$ teaspoon salt | consommé |
| 1 tablespoon Dijon | lettuce leaves |
| mustard | |

► Wash 2 large green peppers, slice off the tops. Remove seeds and white membranes.

► Mash the yolks of 5 hard-boiled eggs. Add 1 breakfast cup chopped tinned pimentoes.

► Into a liquidizer put 1 whole egg, $\frac{1}{8}$ teaspoon salt, 1 tablespoon Dijon mustard and 1 tablespoon salad oil. Cover and blend for 2 minutes. Remove cover and slowly pour in the rest of the oil, blend until thick. Measure mayonnaise, do not use more than 8 oz., add 1 teaspoon curry powder. Mix well.

► Soak 1 tablespoon gelatine in 2 tablespoons cold water. Let it stand 5 minutes. Dissolve over hot water and add to the curry mayonnaise. Mix well.

► Combine the hard-boiled egg mixture with the curry mayonnaise. Fill the peppers with this mixture and chill.

► Poach 6 eggs. Chill and trim evenly and place on the peppers which have been already cut each into 6 slices. Arrange the eggs on top of them.

► Make an aspic by soaking 2 tablespoons gelatine in 2 tablespoons of cold water. Let stand for 5 minutes. Pour into 12 oz. of boiling tinned consommé. Allow to cool until almost on the point of setting and then pour over the eggs and peppers. Put into the refrigerator. Keep there until ready to serve.

► Arrange the eggs on a bed of lettuce leaves, and serve from a large flat dish.

## Suprême of Sweetbreads

| | |
|---|---|
| 3 pairs sweetbreads | $\frac{1}{2}$ tablespoon sherry |
| 1 tablespoon vinegar | 12 tinned artichoke |
| 12 oz. single cream | hearts |
| $\frac{1}{2}$ oz. butter, and a | 2 oz. brandy |
| little extra | salt and pepper to |
| 1 heaped teaspoon | taste |
| plain flour | shredded pistachio nuts |

► Soak 3 pairs sweetbreads in cold water for 1 hour. Change water during this time. Blanch by putting them into 3 pints of cold water containing 1 tablespoon vinegar, and bringing them slowly to the boil. Simmer for 10 minutes. Drain. Firm by plunging them immediately into ice water. When cold, drain again. Trim them by removing cartilage, tubes, tougher membranes and connective tissue. Store covered in refrigerator overnight.

▶ Next day, break the sweetbreads into small pieces. Poach them over low heat in a tightly covered saucepan in 12 oz. single cream until tender; it will take about ten minutes. Remove the sweetbread pieces, reserving the cream sauce.

▶ Sauté in a little butter 12 tinned artichoke hearts. Salt and pepper them. Place in a buttered ovenproof dish. Fill them with the pieces of sweetbreads.

▶ Cream ½ oz. butter with 1 heaped teaspoon plain flour until smooth.

▶ Heat the cream in which the artichokes were cooked. Add ½ tablespoon sherry. Pour a small amount at a time over the creamed butter, stirring continuously. Return to stove. Continue stirring over low heat until slightly thickened. Salt and pepper to taste. Pour over the sweetbreads. Sprinkle with shredded pistachio nuts.

▶ To serve. Reheat in oven at 400°F, Reg 5. Pour a little warm brandy in a ring around the dish and light. Serve flaming.

## Purée of Peas

| | |
|---|---|
| 3 packets frozen peas | ½ level teaspoon sugar |
| 2 hearts of lettuce | 1 oz. butter |
| ½ small onion | 2 oz. double cream or more |
| | salt and pepper to taste |

▶ Put 3 packets frozen peas in a small saucepan. Add 2 shredded hearts of lettuce, ½ of a thinly sliced small onion, and ½ level teaspoon sugar. Add boiling water to just cover. Simmer uncovered until the peas are tender. Drain, reserving the water in which the peas were cooked. Boil it down until it is reduced to 4 oz.

▶ Blend peas and lettuce in a liquidizer or put through a fine sieve. Stir in the 4 oz. of reduced liquid and 1 oz. butter. Cook over a low heat until butter melts, stirring continuously. Cool and store in the refrigerator. Salt and pepper to taste.

▶ To serve. Stir in 2 oz. double cream. Reheat in a double boiler. If it is too thick add another tablespoon cream.

## Alexander's Nut Cake

| | |
|---|---|
| 4 eggs | 1½ oz. butter, unsalted |
| 7 oz. castor sugar | 9 oz. icing sugar |
| ¼ lb. shelled walnuts | 2 tablespoons strong |
| ¼ lb. shelled hazelnuts | black coffee |
| 2 teaspoons instant coffee powder | 2 tablespoons brandy |

▶ Separate the yolks and whites of 4 eggs.

▶ Out of ¼ lb. shelled walnuts reserve 10 halves. Put the rest through a fine mincer with a ¼ lb. of shelled unpeeled hazelnuts. Pound into a paste-like consistency.

▶ Beat the egg yolks until creamy. Slowly add 7 oz. castor sugar and continue beating until thick and smooth. Stir in 2 teaspoons powdered coffee and 1 tablespoon of brandy. Add the nuts. Mix well.

▶ Beat the whites of eggs until stiff. Fold into the nut mixture. Lightly butter and flour a 10-inch cake tin. Pour in the batter and bake in a pre-heated moderate oven 350°F, Reg 4 for 25 minutes, or until cooked. Turn out on a cake rack to cool.

▶ Cream 1½ oz. unsalted butter. Add 9 oz. icing sugar, a little at a time, alternating with 2 tablespoons very strong black coffee and 1 tablespoon brandy mixed together. Beat well after each addition.

▶ Divide the cake into 2 layers by cutting through the middle with a sharp knife. Cover the bottom layer with half of the butter icing. Place the top layer on it and spread with the rest of the icing. Decorate with the reserved walnut halves.

# 28

## MENU

*Sweet Peppers and Cucumbers*

*Clarita's South American Fish*

*Melon Ice Cream*

## Sweet Peppers and Cucumber

3 sweet red peppers    1 cucumber
3 sweet green peppers    vinaigrette sauce
         (Menu 30)
         chopped parsley and
         chives

▶ Put 3 sweet red peppers and 3 green peppers, 2 at a time on a skewer and hold them over a gas flame, turning them round and round until their skin is charred quite black. Run them under cold water and the charred skins rub off quite easily. Remove every bit of the blackened skin, the seeds and membranes. Cut in thin lengthwise slices and marinate overnight in an olive-oil vinaigrette sauce.

▶ Peel and slice thinly 1 cucumber. Marinate in vinaigrette sauce for at least two hours.

▶ Serve the peppers heaped in the centre of a large round plate surrounded by thinly sliced cucumbers and sprinkled with chopped parsley and chives.

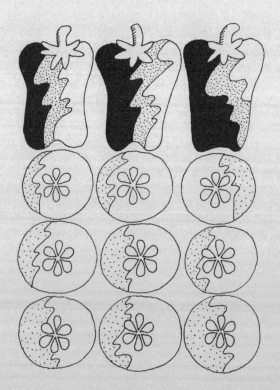

# Clarita's South American Fish

| | |
|---|---|
| 2½ lb. piece of fresh cod | 1 large tin tomato |
| 10 medium-sized | purée |
| potatoes | ¼ teaspoon sugar |
| 5 onions | ½ teaspoon cayenne |
| 4 oz. olive oil | pepper |
| salt and pepper | lemon juice |

*Court Bouillon*

| | |
|---|---|
| 2½ pints water | 1 onion studded with |
| ½ bottle dry white wine | 1 clove |
| 2 carrots | 6 sprigs parsley |
| 4 sticks celery | 1 bay leaf |
| | ½ teaspoon salt |

▶ Make court bouillon by bringing to a boil 2½ pints water, and ½ bottle dry white wine. Chop and add 2 carrots and 4 sticks of celery. Add 6 sprigs parsley, tied together, 1 bay leaf, 1 onion studded with clove and ½ teaspoon salt. Continue to boil 10 minutes.

▶ Rub a 2½ lb. piece of fresh cod with lemon juice. Put it in the boiling stock. Reduce heat and simmer, uncovered, until the fish is tender. Cool in the court bouillon. Take out fish, remove the skin and bones, and flake. Reserve the court bouillon.

▶ Boil 10 medium-sized potatoes in their jackets. Drain, peel and cut into slices ¼ inch thick.

▶ Slice 5 onions in thin slices lengthwise, not in rounds. Heat olive oil in a sauté pan or saucepan. Add onions, cook until golden. Add 1 large tin of tomato purée, ¼ teaspoon sugar, ½ teaspoon cayenne pepper and 4 tablespoons court bouillon. Mix well. Add the potatoes and cook over low heat, stirring gently until the potato slices are well coated with tomato sauce. Add the fish, being careful not to break up the fish flakes. Put in an ovenproof dish. Cover and keep in the refrigerator.

▶ Next evening pour over the fish 4 oz. of the reserved court bouillon (if the mixture seems dry) and reheat, covered in a moderate oven, 350°F, Reg 4, for 20–30 minutes.

# Melon Ice Cream

| | |
|---|---|
| 1 large canteloupe | ½ tablespoon lemon |
| melon | juice |
| 8 oz. castor sugar | 12 oz. double cream |
| 4 egg yolks | green leaves |

▶ Cut a slice off the stalk end of a canteloupe melon. Remove seeds. Scoop out its flesh, being careful not to damage the shell. Blend in a liquidizer with 8 oz. castor sugar. Put in a double boiler. Add 4 well-beaten egg yolks. Stirring continuously, cook over hot but not boiling water until the consistency of a thin custard. Remove from heat. When cold stir in ½ tablespoon lemon juice. Whip 12 oz. double cream and fold into the mixture. Pour into a refrigerator tray and freeze until the outer edge is solid. Transfer to a bowl and beat with a rotary beater until smooth. Return to refrigerator tray, cover with foil and freeze until firm.

▶ Fill the shell of the melon, replace its top slice and serve on a bed of green leaves.

## MENU

*Hot Potted Shrimps*

*Boeuf Miroton*

*German Potato Salad*

*Biscuit Tante Marie*

## Hot Potted Shrimps

| | |
|---|---|
| 1 large carton potted shrimps | 6 hard-boiled eggs parsley or watercress melba toast and butter |

▶ Chop the shrimps finely. Put them in an ovenproof dish in a medium oven, 350°F, Reg 4, until the butter melts. Remove immediately.

Chop finely 6 hard-boiled eggs. Mix thoroughly with the shrimps. Make a mound of them in the centre of a serving plate and surround with parsley or watercress. Serve with slices of melba toast and butter.

## Boeuf Miroton

| | |
|---|---|
| 1½ lb. boiled beef | 2 teaspoons wine or |
| 2 oz. butter | cider vinegar |
| 3 onions | ½ teaspoon dry |
| ½ oz. flour | mustard |
| 12 oz. beef stock, fresh or cubes | 2 level teaspoons horseradish |
| | 3 small dill gherkins |
| | 2 tablespoons chopped parsley |
| salt and pepper to taste | |

▶ Cut 1½ lb. of left-over boiled beef into ¼-inch slices.

▶ Melt 2 oz. butter in a saucepan. Add 3 onions finely chopped. Cook until golden. Add ½ oz. plain flour, cook 5 minutes longer. Add 12 oz. stock slowly, stirring constantly, cook for 10 minutes. Add 1 teaspoon vinegar, salt and pepper to taste. Add ½ teaspoon dry mustard dissolved in 1 teaspoon vinegar, 2 teaspoons of horseradish, and 3 small gherkins sliced thinly. Cook until well mixed but do not let it boil. Take the sauce off the heat, add 1 tablespoon chopped parsley.

▶ Pour some of the sauce in the bottom of a buttered heat-proof serving dish. Lay the slices of meat on the sauce and cover with the rest of the sauce. Put in refrigerator.

▶ To serve, reheat, covered, in a warm oven, 330°F, Reg 3 for $\frac{1}{2}$–$\frac{3}{4}$ hour. Sprinkle with the remaining tablespoon of chopped parsley. Serve with German Potato Salad.

## German Potato Salad

| | |
|---|---|
| 6 medium-sized waxy potatoes | $\frac{1}{2}$ teaspoon sugar |
| 2 sticks celery | $\frac{1}{4}$ teaspoon dry mustard |
| 1 onion | 2 teaspoons caraway seeds |
| 4 oz. wine vinegar | |
| 2 oz. stock, fresh or cubes | salt and pepper |
| $\frac{1}{2}$ teaspoon salt | chopped chives |
| | 6 thin slices lean bacon |

▶ Cook in their jackets 6 medium-sized waxy potatoes, until tender. Drain. When cool, remove the skins and cut into smallish cubes. Thinly slice crosswise 2 celery sticks. Add to the potatoes. Store in a covered container in the refrigerator.

▶ Mince and fry until crisp 6 slices of lean bacon. Remove from the frying pan, reserving the fat, and drain on absorbent paper. When all the fat is absorbed, put aside in a plastic bag or container.

▶ In the bacon fat fry 1 finely chopped onion until golden brown—you need at least 1 heaped tablespoon of fat, and may have to add more if necessary.

▶ Heat to boiling point 4 oz. wine vinegar, 2 oz. stock, $\frac{1}{2}$ teaspoon salt, $\frac{1}{2}$ teaspoon sugar, and $\frac{1}{4}$ teaspoon dry mustard. Add to the hot onions. When cool, store in a screw-top jar.

▶ Next day, in a bowl, mix the potatoes, the bacon, celery and 2 teaspoons of caraway seeds.

▶ To serve, reheat the onion mixture to boiling point. Pour over the potatoes.

Mix well. Add salt and pepper if necessary. Put in a serving bowl and sprinkle with chopped chives.

## Biscuit Tante Marie

| Cake | Filling |
|---|---|
| 6 eggs | 6 oz. unsalted butter |
| 5 oz. castor sugar | $3\frac{1}{2}$ oz. icing sugar |
| 3 oz. plain flour | 1 egg yolk |
| | 3 tablespoons strong black coffee |
| | icing sugar to finish |

▶ Separate the yolks and whites of 6 eggs.

▶ Beat the yolks and slowly beat in the sugar until the whole is a creamy yellow. Add the flour a bit at a time and beat the mixture until it is smooth.

▶ Beat the whites of 6 eggs until stiff and standing in a peak. Fold into the above mixture.

▶ Grease and flour a 9-inch cake tin. Pour in the batter and bake for approximately 40–50 minutes in an oven at 275°F, Reg $\frac{1}{2}$–1. Test with a skewer. When cool, cut into 2 layers.

### Coffee Cream Filling

▶ Cream until soft 6 oz. unsalted butter. Add $3\frac{1}{2}$ oz. icing sugar gradually and cream until light and smooth. Add slightly beaten egg yolk and stir until thoroughly mixed. Add 3 tablespoons strong black coffee and mix thoroughly. Spread between the cake layers and dust the top with icing sugar.

# 30

## MENU

*Artichokes Vinaigrette*

*Chicken San Remo*

*Italian Courgettes*

*Peach Clafouti*

## Artichokes Vinaigrette

| | |
|---|---|
| 6 artichokes | 1 clove garlic |
| 3 tablespoons olive oil | ½ lemon |

▶ Wash 6 artichokes—hold each by its stalk and dash up and down in a deep bowl of water. Cut off the stalks. Pull off the tough bottom row of leaves. Using scissors, cut off half the tops. Rub each artichoke with a lemon to avoid discoloration. Heat 3 tablespoons olive oil in a large pan with 1 clove unpeeled garlic. Place the artichokes upright in the pan. Cover and cook over a low medium heat for 10 minutes. Now pour boiling water over them, until the artichokes start to float. Cover and cook over medium heat for 45 minutes. Remove from water and drain upside down. When cool remove the inner core with a teaspoon.

▶ Place in refrigerator until needed. To serve, pour vinaigrette sauce in the well of each artichoke. Have a bowl of vinaigrette on the table if additional sauce is needed.

## Vinaigrette Sauce

| | |
|---|---|
| 6 tablespoons olive oil | white pepper |
| 3 tablespoon wine vinegar | ½ teaspoon made mustard |
| 1 tablespoon tarragon vinegar | |

▶ Mix salt, pepper and mustard together, add the oil, add the vinegars. Pour into a jar with a screw top and shake vigorously.

## Chicken San Remo

| | |
|---|---|
| 1 3-lb. to 4-lb. chicken | 4 carrots |
| 2 oz. plain flour | 1 small tin pimentoes |
| 2 oz. paprika (sweet, Hungarian) | 7 oz. green and black olives, mixed |
| 2 teaspoons salt | 1 teaspoon chopped tarragon, fresh or dried |
| 4 oz. butter | |
| 2 oz. olive oil | |
| 3 large onions | 1 teaspoon chopped basil, fresh or dried |
| 2 cloves garlic | |
| ¼ lb. mushrooms | 2 tablespoons chopped parsley |
| 1 large tin whole tomatoes | |
| | 1 small tin Italian tomato purée |
| 1 tin beef consommé or ¾ pint chicken or beef stock or cubes | ½ teaspoon celery seed |
| | ½ teaspoon sugar |
| | salt and pepper to taste |

▶ Have a 3-lb. or 4-lb. roasting chicken cut into pieces. Mix 2 oz. plain flour, 2 oz. paprika and 2 teaspoons salt, spread on a piece of kitchen paper. Roll each piece of chicken in the mixture until thoroughly covered. Reserve the giblets.

▶ In a frying or sauté pan heat 4 oz. butter and 2 oz. olive oil. Fry the chicken in it until well browned on all sides. Remove from the frying pan to a well-buttered casserole with a tight-fitting lid.

▶ Chop very finely 3 large onions and 2 cloves of peeled garlic. Brown in the fat left in the frying pan. Add ¼ lb. mushrooms, washed and sliced thinly, then the giblets, chopped and sautéed for a few minutes. Pour in 1 tin consommé or substitute and 1 large tin whole tomatoes, simmer slowly. Peel and chop coarsely 4 carrots, chop 1 small tin pimentoes and 7 oz. black and green olives. Chop tarragon and basil. Chop parsley. Add all of these chopped ingredients to the sauce. Stir in contents of 1 small tin tomato purée, add ½ teaspoon sugar and ½ teaspoon celery seed. Season to taste and simmer for 10 minutes.

▶ Pour the sauce over the chicken in the casserole, cover and cook in a moderate oven 350°F, Reg 4 for 50 or 60 minutes or until the chicken is tender, adding a little consommé from time to time if it seems to be getting dry.

▶ Remove from oven and when cool put into the refrigerator until next day.

▶ Reheat in a moderate oven 350°F, Reg 4 for 20–30 minutes. Serve in the casserole, with a dish of rice separately.

## Italian Courgettes

| | |
|---|---|
| 4 courgettes | 1 clove garlic |
| 1 onion | 3 tablespoons olive oil |
| 1 green pepper | salt and pepper to taste |

▶ Wash and slice in ½-inch slices 4 courgettes. Sprinkle them with salt and let them drain for ½ hour. Dry with a soft cloth or on kitchen paper. Peel the onion and slice very thinly crosswise. Wash and cut in half 1 green pepper. Remove seeds and white membranes. Cut in thin strips. Heat 3 tablespoons olive oil in a saucepan, add sliced onion and pepper and 1 crushed clove of garlic. Cook for 5 minutes, stirring continuously. Add the courgettes. Season to taste with very little salt and some pepper. Cook over low heat until tender. Store in refrigerator.

▶ In the evening reheat over low heat and serve in heated vegetable dish.

## Peach Clafouti

| | |
|---|---|
| 8 peaches | 3 egg yolks |
| ½ lemon | 1½ oz. sugar |
| 12 macaroons | 8 oz. single cream |
| 4 oz. kirsch | |

▶ Remove the skins from 8 peaches by scalding with boiling water. Tinned may be used if fresh ones not available. Cut in ½ and place in a buttered shallow baking dish. Sprinkle with the juice of ½ a lemon.

▶ Soak 12 macaroons in 4 oz. kirsch. Crumble and fill the centres of the peaches. Dust with sugar. Beat 3 egg yolks with 1½ oz. sugar. Fold in 8 oz. single cream. Pour mixture over peaches. Bake in a moderate oven 350°F, Reg 4 about 30 minutes or until the peaches are tender. This may be prepared 1 day before or in the morning. Serve chilled.

# 31

## MENU

*Cold Green Bean Soup*

*Roumanian Lamb Pie with Tomato Sauce, Buttered Peas*

*Gorgonzola Cream*

## Cold Green Bean Soup

| | |
|---|---|
| 1 lb. French beans | 4 oz. single cream |
| 16 oz. tinned consommé | 1 egg yolk |
| 1 teaspoon salt | 1 teaspoon lemon juice |
| 1 bay leaf | 4 oz. double cream |
| 1 oz. plain flour | chopped parsley |
| fresh ground pepper | chopped chives |
| 12 oz. milk | 1 tablespoon Bovril |

▶ Cut 1 lb. French beans in small pieces crosswise after removing the ends and strings. Cook in 16 oz. tinned consommé with the bay leaf and 1 teaspoon salt until tender. Drain. Reserve the stock.

▶ Thicken the stock by adding 1 oz. plain flour mixed smooth in 3 tablespoons cold water. Add pepper to taste.

▶ Bring to boil. Add 12 oz. milk, 4 oz. single cream and drained beans. Cook gently 3 minutes, add 1 egg yolk beaten with 2 or 3 tablespoons of the boiling soup. Add 1 tablespoon Bovril and continue cooking on a low heat for 5 minutes, stirring continuously, but do not reboil.

▶ Cool. Stir in 1 teaspoon lemon juice and 4 oz. double cream. Chill thoroughly. Sprinkle with chopped chives and parsley when serving.

## Roumanian Lamb Pie

*Filling*

| | |
|---|---|
| 2 lb. lamb, boned shoulder or leg | 8 large mushrooms |
| 1½ oz. butter | 3 slices white bread |
| 4 oz. stock, fresh or cubes | 2 oz. raisins |
| 1 teaspoon salt | 3 oz. almond slivers |
| ½ teaspoon pepper | ½ tablespoon chopped parsley |
| 2 onions | juice of ½ lemon |

2 packets frozen peas and a little butter

*Crust*

| | |
|---|---|
| 1¼ lb. plain flour | 2 egg yolks |
| 8 oz. butter | 3–4 tablespoons single |
| pinch of salt | cream |

▶ Cut 2 lb. of lamb into slices. Melt 1 oz. butter and, over a moderate heat, fry slices on both sides. Add 4 oz. stock, 1 teaspoon salt and ½ teaspoon pepper. Simmer until lamb is tender. Remove slices and cut into small pieces. Reserve sauce.

▶ Remove the stalks and wash thoroughly 8 large mushrooms. Chop coarsely. Chop 2 onions and fry until lightly browned in ½ oz. butter. Add mushrooms and 2 oz. raisins. Cook 5 minutes.

▶ Cut crusts from 3 slices white bread and soak in a little milk. Squeeze dry.

▶ Add meat, bread, 3 oz. slivered almonds, and ½ tablespoon chopped parsley to the onions. Pour over the reserved sauce and the juice of ½ lemon, mix thoroughly. Correct seasoning if necessary.

▶ Put 1¼ lb. plain flour in a bowl and with a pastry cutter or 2 knives cut 8 oz. butter into it. Add 2 egg yolks, a pinch of salt, and 3 or 4 tablespoons single cream. With your hand, knead lightly so that the dough barely holds together. Chill.

▶ Take a little more than a third of the dough and roll out to make a very thin lining for a 9-inch pie plate. Prick generously with a fork and line with crumpled tin foil. Bake about 12 minutes in a pre-heated oven at 420°F, Reg 7, and remove the foil after about 5 minutes. Cool.

▶ Roll out the remaining dough to the size of the pie plate—it will make a thicker crust than the bottom. Fill the shell with the meat. Cover with the unbaked crust, press the edges firmly together. Wrap in foil and put in refrigerator overnight.

▶ Next night bake in a pre-heated oven at 400°F, Reg 6 until thoroughly heated and top is a light brown, about 12 to 15 minutes. To protect the baked crust from over-browning put the pie in an extra pan to keep it from too much heat. Serve with Tomato Sauce.

## Tomato Sauce

| | |
|---|---|
| 12 oz. tomato purée | ½ teaspoon salt |
| 4 oz. stock, fresh or | ½ teaspoon sugar |
| cubes | 1 tablespoon |
| 1 onion | chopped basil |
| 1 tablespoon olive oil | pepper to taste |

▶ In a saucepan fry 1 finely chopped onion in 1 tablespoon olive oil until slightly browned. Add 12 oz. tomato purée, 4 oz. stock, ½ teaspoon salt, ½ teaspoon sugar and 1 tablespoon chopped basil. Cook over low heat 30 minutes, stirring occasionally. If it becomes too thick add a little more stock. Correct seasoning. Put aside until next evening. Reheat over low heat.

▶ Before the guests arrive cook 2 packets of frozen peas. Reheat in melted butter, and serve with the pie.

## Gorgonzola Cream

| | |
|---|---|
| 5 oz. gorgonzola | salad leaves |
| cheese | sliced pumpernickel |
| 5 oz. mayonnaise | butter |
| (Menu 48) | |

▶ Blend the mayonnaise with the cheese, rind removed, and stir until the mixture has a smooth, creamy consistency.

▶ Serve on a bed of, and surrounded by, salad leaves, accompanied by thinly sliced buttered pumpernickel.

# 32

## MENU

*Avocados with Grapes*

*Saddle of Hare in Sour Cream*

*Purée of Lentils*

*Kissel*

## Avocados with Grapes

| | |
|---|---|
| 3 avocados | 1 bunch grapes, about |
| ½ cucumber | ¾ lb. |
| | 4–5 oz. dry white wine |
| | freshly ground pepper |

▶ Peel ½ cucumber. Cut in ½ lengthwise and remove seeds. Chop very fine. Sprinkle with a little freshly ground pepper.

▶ Skin and pip 1 bunch grapes. Soak in 4–5 oz. dry white wine for ½ hour.

▶ Drain grapes and combine with the cucumber. Chill.

▶ Cut the avocados in half just before serving—to avoid discoloration. Fill with the grape mixture and serve.

## Saddle of Hare in Sour Cream

| | |
|---|---|
| 1 saddle of a hare | 1¼ pints stock, |
| 4 tablespoons oil | fresh or |
| (vegetable) | cubes |
| 4 carrots | 8 oz. red wine |
| 2 leeks | 6 oz. sour cream |
| 1 cup parsley sprigs | 2 bay leaves |
| 1 onion | salt and pepper |
| level tablespoon red- | juice ½ lemon |
| currant jelly | |

▶ Ask the butcher to lard the saddle of a hare and cut it in 2-inch slices.

▶ Chop 4 carrots, 2 leeks, 1 cup parsley sprigs and 1 onion.

▶ Heat 3 tablespoons oil in a saucepan or deep sauté pan and sauté the pieces of hare on a slow heat for 10 minutes. Take them out and put aside on a warm plate.

▶ Add another tablespoon of oil to the oil in which the hare has cooked, add the chopped vegetables and sauté, on gentle heat, until they are soft, stirring them from time to time so they do not stick to the pan, for about 10 minutes.

▶ Put the vegetables and hare in an iron or enamelled pot. Add 1¼ pints of stock and 4 oz. red wine, stir well and add only 2 oz. sour cream and stir again. Salt and pepper and put in 2 bay leaves. Cover the pot and put in a medium oven at 350°F, Reg 4 for 1 hour and 40 minutes. If the liquid reduces too much, add the rest of the wine and a little water. Remove from the oven, remove the pieces of hare and put aside. When they are cool, wrap them in tin foil and put in the refrigerator until they are to be served. Strain the sauce and place in a covered bowl in the refrigerator.

▶ Next evening, put the hare and the strained sauce in a saucepan, add the juice of ½ a lemon and reheat. Stir in a level tablespoon of red-currant jelly, 4 oz. of sour cream, heat to the boiling point and serve.

# Purée of Lentils

11 oz. lentils
16 oz. water
8 oz. stock, fresh or cubes
1 carrot
1 stick of celery
1 onion

$1\frac{1}{2}$ teaspoons salt
$\frac{1}{4}$ teaspoon pepper
1 bay leaf
butter
dash of powdered clove

▶ Soak the lentils overnight or 6 hours in 16 oz. water. Add 8 oz. stock, 1 carrot, 1 stick celery, 1 onion, $1\frac{1}{2}$ teaspoons salt, $\frac{1}{4}$ teaspoon pepper and 1 bay leaf. Simmer until tender.

▶ Drain the lentils and vegetables and put through a fine sieve or into a liquidizer. Allow for every cup of purée, tea-cup size, $\frac{1}{2}$ tablespoon of butter and a dash of powdered clove, mix well.

▶ Whip the purée over a high heat until thoroughly hot and serve.

# Kissel

$1\frac{1}{4}$ pints cranberry juice
8 oz. juice tinned blue plums

scant 1 oz. potato flour
$1\frac{1}{2}$ tablespoons cold water
double cream for serving

▶ Heat the cranberry and plum juice together, sweetening to taste if the cranberry juice is of the unsweetened variety.

▶ Mix the potato flour and water and add to the hot juice, stirring constantly. Remove from the fire as soon as the mixture thickens and becomes transparent. It must never boil as it becomes sticky and tasteless if it does.

▶ Chill and serve with cream.

# 33

## MENU

*Prawns and Artichokes, Pepperoni Relish*

*Veal Gulyas*

*Gnocchi Loaf*

*Apple Pudding*

## Prawns and Artichokes

| | |
|---|---|
| 1 tin artichoke hearts | 2 tablespoons wine |
| 1 packet frozen | vinegar |
|   prawns | ½ teaspoon salt |
| 6 tablespoons olive oil | ¼ teaspoon pepper |
| | chopped parsley |
| | bunch of watercress |

▶ Drain 1 tin artichoke hearts in a colander. Pour over hot and then cold water and thoroughly drain. Shake vigorously in a jar with a screw top 6 tablespoons olive oil, 2 tablespoons wine vinegar, ½ teaspoon salt and ¼ teaspoon pepper. Pour dressing over the artichoke hearts and marinate overnight.

▶ Following instructions on the packet, prepare 1 packet of frozen prawns. Mix cold prawns with 4 tablespoons Pepperoni Relish.

▶ To serve, mix the marinade from the artichoke with the prawns and fill each heart. Sprinkle with chopped parsley and serve on a bed of watercress and parsley.

## Pepperoni Relish

| | |
|---|---|
| 12 red peppers | 8 oz. granulated sugar |
| 2 large onions | 1 tablespoon salt |
| 16 oz. of wine vinegar | |

▶ This will be much more than you need; keep the rest in jars with screw tops. It will keep indefinitely in a cold place. Note that it is also used in Menu 65.

▶ Split 12 red peppers and remove the seeds. Chop peppers coarsely, pour boiling water over them and let stand for 5 minutes. Drain. Pour more boiling water over them and let stand for 10 minutes. Drain. Add 2 chopped onions.

▶ Boil 16 oz. wine vinegar, 8 oz. granulated sugar and 1 tablespoon salt for 5 minutes. Pour over the peppers. Cook for 10 minutes after the mixture has come to the boil. Put into hot glass jars. Store in refrigerator or cool place.

▶ Use sufficient relish to moisten the prawns and artichokes thoroughly.

## Veal Gulyas

3-lb. shoulder or other boneless joint of veal
  cut into 1-inch cubes
1 lb. finely cut onions
3 tablespoons paprika or more to taste
chicken stock to cover
1 carton sour cream (5 oz.) or 1 carton cream
  and ½ tablespoon of lemon juice
1 oz. lard
1 scant teaspoon salt

▶ Melt 1 oz. lard in a flameproof casserole. Add 1 lb. finely cut onions and fry 10–15 minutes on a low heat until soft and pale yellow. Now add the 1-inch cubes of veal and cook, stirring all the time until the veal looks whitish. Shake over the 3 tablespoons paprika and the scant teaspoon salt. Cover with boiling chicken stock and cook over low heat until the meat is soft, which should be approximately 50 minutes to 1 hour. Add more stock if necessary, as a Veal Gulyas should have plenty of gravy.

▶ Remove the cubes of meat, scraping off all the onions. Press the onions and sauce through a sieve, or liquidizer, and let it stand for an hour. Skim off any fat and taste for seasoning. It should taste slightly sharp. Place the sauce and meat in an ovenproof serving dish and keep in refrigerator.

▶ Next evening add the sour cream, before reheating. Pour the cream in slowly and taste again and again, as a whole carton of sour cream added may not be to your liking. Reheat, covered, either on top of the stove or in the oven at 350°F, Reg 4 for 20–30 minutes.

▶ Serve in a deep serving dish.

## Gnocchi Loaf

| | |
|---|---|
| 1 small loaf white bread | 1 teaspoon salt |
| 4 oz. milk | $\frac{1}{4}$ teaspoon pepper |
| 3 egg yolks | 4 oz. olive oil |

▶ Cut the crusts from 1 loaf of white bread. Break loaf into pieces and pour over 4 oz. milk. When bread is thoroughly saturated, using a cheesecloth gently squeeze out the milk, leaving the bread very moist. Add 3 beaten egg yolks, 1 teaspoon salt, and $\frac{1}{4}$ teaspoon pepper. Mix well. Stir in 4 oz. olive oil, beat with a wooden spoon until all of the oil is absorbed. Put aside for an hour at least.

▶ Form bread mixture into a loaf 2 to 2$\frac{1}{2}$ inches in diameter. Grease a large piece of tin-foil. Wrap the loaf in the foil, turning in the sides, and secure with a lot of rubber bands, not too tight as it will expand as it cooks. You will find the loaf mixture very

liquid, but it keeps the loaf from being too heavy. Simmer gently in a large pan of boiling water for 1 hour. Take it out of the water and, as soon as it is cool enough to handle, remove the rubber bands and the foil. When cold, wrap in another piece of foil and store in the refrigerator.

▶ Next day, cut into slices half an inch thick and reheat in steamer. Serve separately, at the same time as the Gulyas.

## Apple Pudding

| | |
|---|---|
| 8 cooking apples | $\frac{1}{2}$ rounded teaspoon cinnamon |
| 2$\frac{1}{2}$ oz. butter | 4 oz. orange juice |
| 5 oz. brown sugar | 2 oz. lemon juice |
| 2 oz. plain flour | grated orange and lemon rind |
| | jug of cream |

▶ Pare, core and cut 8 cooking apples lengthwise into thin slices.

▶ Combine 2$\frac{1}{2}$ oz. butter, 5 oz. brown sugar, 2 oz. plain flour and $\frac{1}{2}$ teaspoon cinnamon. Work into a crumb-like mixture.

▶ Alternate layers of sliced apples and crumb mixture in a buttered ovenproof dish until all of it is used.

▶ Pour 4 oz. orange juice and 2 oz. lemon juice over the pudding and sprinkle with the grated rind. Cover and store in the refrigerator.

▶ To serve, bake in a moderate oven, 350°F, Reg 4, for 1 hour. If necessary turn the oven off and let it stand until serving time. Serve warm with a small jug of cream.

# 34

## MENU

*Corn and Bean Sprout Salad*

*King's Moussaka*

*Lemon Water Ice with
Raspberry Sauce*

## Corn and Bean Sprout Salad

| | |
|---|---|
| 1 large tin sweet-corn kernels | $\frac{1}{2}$ teaspoon salt |
| 3 small onions or 3 big spring onions | $\frac{1}{8}$ teaspoon pepper |
| | 2 mint leaves |
| 4 tablespoons olive oil | 2 tablespoons chopped parsley |
| 2 tablespoons lemon juice | $\frac{1}{4}$ lb. Chinese bean sprouts or tin of bean sprouts |

salt and pepper to taste
lettuce leaves for serving

▶ Drain 1 large tin of sweet-corn kernels. Cut in paper-thin slices 3 small onions or 3 big spring onions. Add to corn with 2 tablespoons chopped parsley and 2 chopped mint leaves.

▶ Shake well in a jar 4 tablespoons olive oil, 2 tablespoons lemon juice, $\frac{1}{2}$ teaspoon salt and pinch of pepper. Pour over the corn.

▶ Cook in boiling salt water for 10 minutes $\frac{1}{4}$ lb. of fresh Chinese bean sprouts or tinned. Drain. Run cold water over them if using fresh and drain again. Add to the corn, mix well, correct seasoning if necessary and marinate overnight in the refrigerator.

▶ Serve thoroughly chilled on a bed of lettuce leaves.

# King's Moussaka

| | |
|---|---|
| 4 medium-sized aubergines | 12 oz. stock, fresh or cubes |
| ½ lemon | 3 tablespoons tomato purée |
| 2 lb. minced veal | |
| 8 tablespoons olive oil | pinch of sugar |
| 4 large onions | 2 egg yolks |
| 8 oz. cream | ½ teaspoon flour |
| | 2 oz. parmesan cheese |
| salt and pepper to taste | |

▶ Cut 4 unpeeled, medium-sized aubergines into slices ½ inch thick. To prevent discoloration, rub each slice with the ½ lemon and then with salt. Stack the slices on absorbent paper, cover with a plate, put a weight on top and let stand until the moisture is squeezed out, at least ½ hour.

▶ Chop 4 large onions. Fry in 4 tablespoons hot olive oil until slightly brown. Add 2 lb. minced veal. Stirring with a wooden spoon so that it does not stick to the pan, cook until the meat is slightly browned. Dilute 3 tablespoons tomato purée and a pinch of sugar with 12 oz. stock. Add to the meat and onions only 4 oz. of this mixture, salt and pepper to taste. Mix well and set aside.

▶ Dry each slice of aubergine with a cloth, dust lightly with flour and fry 4 at a time in 4 tablespoons of hot olive oil. Add more oil if you need towards the end of the frying. Cook 2 minutes on each side, and put on an absorbent paper to drain off excess grease.

▶ Grease lightly with a bit of olive oil the bottom of a large ovenproof dish. Put in a layer of aubergines and, over them, a layer of meat. Continue with alternate layers until used. Last layer must be meat. Pour over the remaining 8 oz. of tomato stock. Bake in a moderate oven 350°F, Reg 4 until sauce is reduced, at least ½ hour. Remove from oven and when cooled store in a refrigerator or a cool place.

▶ Next day beat the egg yolks with the flour and pour the egg mixture over the Moussaka. Sprinkle with 2 oz. parmesan cheese. Reheat in a moderate oven 350°F, Reg 4 about ¾ of an hour. Increase the oven heat at the end if necessary. It must be golden brown.

▶ A Moussaka must be made 24 hours in advance.

# Lemon Water Ice with Raspberry Sauce

| | |
|---|---|
| 6 oz. lemon juice | 1 packet frozen raspberries |
| 6 oz. castor sugar | |
| 12 oz. milk | 1 tablespoon framboise liqueur or kirsch |
| 8 oz. double cream | |
| grated rind 2 lemons | |

▶ In a bowl combine 6 oz. of lemon juice and 6 oz. castor sugar. Mix thoroughly with a wooden spoon, and mix in the lemon rind. Gradually pour in 12 oz. milk and 8 oz. double cream. Stir until the sugar is dissolved. Pour into a refrigerator tray and freeze until it is solid around the edges. Put mixture in the bowl of an electric mixer and beat until it is smooth. Return the mixture to the refrigerator tray, cover the tray with foil and freeze until the mixture is firm.

▶ In a liquidizer purée 1 packet of frozen raspberries that have been partially thawed. Stir in 1 tablespoon framboise liqueur or 1 tablespoon kirsch.

▶ Serve the Lemon Water Ice in chilled glasses with the raspberry purée as a sauce.

# 35

MENU

*Fried Stuffed Artichokes, Dipping Sauce*

*Boeuf Bourguignon*

*Purée of Cabbage*

*Stella's Cheese and Almond Cake*

½ tablespoon salt. Cook for 30 to 40 minutes or until tender. Drain. When cool enough to handle, slice the artichokes in half lengthwise, remove fuzzy choke.

▶ Mix 4–5 oz. coarse breadcrumbs, 1 oz. grated parmesan cheese, 3 tablespoons chopped parsley, celery salt to taste and 1 teaspoon lemon juice. When well mixed fill each artichoke cavity with this stuffing. Store in refrigerator until next day.

▶ To serve, sprinkle the 2 oz. melted butter over the stuffed artichokes. Grill 4 inches away from the heat for 5 minutes until the stuffing is golden brown. Serve hot with Dipping Sauce.

## Dipping Sauce

| | |
|---|---|
| 4 oz. butter | 1 teaspoon lemon juice |
| 1 oz. grated parmesan cheese | ¼ teaspoon pepper |

▶ Melt 4 oz. butter in a saucepan. Stir in 1 oz. grated parmesan cheese, 1 teaspoon lemon juice and ¼ teaspoon pepper. Set aside. To serve, reheat over high heat, stirring constantly. Serve immediately.

## Fried Stuffed Artichokes

| | |
|---|---|
| 3 large artichokes | 1 oz. grated parmesan cheese |
| 1 clove garlic | |
| 6 tablespoons olive oil | 3 tablespoons chopped parsley |
| ½ tablespoon salt | |
| 4–5 oz. coarse breadcrumbs | celery salt to taste |
| | 1 teaspoon lemon juice |
| | 2 oz. melted butter |

▶ Wash 3 large artichokes. Cut off prickly leaf-tips. Trim stems.

▶ Heat 6 tablespoons olive oil and 1 clove of peeled garlic in a deep pan. Put in the artichokes. Cover. Cook over moderate heat for 10 minutes, and then pour over boiling water until they float. Add

## Boeuf Bourguignon

| | |
|---|---|
| 2 lb. topside beef | 1½ tablespoons flour |
| 2 large onions | |
| 2 carrots | 8 oz. stock, fresh or cubes |
| 1 clove garlic | |
| 2 sprigs thyme | 3 sprigs of parsley |
| 3 bay leaves | 2 sticks of celery |
| 2 tablespoons olive oil | ½ lb. button mushrooms |
| ¼ pint red wine | |
| 1 teaspoon salt | 1 tablespoon tomato purée |
| ¼ teaspoon pepper | |
| 2 ¼-inch thick rashers streaky bacon | 2 oz. brandy |
| 12 button or pickling onions | |
| 1½ tablespoons beef dripping | |

▶ Cut 2 lb. topside beef into 2-inch cubes. Put in a china dish, season with 1 teaspoon salt and ¼ teaspoon pepper. Cover with 2 large onions thinly sliced, 2 sliced carrots, 1 crushed garlic clove, 1 sprig of thyme and 2 bay leaves. Shake 2 tablespoons olive oil and ¼ pint red wine in a bottle until well mixed. Pour over the meat. Marinate for at least 6 hours or overnight.

▶ Cut 2 ¼-inch thick rashers of bacon into ¼-inch strips crosswise. Melt 1½ tablespoons beef dripping in a heavy stewing pan. Cook bacon strips and 12 button onions in this fat until bacon becomes transparent and onions are nicely coloured. Take out and set aside. Reserve the fat.

▶ Drain the meat cubes, reserving the marinade. Dry each cube carefully, heat fat and brown quickly on all sides in the hot fat. Sprinkle with 1½ tablespoons flour. Shake the pan so that the flour mixes with the fat and absorbs it. Pour over the strained marinade and 8 oz. stock. Put in 1 bouquet garni (3 sprigs parsley, 2 sticks of celery, 1 sprig thyme, and 1 bay leaf tied together with a string). Add the brandy, previously heated and flamed in a small pan. Bring to a boil. Cover with a tight lid. Reduce heat and simmer for 2 hours. Remove the bouquet garni and set aside until next day.

▶ Next day remove fat from the top of the Bourguignon and reheat slowly over low heat.

▶ Wash carefully ½ lb. button mushrooms. Cut off stalks. Fry for a few minutes in a little butter to remove moisture. Add to the meat with the reserved bacon and onions. Stir in 1 tablespoon tomato purée. Cook slowly over low heat for ½ hour. Set aside until serving time.

▶ To serve. Reheat over low heat. Serve with Purée of Cabbage.

## Purée of Cabbage

| 1 head green cabbage | 1 oz. butter |
| 2 oz. single cream | salt and pepper |

▶ Wash 1 head of green cabbage. Cut in half. Cut out the core. Slice each half into thin shreds. Put in a medium-sized saucepan. Pour over boiling water to cover. Cook for 7 minutes. Drain. Blend in a liquidizer with 2 oz. single cream. Add 1 oz. butter. Salt and pepper to taste. Set aside in a cool place.

▶ To serve. Reheat in the top of a double boiler. Add more cream if necessary.

## Stella's Cheese and Almond Cake

| 7 oz. cottage cheese | 7 oz. ground almonds |
| 10 oz. butter | 1 lemon |
| 8 oz. castor sugar | 1 pinch salt |
| 6 eggs | icing sugar |

▶ Put 7 oz. cottage cheese through a fine sieve.

▶ Cream 10 oz. butter. Slowly add 8 oz. castor sugar and cream until light and fluffy. Beat in one by one the yolks of 6 eggs. Beat well after the addition of each egg yolk. Stir in 7 oz. ground almonds. Mix well. Stir in the cottage cheese; mix well. Stir in the grated rind and juice of 1 lemon.

▶ Beat 6 egg whites, with a pinch of salt added, until stiff. Fold whites into the cake batter. Pour into a well-buttered and -floured baking tin, which has a removable bottom or rim. Bake in a pre-heated oven at 350°F, Reg 4 for ¾ of an hour. Remove from oven. Keep in the tin on a rack until cake is slightly cooled. Remove from tin and sprinkle with icing sugar.

# 36

## MENU

*Andalusian Soup*

*Cold Fried Chicken*

*Potato Salad*

*Barbara's Golden Syrup Delight*

## Andalusian Soup

| | |
|---|---|
| 2 medium onions | 1 bay leaf |
| 2 oz. butter | 3 sticks of celery with |
| 1½ pints stock, fresh or | leaves |
| cubes | 6 sprigs parsley |
| ¾ lb. peeled sliced | 1 sprig thyme |
| potatoes | 4 tablespoons |
| 2 tablespoons tomato | parmesan cheese |
| purée | salt and pepper |
| 1 teaspoon sugar | |
| 1 teaspoon oregano | |

▶ Slice finely 2 medium onions. Sauté in 2 oz. butter until soft. Do not let them brown. Add 1½ pints stock, 2 tablespoons tomato purée, ¾ lb. sliced potatoes, 1 teaspoon sugar, 1 teaspoon oregano, and a bouquet garni of 1 bay leaf, 3 sticks celery, 6 sprigs parsley, 1 sprig thyme tied together. Simmer for 1 hour. Remove bouquet and blend soup in a liquidizer until smooth. Cool and store in the refrigerator.

▶ To serve, reheat in a double boiler and just before serving stir in 4 tablespoons parmesan cheese. Salt and pepper to taste.

## Cold Fried Chicken

| | |
|---|---|
| 2 roasting chickens | 12 oz. butter |
| (2½–3 lb. each) | 4 oz. cooking oil |
| flour | milk |
| salt and pepper | |

▶ Ask the butcher to cut 2 roasting chickens, weighing 2½ lb. to 3 lb. each, as for a fricassee, wings, breasts, second joints and drumsticks. Salt and pepper them and place in the refrigerator for 1 hour.

▶ Roll the pieces of chicken in flour to which you have added salt and pepper. Dip the pieces one by one in milk and roll in flour again.

▶ Melt 12 oz. butter and 4 oz. cooking oil in a heavy saucepan. When both are very hot put in the pieces of chicken. As soon as the mixture of oil and butter foams around them, reduce the heat and fry on each side until tender, 20 to 30 minutes in all, being careful not to let them burn. Place the pieces on absorbent paper. When cold, store in the refrigerator. Strain the fats and keep in the refrigerator for further use.

▶ Serve with Potato Salad.

## Potato Salad

| | |
|---|---|
| 6 medium waxy potatoes | 1 medium onion |
| 8 oz. consommé, fresh or tinned | 8 oz. mayonnaise (Menu 48) |
| | salt and pepper to taste |
| | paprika |

▶ Cook in their jackets 6 medium waxy potatoes. Remove the skins and slice while they are hot.

▶ Grate 1 medium onion into 8 oz. hot consommé. Pour over sliced potatoes. Cool and put in covered dish in refrigerator overnight.

▶ Next day pour off liquid which has not been absorbed. Pour over 8 oz. mayonnaise and mix carefully so as not to break the slices. Serve in a bowl. Sprinkle with paprika.

## Barbara's Golden Syrup Delight

| | |
|---|---|
| 14 oz. light brown sugar | 9 oz. butter |
| 9 oz. golden syrup | 1 small loaf stale white bread |
| | $\frac{1}{4}-\frac{1}{2}$ pint double cream |

▶ Although this pudding needs a little last-minute preparation it is well worth the effort.

▶ Put 14 oz. light brown sugar, 9 oz. golden syrup and 9 oz. butter in a heavy saucepan. Cook over moderate heat until all the sugar has dissolved and you have a thick syrup. Set aside.

▶ Remove the crusts from 1 loaf of stale white bread. Cut into large cubes. Dip each cube in milk and put aside.

▶ To serve, reheat syrup until golden brown. Quickly but carefully stir in cubes of bread so they do not break too much. Serve immediately accompanied with a bowl of whipped cream.

# 37

## MENU

*Avocado Mousse*

*Poached Salmon, Sauce Mousseline*

*Cucumber Salad*

*Malakoff Cake*

## Avocado Mousse

| | |
|---|---|
| 2 large ripe avocados | $\frac{3}{4}$ oz. powdered |
| 1 teaspoon salt | gelatine |
| 1 teaspoon Dijon | 2 oz. boiling water |
| mustard | 4 oz. mayonnaise |
| 2 teaspoons | (Menu 48) |
| Worcester sauce | 6 oz. whipped cream |
| 1 teaspoon finely | watercress |
| grated onion | |

▶ Cut avocados through lengthwise. Remove stone and peel. Mash them to pulp with a fork. Put them into a basin with 1 teaspoon salt, 1 teaspoon mustard, 2 teaspoons Worcester sauce, 1 teaspoon finely grated onion. Stir well. Add 4 oz. mayonnaise, 6 oz. whipped cream and stir until smooth.

▶ Dissolve $\frac{3}{4}$ oz. powdered gelatine in 2 oz. boiling water. When gelatine is cool but not cold, add to ingredients in the basin. Rinse out a ring mould with cold water, fill with avocado mousse. Chill overnight. Turn out, garnish centre with watercress and keep in refrigerator until you serve.

## Poached Salmon

| | |
|---|---|
| 6 salmon steaks | 4 celery sticks, leafy |
| 1 pint water | part |
| 1 pint dry white wine | 8 sprigs parsley |
| 2 carrots | 1 sprig thyme |
| 2 onions | 1 bay leaf |
| 1 teaspoon salt | juice of 1 lemon |
| 2 cloves | $\frac{1}{2}$ a cucumber, sliced |
| a few peppercorns | fresh dill |

▶ Bring to a boil 1 pint water, 1 pint dry white wine, 2 carrots, 2 onions, sliced thinly, 2 cloves, 1 teaspoon salt, a few peppercorns, and a bouquet garni of the leafy parts of 4 celery sticks, 8 sprigs of parsley, 1 sprig of thyme and 1 bay leaf tied together. Simmer for $\frac{1}{2}$ hour. Strain. Add juice of 1 lemon. Poach 6 salmon steaks 1 inch thick in the court bouillon for 10 minutes. Cool in the court bouillon.

Remove and place in a covered dish in refrigerator until next evening. Serve thoroughly chilled with the cold Sauce Mousseline. Garnish with cucumber slices sprinkled with fresh dill.

▶ An old fishmonger told us that if you are pressed for time you can pack each salmon steak into greaseproof paper, tied up with string. Place into boiling water to boil for 6 minutes. Turn off heat and let them get cold in the water. It is definitely a success.

## Sauce Mousseline

| | |
|---|---|
| 4 egg yolks | $\frac{1}{4}$ teaspoon salt |
| 2 tablespoons lemon juice | 6 oz. butter |
| | $\frac{1}{4}$ pint double cream |

▶ Blend in your liquidizer the yolks of 4 eggs, 2 tablespoons lemon juice and $\frac{1}{4}$ teaspoon salt. Melt 6 oz. butter until it foams but do not let it brown. With your liquidizer at high speed pour the butter in a steady stream over the yolks. By the time you have finished pouring in the butter, the sauce will have thickened and will be ready. Whip $\frac{1}{4}$ pint double cream until thick and fold into the sauce. Serve cold but do not refrigerate.

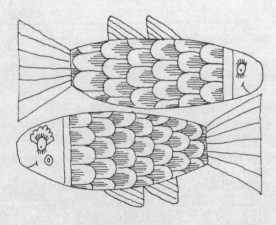

## Cucumber Salad

| | |
|---|---|
| 2 cucumbers | salt |
| 3 tablespoons olive oil | 3 tablespoons wine vinegar |
| 2 tablespoons chopped chervil, or parsley | pepper |

▶ Peel 2 cucumbers and cut in two lengthwise. Remove seeds and slice crosswise into very thin slices. Place on a wooden board and salt generously. Leave for $\frac{1}{2}$ hour. Drain and press in a soft towel or kitchen paper to remove liquid.

▶ Shake vigorously in a screw-topped jar 3 tablespoons olive oil, 3 tablespoons wine vinegar, 2 tablespoons chopped chervil or parsley, and a quantity of freshly ground pepper. Pour over cucumbers.

## Malakoff Cake

| | |
|---|---|
| 8 oz. butter | 3 oz. rum |
| 8 oz. castor sugar | 8 oz. water |
| 1 egg yolk | 30 sponge fingers |
| 3 oz. bitter chocolate | 8 oz. double cream |
| 3 tablespoons strong black coffee | |

▶ Cream 8 oz. butter. Add gradually 8 oz. castor sugar and cream until smooth and light. Stir in the beaten yolk of 1 egg. Mix thoroughly. Melt 3 oz. bitter chocolate in a double boiler, add the 3 tablespoons coffee, mix well and cool. Then stir into the cream mixture.

▶ Combine 3 oz. rum and 8 oz. water. Line the bottom of a rectangular cake tin with foil. Dip the sponge fingers one by one in the rum and line the bottom of the cake tin. Add a layer of chocolate mixture, then alternate layers, ending with sponge fingers, until all are used. Put in refrigerator overnight, covered in tin-foil.

▶ Beat 8 oz. double cream until stiff. Unmould the cake. Remove the layer of foil and mask, covering completely, with the stiffly beaten cream.

# 38

## MENU

*Halibut Salad*

*Esterhazy Rumpsteak,
Noodles in Brown Butter*

*Bombe Baur Au Lac*

## Halibut Salad

| | |
|---|---|
| $\frac{3}{4}$ pint dry white wine | 2 lb. halibut |
| $\frac{3}{4}$ pint water | 4 oz. lemon juice |
| 2 carrots | 8 oz. olive oil |
| 2 onions | $\frac{1}{2}$ teaspoon black |
| 2 sticks celery | pepper |
| 1 bay leaf | 1 tablespoon green |
| 4 sprigs parsley | chutney |
| 2 teaspoons salt | $\frac{1}{2}$ pint shelled shrimps |
| 6 peppercorns | 1 green pepper |
| | 1 round lettuce |

▶ Combine $\frac{3}{4}$ pint wine and $\frac{3}{4}$ pint water in a saucepan big enough to contain the fish. Peel and quarter 2 carrots and 2 onions. Put them into the wine mixture with 2 sticks celery, 1 bay leaf, 4 sprigs parsley, 1 teaspoon salt and 6 peppercorns. Simmer over moderate heat with the pan covered for $\frac{1}{2}$ hour.

▶ Place the fish in the hot liquid and over reduced heat simmer until the fish is opaque, about 20 minutes. Take off stove and cool in its cooking liquid. When cold, remove from liquid, skin, bone, flake, and put into a bowl with a spoonful or two of the liquid poured over to prevent drying. Refrigerate.

▶ Make the sauce by combining 4 oz. lemon juice, 8 oz. olive oil, $\frac{1}{2}$ teaspoon freshly ground pepper, 1 teaspoon salt and 1 tablespoon green chutney in a jar with a screw top. Shake until thoroughly mixed. Store in a cool place.

▶ Shell and refrigerate $\frac{1}{2}$ pint shrimps.

▶ Seed and cut 1 green pepper lengthwise in thin strips. Place strips in a plastic bag in the vegetable crisper of refrigerator. Wash lettuce leaves, drain carefully, wrap lightly in a towel and keep in the crisper.

▶ To serve, line a chilled salad bowl with lettuce leaves. Pile fish in centre and sprinkle with the shrimps and pepper strips on top. Shake the chutney mixture again thoroughly and pour over the salad.

# Esterhazy Rumpsteak, Noodles in Brown Butter

| | |
|---|---|
| 3 lb. rumpsteak | 10 oz. beef stock or |
| 2 oz. beef dripping | cubes |
| 4 carrots | 4 oz. sour cream |
| 2 onions | ½ teaspoon salt |
| 2 parsnips | ½ teaspoon pepper |
| 2 sticks of celery | 1 teaspoon paprika |
| ½ lb. butter | 2 level teaspoons |
| 1 oz. plain flour | capers |
| | 3 tablespoons madeira |
| | or sherry |
| | ½ lb. broad egg |
| | noodles |

▶ Heat 1 oz. dripping in a heavy frying pan and rapidly sear 3 lb. rumpsteak cut in thick slices. Season with salt and pepper and remove slices to a heavy casserole with a tight-fitting cover. Leave any remaining fat in the frying pan.

▶ Peel 4 carrots, 2 parsnips, 2 onions, 2 sticks of celery and chop them coarsely. Add 1 oz. more dripping to frying pan and sauté the vegetables for 10 minutes. Sprinkle with 1 teaspoon paprika, ½ oz. flour, mix well and slowly stir in 8 oz. bouillon, reserving 2 oz. Continue cooking slowly. Brown ½ oz. flour in ½ oz. butter in a small saucepan. When well coloured, add the remaining 2 oz. stock, mix well and stir the brown sauce into the vegetables with 4 oz. sour cream and 2 level teaspoons capers. Taste for seasoning and pour over meat. Cover the casserole tightly and bake in moderate oven 350°F, Reg 4 for 25 minutes. Remove from oven, uncover, cool, recover and chill.

▶ Cook ½ lb. noodles in large quantity of boiling salted water until cooked but still quite firm (reheating will cook them slightly more); drain in colander, rinse copiously under hot water and set aside in colander to reheat.

▶ Next evening stir 3 tablespoons madeira or sherry into the casserole, cover and put into moderate oven 350°F, Reg 4 until piping hot, about 20–30 minutes. At the same time place the noodles in a steamer over boiling water to reheat thoroughly; it will only take 5 minutes. Brown the remaining butter in a small saucepan. Put a little in the bottom of a heated serving dish, add the hot noodles and pour the rest of the sizzling butter on top. Toss and keep in oven.

▶ Serve the steaks in the casserole or in a heated serving dish at the same time as the noodles.

# Bombe Baur Au Lac

| | |
|---|---|
| 12 macaroons | grated rind of 1 |
| 12 tablespoons Grand | orange |
| Marnier | pinch salt |
| 5 eggs | 16 oz. double cream |
| 3 oz. castor sugar | 1½ tablespoons cocoa |

▶ Crumble 12 macaroons and soak in 4 tablespoons Grand Marnier. Stir until it becomes a paste.

▶ Beat 5 egg yolks. Add 3 oz. castor sugar and a pinch of salt and beat until lemon-coloured and thick. Stir in 4 tablespoons Grand Marnier and grated rind of 1 orange. Fold in 16 oz. double cream whipped and 4 egg whites beaten until stiff.

▶ Fill a mould with half of the cream mixture. Add the macaroon mixture, then the rest of the cream mixture. Cover with foil and freeze. If your freezing compartment is large enough this can be done in individual custard cups.

▶ To serve, dust lightly with cocoa and pour over remaining 4 tablespoons Grand Marnier.

# 39

## MENU

*Yoghourt Prawn Soup*

*Simla Chicken Curry*

*Rice and Green Pepper*

*Pineapple Water Ice*

## Yoghourt Prawn Soup

| | |
|---|---|
| ¾ lb. cooked prawns | 2 teaspoons mustard |
| 1 small cucumber | dash nutmeg |
| 1 tablespoon chopped chives | 1¾ pints yoghourt |
| 1 tablespoon chopped parsley | salt and pepper to taste |
| | chives for garnishing |

▶ Blend in a liquidizer only 10 oz. chopped cooked prawns, the small cucumber, peeled and chopped, seeds removed, 1 tablespoon chopped chives, 1 tablespoon chopped parsley, 2 teaspoons mustard and a pinch of nutmeg. Add only ¾ pint yoghourt and blend a minute longer. Season to taste with salt and pepper. Chill and stir in the remaining 1 pint yoghourt.

▶ Serve in individual cups garnished with the remaining 2 oz. prawns. Sprinkle with chives.

## Simla Chicken Curry

| | |
|---|---|
| 1 3-lb. chicken | 16 oz. chicken stock |
| 2 oz. butter | 1 coconut or 2 tablespoons desiccated coconut and 5 oz. hot milk |
| 2 tablespoons cooking oil | |
| 4 large onions | |
| 2 cloves garlic | 1 teaspoon turmeric |
| 2 tablespoons fresh ginger root | 1 teaspoon cumin |
| | 1 teaspoon powdered coriander |
| 3 tablespoons curry powder | |
| | 1 bay leaf |
| 4 tomatoes | 3 oz. raisins |
| 2 cooking apples | ground peanuts |
| | ½ lb. desiccated coconut if no fresh coconut available |
| | 2 or 3 varieties chutney |

▶ Ask the butcher to cut chicken in pieces as for a fricassée.

▶ Melt 2 oz. butter and 2 tablespoons cooking oil. Add 4 large onions chopped, 2 peeled chopped cloves garlic, and 2 tablespoons chopped fresh ginger root. If not available use ½ teaspoon ground ginger. Cook 5 minutes. Add 3 tablespoons curry powder. Cool 5 minutes. Add the pieces of chicken and let them brown all over without burning the vegetables. Add 4 chopped tomatoes, skin removed; and 2 peeled, cored and diced cooking apples. Pour over 16 oz. warm chicken stock and the milk from 1 fresh coconut. (Bore a hole in the eyes of the coconut and drain off milk. Afterwards remove shell and skin from the coconut, and grate to serve with the curry. If fresh coconut not available, pour 5 oz. hot milk over 2 tablespoons desiccated coconut, let stand and squeeze out the liquid through a fine cloth. Add liquid to the other ingredients.) Now add 1 teaspoon each of turmeric, cumin, and powdered coriander, 1 bay leaf and 3 oz. raisins. Simmer on moderate heat, stirring occasionally, for 40 minutes. Set aside.

▶ Reheat on a slow heat. Serve with grated fresh coconut (or desiccated), 2 or 3 varieties of chutney, ground peanuts and hot Rice and Green Pepper.

## Rice and Green Pepper

| | |
|---|---|
| ¾ lb. patna rice | 1 lemon |
| boiling water | ½ oz. butter |
| ½ teaspoon salt | 1 green pepper |

▶ Put ½ teaspoon salt in a large saucepan of rapidly boiling water. Slowly stir in ¾ lb. patna rice. Wash the green pepper, remove membrane and seeds, chop up into small pieces, add to rice. Stirring occasionally, cook for 20 or 30 minutes. Drain in a colander and run cold water over it until it is thoroughly chilled. Leave in colander until completely drained. Place in a buttered ovenproof dish and put aside.

▶ Next day sprinkle with the juice of 1 lemon and dot with ½ oz. butter. Reheat lightly covered in a slow oven 310°F, Reg 2 until rice is thoroughly hot, taking 20–30 minutes.

## Pineapple Water Ice

| | |
|---|---|
| 1 pint water | 1 teacupful freshly |
| 6 oz. granulated sugar | grated pineapple |
| 3 oz. golden syrup | 8 oz. orange juice |
| | juice 1 lemon |

▶ Boil 1 pint water, 6 oz. granulated sugar and 3 oz. golden syrup to a light syrup.

▶ Peel, core, and cut out the eyes of 1 fresh pineapple. Grate on a fine grater or blend, previously cut up, in the liquidizer. Add 8 oz. orange juice and the juice of 1 lemon. Stir in the syrup. Pour into the refrigerator tray. Set the freezing unit at high and freeze. When firm, return the freezing unit to normal.

# 40

## Cream of Carrot Soup

| | |
|---|---|
| 12 medium-sized carrots | 1½ pints chicken stock |
| 2 medium-sized onions | 2 oz. plain flour |
| 4 cloves | 1½ pints milk |
| 4 oz. butter | 8 oz. single cream |
| | paprika |
| salt and pepper to taste | |

▶ Peel and slice thinly 12 medium-sized carrots and 2 medium-sized onions. Sauté in 2 oz. butter until vegetables are well coated. Add 8 oz. chicken stock and 4 cloves and simmer over low heat until vegetables are tender.

▶ In another saucepan melt 2 oz. butter, blend with 2 oz. flour. Stirring constantly, cook until smooth. Add 1½ pints milk and 16 oz. chicken stock. Cook until it thickens.

▶ Combine the 2 mixtures and cook over low heat for 10 minutes, stirring continuously. Pour into a liquidizer and blend until smooth. Season with salt and pepper to taste. Put aside.

▶ Next day add 8 oz. single cream and reheat in a double boiler. Serve with a sprinkling of paprika. It is a thick soup but should it be too thick, add a little cream or milk.

## Jambon Persille

| | |
|---|---|
| 1 2-lb. tin Danish ham or left-over ham | 1 bay leaf |
| | 8 sprigs parsley |
| 1½ pints tinned beef consommé | 4 tablespoons gelatine |
| | 2 tablespoons tarragon vinegar |
| 8 oz. dry white wine | |
| 3 shallots or small onions | 6 tablespoons chopped parsley |
| 2 teaspoons tarragon | |
| 4 short sticks of celery | |

▶ Cut a 2-lb. tinned Danish ham, or left-over ham, into smallish chunks. Put into a glass serving dish.

▶ Simmer only 1¼ pints of the tinned consommé, 8 oz. dry white wine, 3 shallots chopped fine, 2 teaspoons tarragon and a bouquet garni made of 4 short sticks of celery, 8 sprigs of parsley and 1 bay leaf tied together, for ½ hour. Remove bouquet garni and strain through a cheesecloth.

▶ Soak 4 tablespoons gelatine in the remaining ¼ pint of cold consommé. After 5 minutes, heat to dissolve and add to the strained hot consommé. Add 2 tablespoons tarragon vinegar. Pour over the ham enough consommé to half cover it. Put rest of consommé in the refrigerator until it starts to thicken. Stir in 6 tablespoons finely chopped parsley and pour over ham. Put in refrigerator overnight.

▶ In France, this is always served at table in a glass bowl, and cut into slices there. Serve it with a green salad, such as Salad Pitoeff, and Baked Potatoes.

## Baked Potatoes

6 even-sized large potatoes

▶ Wash and scrub the potatoes in lukewarm water. Dry. Bake in a moderate oven 350°F, Reg 4 for about 1½–2 hours, according to size.

▶ When they are half cooked, prick them with a fork to allow the steam to escape. This will prevent them from bursting.

## Salad Pitoeff

2 heads of crisp lettuce with tightly packed
  leaves, Webb's if possible
¼ teaspoon salt
¼ teaspoon castor
  sugar
¼ teaspoon Dijon
  mustard

3 tablespoons single
  cream
½ tablespoon lemon
  juice
chopped tarragon and
  chervil or parsley

▶ Mix ¼ teaspoon castor sugar and ¼ teaspoon Dijon mustard smoothly together, stir in the 3 tablespoons of single cream, then add the lemon juice drop by drop. Season with the ¼ teaspoon salt. Stir in the herbs. Keep dressing in a screw-top jar in the refrigerator.

▶ Next day wash each lettuce leaf, dry lightly in a soft absorbent cloth. Chill in refrigerator until the lettuce is crisp, when ready to serve. Mix dressing into the salad— it should look as if covered with snow.

▶ Keep in refrigerator for at least a ¼ of an hour before serving.

## Junket

16 oz. double cream
8 oz. milk
2 rounded teaspoons
  castor sugar

rennet, use according
  to directions on the
  bottle

▶ Heat 16 oz. double cream, and 8 oz. milk together. Away from the fire stir in 2 rounded teaspoons castor sugar and the rennet. Pour into a serving bowl. Let it stand for 2 hours until it coagulates. Chill in the refrigerator overnight.

## Kissel Sauce

scant 11 oz. cranberry
  sauce
5 oz. juice from tinned
  red plums

2 teaspoons potato
  flour
2 tablespoons cold
  water

▶ Heat the scant 11 oz. cranberry juice and 5 oz. juice tinned red plums. Add sugar to taste if the cranberry juice is unsweetened.

▶ Mix 2 teaspoons potato flour and 2 tablespoons cold water. Add to the hot juice. Cook, stirring constantly, over low heat. Remove from the fire as soon as the mixture thickens and becomes transparent. Cool and store in refrigerator.

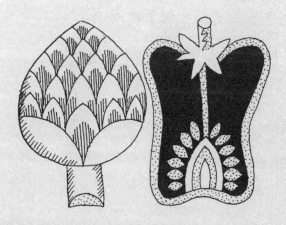

**41**

MENU

*Gnocchi*

*Cider Duck*

*Sauté Apples*

*Honey Mousse*

## Gnocchi

| | |
|---|---|
| 1½ pints milk | 1 oz. butter |
| 1 teaspoon salt | 2 eggs |
| 8 oz. farina | ½ lb. cheddar cheese |
| | paprika |

▶ Scald 1½ pints milk in a double boiler. Add 1 teaspoon salt and pour in 8 oz. farina slowly, stirring constantly to avoid lumps. Cook until thickened. Add 1 oz. butter and the beaten yolks of 2 eggs. Continue cooking for 2 minutes, remove from heat, cool slightly and fold in the stiffly beaten whites of 2 eggs.

▶ Spread ½ inch thick in a buttered baking tin and chill. When cold, cut into 2 inch cubes.

▶ Grate ½ lb. cheddar cheese.

▶ Butter a shallow baking dish generously. Put in layer of cubes on the bottom, cover with a layer of cheese and repeat, alternating layers, with cheese last. Sprinkle with paprika, dot with butter. Place in refrigerator.

▶ Next day place dish in a pan of hot water and bake in a moderate oven 350°F, Reg 4 for ½ hour. Serve in the baking dish.

# Cider Duck

| | |
|---|---|
| 1 duckling (5 or 6 lb.) | 6 oz. calvados or |
| 1 cooking apple | brandy |
| ½ teaspoon salt | 16 oz. cider |
| 1½ oz. butter | 8 oz. double cream |

▶ Season duckling inside and out with ½ teaspoon salt. Stuff with 1 apple, quartered. Truss legs and wings close to the body. Rub all over with 1½ oz. softened butter. Put in a pre-heated hot oven, 425–450°F, Reg 7–8. Roast for 15 or 20 minutes until a golden brown. Remove duckling from pan. Pour off all fat in the pan except about 3 tablespoons. Return duckling to pan and flambé with 6 oz. warmed calvados, or with 6 oz. warmed brandy. Cover immediately and let stand for 5 minutes. Pour over 16 oz. heated cider. Cover and cook 25 to 30 minutes with oven heat reduced to 400°F, Reg 6.

▶ Remove duckling, and on top of the stove over a high heat reduce the cider by one-half. Return duckling to pan and put aside in a cool place.

▶ Next day carve duckling, pour over the sauce and reheat in a moderate oven 350°F, Reg 4 for 20–30 minutes. When thoroughly heated, add 8 oz. double cream and continue cooking for 10 minutes.

▶ To serve, put on a serving dish. Pour over some of the sauce and surround with Sauté Apples. Serve the rest of sauce separately in a sauceboat.

# Sauté Apples

| | |
|---|---|
| 2 lb. cooking apples | 4 oz. calvados or |
| 4 oz. butter | brandy |
| | 1 lemon |

▶ Core and cut in thick round slices 2 lb. of cooking apples.

▶ Melt 4 oz. butter in a frying pan. Sauté apples until slightly browned, being careful not to break the slices. Put aside.

▶ Next day, reheat on a low heat. Flambé with 4 oz. calvados or brandy. Pour over the juice of 1 lemon. Serve around the carved duckling.

# Honey Mousse

| | |
|---|---|
| 6 egg yolks | 3 egg whites |
| 1 lb. strained dark | 16 oz. double cream |
| honey | |

▶ Beat the yolks of 6 eggs until lemon yellow. Beat in 1 lb. strained honey, the dark variety as it has more taste. Put in a double boiler over hot water but not boiling. Stirring constantly, cook until it thickens. Chill.

▶ Beat 3 egg whites stiff and fold into the honey mixture. Whip 16 oz. double cream and fold in. Pack in a mould or moulds and store in the freezing chamber of refrigerator. Turn out of mould on a plate to serve.

## MENU

*Artichoke Hearts Au Gratin*

*Braised Beef*

*Austrian Fried Potatoes*

*Cherry Cake*

## Artichoke Hearts Au Gratin

| | |
|---|---|
| 1 or 2 jars artichoke hearts | 12 oz. chicken bouillon, stock or cubes |
| 1 lemon | |
| 4 oz. butter | 4 oz. dry white wine |
| 2 tablespoons flour | 5 oz. grated parmesan paprika |

▶ Scald 12 small or 9 medium artichoke hearts in boiling water and the juice of 1 small lemon. If they are a little hard they may simmer gently until just tender. Drain carefully and arrange in a well-buttered, shallow, ovenproof serving dish. Keep warm.

▶ Heat 12 oz. chicken stock with 4 oz. white wine. Keep warm.

▶ Melt 2 oz. butter in a saucepan, stir in 2 tablespoons of flour and cook on low heat for a few minutes until well mixed. Do not allow to brown. Slowly pour in the hot wine and bouillon and continue cooking, stirring constantly for 10 minutes until thickened. Fold in 3 oz. grated parmesan, remove from heat when cheese has melted and pour over warm artichokes. Cool.

▶ Sprinkle the remaining 2 oz. grated cheese on top, dot with 1 oz. butter, dust with paprika, cover tightly and chill.

▶ Next evening reheat in hot oven 420°F, Reg 7 until sizzling, then reduce heat to minimum to keep hot. Just before serving, place under grill for 2 or 3 minutes to brown.

## Braised Beef

| | |
|---|---|
| 3½ lb. piece topside of beef | 1½ oz. lard or beef dripping |
| 2 cloves garlic | 4 onions |
| 12 peppercorns | 4 carrots |
| 2 oz. plain flour | 3 tomatoes |
| ½ teaspoon salt | 16 oz. beef stock, tin or cubes |
| ½ teaspoon paprika | parsley |

▶ Peel and cut 2 cloves of garlic into 6 slivers each. With the point of a sharp knife incise the meat on all sides, inserting a bit of garlic and 12 peppercorns alternately in each incision. Roll in 2 oz. flour seasoned with ½ teaspoon salt and ½ teaspoon paprika.

▶ Peel and slice 4 large onions.

▶ Put 1½ oz. beef dripping or lard into a heavy iron frying pan on very high heat. When smoking, add meat and sear rapidly on all sides until brown. Reduce heat, add the sliced onions and fry lightly.

▶ Empty contents of frying pan into a heavy pan with a tight-fitting cover (Dutch oven if available). Peel and dice 4 carrots, peel and quarter 3 tomatoes, and add to pan with 8 oz. hot stock. Place pan in pre-heated oven, 350°F, Reg 4 for 5 minutes, then reduce heat to low, 310°F, Reg 2 and roast, covered, for about 2 hours or until meat is tender. Turn meat every ½ hour adding 2 oz. hot stock each time.

▶ When tender, remove meat to a carving board and allow to cool for at least ½ hour to facilitate slicing.

---

▶ Press vegetables and pan liquid through a coarse sieve or blend in a liquidizer and cool.

---

▶ Cut meat into thick slices, arrange in an ovenproof serving dish and cover with the vegetable gravy. Cover and chill overnight.

---

▶ Reheat in moderate oven 350°F, Reg 4 until gravy is bubbling and meat is heated thoroughly. Sprinkle with finely chopped parsley just before serving.

## Austrian Fried Potatoes

| | |
|---|---|
| 6 large potatoes | 3 oz. lard |
| 2 large onions | salt and freshly ground |
| | pepper |
| | chopped parsley |

---

▶ Scrub 6 large potatoes and cook in salted water. When tender, drain, peel, and mash roughly with a fork.

---

▶ Peel, chop and fry 2 large onions in 1½ oz. lard until golden yellow, in a heavy iron saucepan. Add the potatoes, a little freshly ground pepper, more salt if needed, mix and fry gently for a few minutes. Push the potatoes away from the middle towards the sides of the saucepan leaving a round space about 2 inches in diameter uncovered in centre. Put ¾ oz. lard into this space, raise heat and brown the bottom lightly, lifting the potatoes carefully with a spatula to allow lard to flow underneath. Remove from heat, cool and cover saucepan lightly with foil. Do *not* chill.

---

▶ Next evening, place saucepan on high heat, add ¾ oz. more lard if needed into centre and heat through again, lifting potatoes with spatula to let lard flow under. When potatoes are nicely browned, place heated serving dish on saucepan and turn upside down. Keep warm in a very slow oven 290°F, Reg 1 and sprinkle with finely chopped parsley just before serving.

---

▶ Parsley for the Braised Beef and the Austrian Fried Potatoes (or any dish that requires chopped parsley just before serving) can be washed, dried thoroughly in paper towels and chopped the day before using. Wrap in paper towel and store in vegetable crisper of refrigerator until needed.

## Cherry Cake

| | |
|---|---|
| 6 oz. butter | 5 oz. plain flour |
| 6 oz. castor sugar | 5 tablespoons milk |
| 3 eggs | ¼ teaspoon vanilla |
| pinch of salt | extract |
| castor sugar for | ½ lemon |
| dusting | ¾ lb. white cherries or |
| | 1 large tin white |
| | cherries |

---

▶ Cream 6 oz. butter and 6 oz. castor sugar until light.

---

▶ Separate eggs and beat yolks one by one into creamed butter and sugar. Gradually add 5 oz. flour alternately with 5 tablespoons of milk, beating well after each addition. Stir in ¼ teaspoon vanilla and the juice and rind of ½ lemon.

---

▶ Beat 3 egg whites and a pinch of salt until stiff and fold into cake mixture.

---

▶ Pour the batter into a buttered and floured Pyrex cake mould. Cover the surface closely with fresh or well-drained tinned white cherries. Press the fruit very lightly into batter and bake in a slow oven 340°F, Reg 3 about 40 minutes or until skewer, inserted into centre, comes out clean and cake shrinks away from sides of mould. Dust generously with castor sugar while hot and serve next day in baking dish. Do *not* chill.

# 43

## MENU

*Oeufs Mollets Portuguaise*

*Jellied Chicken Loaf*

*Fennel Salad*

*Date Pudding*

## Oeufs Mollets Portuguaise

| | |
|---|---|
| 6 eggs | 1 teaspoon potato flour |
| 3 tablespoons Madeira or Marsala | ½ teaspoon sugar |
| | salt to taste |
| 2 tablespoons tomato purée | 6 rounds fried bread |
| | 1½ tablespoons vinegar |
| 6 oz. beef stock | parsley |
| 1 oz. butter | |

▶ Put 6 eggs in a saucepan, pour boiling water over to cover. Add 1½ tablespoons vinegar and cook over low heat for 6 minutes. Drain and run cold water over them for 5 minutes. Drain again and set aside. Pour 3 tablespoons Madeira or Marsala, 2 tablespoons tomato purée, and 6 oz. stock into a saucepan. Bring to a boil and remove from heat. Blend 1 oz. butter with 1 teaspoon potato flour and stir into the sauce. Add ½ teaspoon sugar. Bring to a boil again stirring constantly. Season to taste with salt. Put in a covered saucepan and set aside.

▶ Next evening shell the eggs. Place in the top part of a steamer and reheat. If the sauce has thickened too much add a little Madeira or Marsala and reheat. Serve the eggs on rounds of fried bread with sauce poured over them, garnished with chopped parsley.

# Jellied Chicken Loaf

| | |
|---|---|
| 2 tablespoons gelatine | 5 tablespoons shredded raw carrots |
| 2 tablespoons cold water | 4 oz. chopped green peppers |
| 12 oz. hot chicken consommé | 3 oz. cold tomato juice |
| 1 teaspoon salt | 12 oz. hot tomato juice |
| $\frac{1}{4}$ teaspoon pepper | $\frac{1}{4}$ teaspoon sugar |
| $1\frac{1}{2}$ lb. diced cooked chicken | 1 teaspoon Worcester sauce |
| 5 tablespoons chopped celery | 8 oz. cooked peas, fresh or frozen |
| 2 tablespoons minced onion | mayonnaise (Menu 48) |

▶ Soften 1 tablespoon gelatine in 2 tablespoons cold water and dissolve in 12 oz. hot chicken consommé. Season with $\frac{1}{2}$ teaspoon salt and $\frac{1}{4}$ teaspoon pepper. Cool. When gelatine begins to thicken, fold in $\frac{3}{4}$ lb. diced cooked chicken, having removed the skin before dicing, 5 tablespoons chopped celery, 5 tablespoons shredded raw carrots and 4 oz. chopped green peppers. Brush a loaf pan with French dressing. Pour in mixture. Chill and allow to stiffen before adding second layer.

▶ Soften the remaining 1 tablespoon of gelatine in 3 oz. cold tomato juice. Let stand 5 minutes. Dissolve in 12 oz. hot tomato juice. Season with the remaining $\frac{1}{2}$ teaspoon salt, 1 teaspoon Worcester sauce and $\frac{1}{4}$ teaspoon sugar. Cool. When the mixture begins to thicken, fold in the remaining $\frac{3}{4}$ lb. chicken, 8 oz. cooked peas, fresh or frozen, and 2 tablespoons minced onion. Pour over the first layer in the loaf pan. Chill overnight or at least 4 hours. Unmould onto a serving dish and surround with watercress. Serve with mayonnaise.

# Fennel Salad

| | |
|---|---|
| 1 lb. fennel | 3 tablespoons olive oil |
| 1 tablespoon lemon juice | $\frac{1}{4}$ teaspoon salt |
| $\frac{1}{8}$ teaspoon pepper | |

▶ Cut the fennel into very thin slices. Make the dressing with 3 tablespoons olive oil, 1 tablespoon lemon juice, salt and pepper. Beat these ingredients with a wire whisk until smooth. Before serving, pour the dressing over the fennel and mix well.

# Date Pudding

| | |
|---|---|
| $\frac{1}{2}$ lb. pitted dates | 4 oz. milk |
| 4 oz. castor sugar | 16 oz. boiling water |
| 5 oz. plain flour | 2 oz. butter |
| 2 teaspoons baking powder | 8 oz. brown sugar |
| $\frac{1}{2}$ teaspoon lemon juice | 1 teaspoon vanilla |
| | cream for serving |

▶ Chop $\frac{1}{2}$ lb. dates. Mix them with 4 oz. castor sugar and 5 oz. plain flour, which has been sifted with 2 teaspoons baking powder.

▶ Add $\frac{1}{2}$ teaspoon lemon juice, and 4 oz. of milk. Put this batter into a well-greased baking dish.

▶ Mix 2 oz. butter, 8 oz. brown sugar and 1 teaspoon vanilla with 16 oz. boiling water. Pour this over the uncooked batter in the baking dish and bake at 350°F, Reg 4 for about 35 to 40 minutes.

▶ Serve hot or cold with cream.

# MENU

*Tuna Fish Santa Barbara*

*Gigot à la Cuillère or
Seven-Hour Leg of Lamb*

*Purée of White Beans*

*Oranges in Red Wine*

## Tuna Fish Santa Barbara

| | |
|---|---|
| 6 small tomatoes | 2 tablespoons |
| 6 celery stalks | vinegar (tarragon) |
| 1 large tin tuna fish | 1 teaspoon mustard |
| 6 tablespoons olive oil | ½ teaspoon salt |
| | ¼ teaspoon pepper |
| | chives |

▶ Remove the skins from 6 small tomatoes by dipping them in boiling water. Store in refrigerator.

▶ Wash 6 celery stalks. Cut crosswise in thin slices. Put in a plastic bag in refrigerator.

▶ In a jar with a screw top, shake well 6 tablespoons olive oil, 2 tablespoons tarragon vinegar, 1 teaspoon mustard, ½ teaspoon salt and ¼ teaspoon pepper.

▶ To serve. Flake 1 large tin tuna fish and toss in the celery and half of the vinaigrette. Place in a salad bowl. Surround with the tomatoes cut in quarters. Pour over the rest of the vinaigrette and sprinkle with chives.

## Gigot à la Cuillère or Seven-Hour Leg of Lamb

| | |
|---|---|
| 1 5-lb. leg of lamb, | 12 small onions |
| 1 small veal knuckle | 4 tomatoes |
| 16 oz. dry white wine | 2 celery sticks |
| 2 medium onions | 6 sprigs parsley |
| 2 cloves garlic | 4 slices lean bacon |
| 4 carrots | 1¼ pints stock or more |
| 2 tablespoons oil | 6 tablespoons brandy |
| salt and pepper | |

▶ Ask your butcher to remove the bones and fat from a 5-lb. leg of lamb and tie it into a melon shape. Save the bones. Also have him split a small veal knuckle.

▶ Marinate the lamb, 6 hours or overnight, in 16 oz. dry white wine, 2 sliced onions, 2 carrots and 1 clove garlic. Turn it from time to time.

▶ Remove lamb. Discard vegetables but save the marinade. Wipe lamb dry. Salt and pepper and brown on all sides in 2 tablespoons hot oil. Brown the veal knuckle, bones and 2 whole carrots in the oil. Put the lamb in a dutch oven or similar heavy pan with veal knuckle and lamb bones. Surround with the carrots, 4 chopped tomatoes, skin removed, 12 peeled small whole onions, 1 clove of garlic and a bouquet garni of 2 celery sticks and 6 sprigs of parsley tied together.

▶ Boil 4 slices of lean bacon in water to cover, for 5 minutes. Drain, rinse with cold water. Place on top of the lamb. Secure with tooth-picks or skewers.

▶ Heat 1¼ pints stock and 4 oz. of the marinade, 3 tablespoons brandy and pour over lamb. Cover with a piece of foil. Cook on top of the stove for 5 minutes. Cover with top of Dutch oven or pan. Pour some water on top of the cover and place the pan in the oven turned to its very lowest heat. Cook for at least 7 hours. If you have your oven at its very lowest it is not necessary to look at the lamb until it is done, but add water to the cover from time to time as it evaporates. If you have no Dutch oven with special cover, cover with greaseproof paper and then a tight-fitting lid. Look at the lamb from time to time, adding more stock if needed.

▶ Carefully remove the gigot and the onions. Discard the bones, bacon and bouquet garni. Remove any excess fat and blend the sauce, vegetables included, in the liquidizer or sieve. Add 3 tablespoons brandy. Correct seasoning if necessary. Remove the strings from the lamb. Put it back in the Dutch oven with the onions. Pour over the liquidizer sauce and put aside in a cool place, covered.

▶ Reheat in its sauce in a moderate oven 350°F, Reg 4 about $\frac{1}{2}$–$\frac{3}{4}$ hour. It is not necessary to slice lamb as it really cuts with a spoon, as the name indicates.

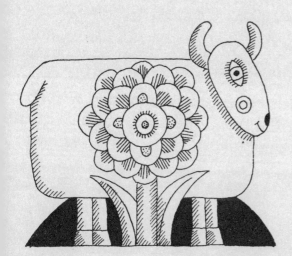

## Purée of White Beans

| | |
|---|---|
| 1 lb. white beans | 1 onion |
| 1 slice bacon | salt and pepper |
| 1 carrot | butter |

▶ Wash 1 lb. white beans. Soak over-night in 3 to 4 times as much water as the beans. Bring slowly to the boil in the water in which they were soaked. Add 1 slice of derinded bacon, 1 carrot and 1 onion. Simmer until done, at least three hours. Halfway through cooking, salt and pepper to taste.

▶ Drain, reserving the liquid they were cooked in. Discard the carrot and onion. Blend beans and slice of bacon in a liquidizer. Add some of the cooking liquid if too thick. Stir in $\frac{1}{2}$ oz. butter for each 8 oz. purée. Correct seasoning.

▶ Reheat in a double boiler, adding more of the liquid if necessary.

## Oranges in Red Wine

| | |
|---|---|
| 6 large oranges | 1 stick cinnamon |
| 6 oz. granulated sugar | 2 cloves |
| 8 oz. red wine | 3 lemon slices |
| 8 oz. water | 3 tangerine slices |

▶ Dissolve 6 oz. sugar in 8 oz. red wine and 8 oz. water. Bring to a boil. Add 1 stick cinnamon, 2 cloves, 3 slices of lemon and 3 slices of tangerine. Simmer for 5 to 10 minutes until of a syrupy consistency. Remove the spices and slices of lemon and tangerine.

▶ Peel with a sharp knife 6 large oranges, cutting well into the fruit so that you slice off every bit of white membrane. Peel the membranes from each segment. Put the segments in a serving bowl. Pour over the hot wine syrup. Cool and put in refrigerator until next evening.

# 45

## MENU

*Everybody's Fish Soup, Garlic Croutons*

*Surprise Salad*

*Apples Poached in Cider*

▶ Ask your fishmonger for heads, tails and bones to make your fish stock, plus 1 small inexpensive fish. Put all of them in a large pan with 1½ pints water, 16 oz. dry white wine, 3 peeled potatoes, 1 large onion studded with 2 cloves, 2 garlic cloves, 1 bay leaf, 1 teaspoon salt and a few peppercorns. Bring to a boil and simmer for 1 hour.

▶ Carefully remove and reserve the potatoes, drain and discard everything except the stock.

▶ Mash the potatoes, liquidize with 4 oz. of the stock and set aside.

▶ Simmer 1½ lb. cod fillets in the remaining stock for 10 minutes. Remove the fillets. Combine the stock and the liquidized potatoes. Stir in 1 teaspoon saffron dissolved in 1 tablespoon hot water. Cool and store in the refrigerator until next day.

▶ Remove the shells from 1 cooked lobster, 6 cooked prawns and ½ lb. cooked shrimps. Cut the lobster into large pieces. Flake the cod. Put all in a covered container in refrigerator until next day.

▶ To serve, add the flaked cod and the shellfish to the cold stock and reheat on a moderate heat. Serve with Garlic Croutons.

## Everybody's Fish Soup

| | |
|---|---|
| 1 small inexpensive fish | 1 teaspoon salt |
| 1½ pints water | a few peppercorns |
| 16 oz. dry white wine | 1 teaspoon saffron |
| 3 medium potatoes | 1½ lb. cod fillets |
| 2 cloves garlic | 1 cooked lobster |
| 1 large onion | 6 cooked prawns |
| 2 cloves | ½ lb. cooked shrimps |
| 1 bay leaf | |

# Garlic Croutons

| | |
|---|---|
| 6 slices stale bread | 2–3 tablespoons olive |
| 2 cloves garlic | oil |

▶ Remove crusts from 6 slices stale bread. Peel and halve 2 cloves garlic. Rub the slices thoroughly with the garlic halves. Cut into cubes. Fry in 2–3 tablespoons hot olive oil until golden brown. Drain on absorbent paper.

# Surprise Salad

| | |
|---|---|
| 1 pair calves brains | 6 tablespoons olive oil |
| 1 small cauliflower | 3 tablespoons wine |
| 2 tomatoes | vinegar |
| 4 hard-boiled eggs | 2 teaspoons Dijon |
| chopped parsley and | mustard |
| sprigs for garnish | 1 teaspoon salt |
| | $\frac{1}{4}$ teaspoon pepper |
| juice of 1 lemon | |

▶ Soak 1 pair calves brains in $1\frac{1}{2}$ pints water and only 1 tablespoon vinegar for 3 hours. Gently skin the brains and soak in lukewarm water for 20 minutes, changing the water at least once to remove all of the blood. Blanch in the water and vinegar, simmer, but do not boil, for 20 minutes. Remove from water carefully, cool and store in refrigerator in a covered container overnight.

▶ Remove the leaves from 1 small head of cauliflower. Soak head down in salted water for 10 minutes. Place it, head up, in 1 inch of boiling water mixed with the juice of 1 lemon. Reduce heat and simmer partially covered for 12 to 15 minutes. Drain. When cool break into flowerets. Put in a covered container in refrigerator.

▶ To serve. Slice the brain. Slice 4 hard-boiled eggs. Arrange alternate slices of brains and eggs around the edge of a serving dish. In the centre arrange a mound of the flowerets surrounded by thin slices of tomato. Pour over a vinaigrette made of 6 tablespoons olive oil, 2 tablespoons vinegar, 2 teaspoons Dijon mustard, 1 teaspoon salt and $\frac{1}{4}$ teaspoon pepper. Shake well in a screw-topped jar before mixing in the salad.

▶ Decorate with a few sprigs of parsley around the edge of the dish and sprinkle with chopped parsley.

# Apples Poached in Cider

| | |
|---|---|
| 6 dessert apples | 4 whole allspice |
| 16 oz. cider | $\frac{1}{4}$ teaspoon nutmeg |
| 12 oz. granulated sugar | juice of $\frac{1}{2}$ lemon |
| 1 cinnamon stick | grated rind of 1 lemon |
| 6 cloves | $\frac{1}{4}$ teaspoon ground |
| | ginger |

▶ Make a syrup, by cooking for 10 minutes 8 oz. sugar with 16 oz. cider, a small stick of cinnamon, 6 cloves, 4 whole allspice, $\frac{1}{4}$ teaspoon nutmeg and $\frac{1}{4}$ teaspoon ground ginger.

▶ Peel, core and quarter 6 apples. Simmer half of them gently in the syrup for 10 minutes or until they are just tender. Carefully remove to a serving dish. Cook the remaining apples in the same way. Place them on the serving dish.

▶ Strain the remaining syrup. Add 4 oz. of sugar, the juice of $\frac{1}{2}$ lemon and the grated rind of 1 lemon, cook until it thickens, 5 to 10 minutes. Pour over all the apples and chill in the refrigerator until serving time.

# 46

## MENU

*Hungarian Liver Sausage Loaf*

*Brunswick Stew*

*Virginian Frozen Plum Pudding*

## Hungarian Liver Sausage Loaf

| | |
|---|---|
| ½ lb. liver sausage | ½ teaspoon made dry mustard |
| 3 eggs | |
| 1 small onion | 1 tablespoon finely chopped parsley |
| 1 teaspoon salt | |
| 1 pinch of pepper | ¼ pint sour cream |
| | 1 tablespoon chopped green olives |

▶ Remove the skin from ½ lb. liver sausage. Cut into chunks. Boil 3 eggs for 7 minutes, run cold water over them until cold. Peel and chop finely. Peel and cut in half 1 small onion. Cook the halves in a little water until soft. Drain and allow to get cold. Liquidize liver sausage, eggs, onions, 1 teaspoon salt, 1 pinch pepper, ½ teaspoon mixed dry mustard in a liquidizer. Fold in ¼ pint sour cream. Form into a loaf and wrap in silver foil and store in the refrigerator.

▶ Garnish with 1 tablespoon chopped green olives when serving.

## Brunswick Stew

| | |
|---|---|
| 1 5-lb. fowl or roasting chicken | 1 lb. corn cut from cob or large tin sweet corn |
| ½ lb. lean salt pork | |
| 3 onions | salt and pepper |
| 18–20 oz. fresh or tinned lima beans (broad beans can be substituted but flavour is different) | 2 oz. tomato ketchup |
| | 1 tablespoon Worcester sauce |
| | 1½ oz. butter |
| | 1 oz. plain flour |
| 1 medium tin whole tomatoes | |
| ¾ pint boiling water | |

▶ Ask the butcher to cut up a 5-lb. fowl or roasting chicken as for a fricassee. Roll each piece of chicken in flour.

▶ Cut ½ lb. lean salt pork into small squares. Scald for 5 minutes in boiling water, drain and rinse with cold water.

▶ Peel and cut vertically in thin slices 3 onions.

▶ Put the salt pork squares on the bottom of a heavy stewing pan. Cover with the onions. Place the pieces of chicken on the onions. Cover with the fresh or tinned lima beans. Pour over a medium-sized tin of whole tomatoes and ¾ pint of boiling water. Bring to a boil. Cover. Reduce heat and simmer gently 1 hour. Add 1 lb. fresh uncooked corn cut from the cob. A drained large tin of golden sweet corn may be substituted if corn is not in season. Salt and pepper to taste. Cover and simmer for ½ an hour or until the chicken is tender.

▶ Correct seasoning. Add 2 oz. tomato ketchup and 1 tablespoon Worcester sauce. Cook 5 minutes longer.

▶ Cream 1½ oz. butter with 1 oz. plain flour. Stir into the stew, and when slightly thickened remove from fire. Store in a cool place or refrigerator.

▶ To serve, reheat on a low heat.

# Virginian Frozen Plum Pudding

| | |
|---|---|
| 12 oz. milk | 3 oz. chopped nuts |
| 4 egg yolks | 2 oz. brandied cherries chopped |
| 3 oz. castor sugar | |
| few grains of salt | 2 oz. chopped preserved pineapple |
| 1 teaspoon vanilla | |
| 5 oz. chopped seedless raisins | 1 level tablespoon orange marmalade |
| | 8 oz. double cream |

▶ Scald 12 oz. milk in the top of a double boiler.

▶ Beat well 4 egg yolks. Gradually beat in the 3 oz. castor sugar. Pour over the milk. Mix well. Return to the double boiler and cook, stirring continuously with a wooden spoon, over hot, not boiling water until the custard coats the spoon. Remove from heat. Add a few grains of salt. Cool. Add 1 teaspoon vanilla. Chill in the refrigerator, covering surface with a piece of wet greaseproof paper.

▶ Remove paper from chilled custard and stir in 5 oz. finely chopped raisins, 3 oz. finely chopped nuts, 2 oz. chopped brandied cherries, 2 oz. chopped preserved pineapple and 1 tablespoon orange marmalade. Fold in 8 oz. double cream. Pour into a refrigerator tray. Freeze quickly. Then turn the regulator to normal.

**47**

MENU

*Senegalese Soup*

*Crabmeat and Cucumber Salad*

*Pears Baked in Cream*

## Senegalese Soup

| | |
|---|---|
| 3 tablespoons butter | 3 egg yolks |
| 3 level teaspoons curry powder | 17 oz. single cream |
| 3 scant tablespoons flour | 6 tablespoons cooked chicken breasts, cut into shreds |
| 2½ pints chicken stock, fresh or cubes | 6 teaspoons chutney chopped chives |
| 1 teaspoon paprika | |

▶ In a large saucepan, melt 3 tablespoons butter. Stir in 3 level teaspoons curry powder, add 3 scant tablespoons flour and blend, add 1 teaspoon paprika. Stir in 2½ pints of strong chicken stock, bring to the boil and simmer for a few minutes. Remove from the heat. Film the top with 2 tablespoons cream to prevent a skin from forming.

▶ In a bowl, beat the yolks of three eggs, add 16 oz. single cream and mix well. Stir into the soup and cook over low heat, stirring constantly until slightly thickened, but do not let it boil, or the eggs will curdle.

▶ Store in refrigerator. Next evening reheat in double boiler. Do not let it boil.

▶ Put a tablespoon of warmed shredded chicken breasts and a teaspoon of chutney into each serving cup. Pour over the soup. Garnish with chopped chives and serve.

▶ It is also excellent served cold.

# Crabmeat and Cucumber Salad

| | |
|---|---|
| 3 tins crabmeat | 4 tablespoons olive oil |
| 2 cucumbers | 2 tablespoons white |
| 2 tablespoons salt | wine vinegar |
| | freshly ground pepper |

▶ Peel and slice into thin slices 2 cucumbers, spread them on a large board, sprinkle with 2 tablespoons of salt and leave for an hour. Then place in a dry cloth and gently squeeze remaining water from them and place in a bowl.

▶ Beat together 4 tablespoons olive oil, 2 tablespoons white wine vinegar and freshly ground pepper. Pour over the cucumbers and let stand until ready to serve. (This salad cannot be made 24 hours earlier.)

▶ Remove the membranes and flake 3 tins crabmeat and keep covered in tin-foil in the refrigerator until next evening. Place in the middle of a serving dish, moisten with some of the liquid in the tin. Arrange the cucumbers around the crabmeat and serve.

# Pears Baked in Cream

| | |
|---|---|
| 6 pears | 4 oz. castor sugar |
| 4 tablespoons butter | $\frac{1}{4}$ pint double cream |
| | cinnamon |

▶ Peel, core and halve the pears. Arrange them in the bottom of a flat buttered ovenware dish. Cover them with 4 oz. castor sugar and pour over 4 tablespoons of melted butter.

▶ Bake in a moderate oven, 350°F, Reg 4, basting frequently until the pears are not quite done. Put aside.

▶ To serve, pour $\frac{1}{4}$ pint double cream over the pears, dust with cinnamon and reheat in oven, 350°F, Reg 4, for at least 10 minutes.

**48**

MENU

*Guacamole Aspic*

*Peasant Partridge*

*Caramel Oranges*

## Guacamole Aspic

| | |
|---|---|
| 3 large avocados | 1 teaspoon salt |
| 1 tomato | dash Tabasco sauce |
| 2 cloves garlic | 1½ pints chicken stock |
| 2 tablespoons lemon | 6 tablespoons gelatine |
| juice | watercress |
| 3 tablespoons | thinly sliced lemon |
| mayonnaise, | |
| (see recipe below) | |

▶ Peel and remove the stones from 3 large ripe avocados. Using a silver fork, crush the flesh and then beat with a wooden spoon until a smooth purée. Combine with 1 tomato peeled, seeded and chopped finely, 2 cloves of garlic crushed with a garlic press (if not available, chopped fine and mashed), 2 tablespoons lemon juice, 3 tablespoons mayonnaise, 1 teaspoon salt and a dash of Tabasco sauce. Stir in 16 oz. chicken stock.

▶ Heat 4 oz. chicken stock. Dissolve 6 tablespoons of gelatine in a cup with 3 tablespoons of cold chicken stock. Add to the hot chicken stock and stir until all the gelatine is dissolved. Cool and stir into the avocado mixture, mixing thoroughly. Pour into a mould. Chill overnight in refrigerator.

▶ To serve, unmould on a serving dish and garnish with watercress and lemon slices.

## Mayonnaise

| | |
|---|---|
| 2 egg yolks | ½ pint olive oil |
| 2 pinches of mustard | 2 or 3 teaspoons of |
| pinch of sugar | lemon juice or |
| salt and white pepper | wine vinegar |

▶ Put the egg yolks into a mixing bowl and add the 2 pinches of mustard, the pinch of sugar and the salt and white pepper. Beat together with a wooden spoon so that the yolks start to thicken. Then begin to add the olive oil, drop by drop, making sure to stir thoroughly after each addition of oil. As soon as the mixture starts to lighten in colour and thicken, the oil can be added more rapidly, about half a teaspoon at a time and stirring thoroughly each time as before. If the mayonnaise becomes too thick to add more oil easily, stir in a little of the measured amount of lemon juice or wine vinegar.

▶ When all the olive oil has been absorbed by the yolks, add the rest of the lemon or vinegar according to taste. Check the seasoning and keep in a cool place until required.

## Peasant Partridge

| | |
|---|---|
| 3 partridges | 2 cloves garlic |
| 6 thick rashers streaky bacon | 2 lumps sugar |
| | 6 juniper berries |
| 2 medium-sized white cabbages | 1 pinch mace |
| | salt and pepper |
| 3 carrots | grated lemon rind |
| 1¼ pints stock, fresh or cubes | 12 chipolata sausages |
| 4 oz. dry white wine | |

▶ Prepare 3 partridges for roasting. Dice 6 thick rashers of bacon. Cook on a low heat until slightly brown. Remove them and reserve fat.

▶ Quarter, core and shred 2 medium-sized white cabbages. Blanch in boiling salted water for 7 minutes. Drain. Mix with the diced bacon, 2 cloves garlic crushed, 6 juniper berries, a pinch of mace, a little grated lemon rind, 2 lumps sugar and salt and pepper to taste. Put a layer of half the cabbage at the bottom of a large flameproof earthenware casserole. Add a layer of 3 thinly sliced carrots. Brown partridges on all sides in the reserved bacon fat. Salt and pepper. Arrange on the layer of cabbage. Cover with the rest of the cabbage. Pour over 16 oz. hot stock and 4 oz. dry white wine. Cover the casserole and cook in a very slow oven 310°F, Reg 2, for 4 hours.

▶ Take out the partridges. Split them in half, and put them back in the casserole on top of the cabbage. If all of the juice seems to have been absorbed, add a little more stock. It must not be dry. Surround with 12 fried chipolata sausages. Cover again and set aside until next day.

▶ Reheat in a slow oven 330°F, Reg 3, 30 or 40 minutes. Serve in the casserole or another earthenware dish.

## Caramel Oranges

| | |
|---|---|
| 6 large oranges | ¼ pint water |
| 12 oz. granulated sugar | ¼ pint hot water |
| | grated coconut or shredded almonds |

▶ Peel 6 large oranges (see Menu 62). Slice each orange crosswise in ¼-inch slices. Carefully remove any pips, and reform as a whole orange. Arrange in a serving dish just large enough to hold them.

▶ Put 12 oz. granulated sugar in a heavy pan. Moisten with ¼ pint cold water. Place pan on a moderate heat and cook without stirring until golden brown. Remove from heat and add ¼ pint hot water. Put back on the heat and stir until the caramel is melted. Continue cooking without stirring until thick and syrupy, from 5 to 10 minutes. Cool. Pour half of the caramel over the oranges and put in the refrigerator until next day.

▶ To serve, trickle the rest of the caramel over the oranges and sprinkle with fresh grated coconut. Shredded almonds can be substituted for the coconut if it is not available.

## MENU

*Ginger Melon*

*Paella Valenciana*

*Cold Cheese Soufflé*

# Ginger Melon

| 2 Casaba or Persian melons or a good large sweet melon | 6 oz. chopped stone ginger |
|---|---|
| | 2 limes or lemons |

▶ Quarter 2 Casaba or Persian melons. Remove seeds. Sprinkle with chopped ginger. Quarter 2 limes or lemons. Serve each quarter of melon with a section of lime or lemon.

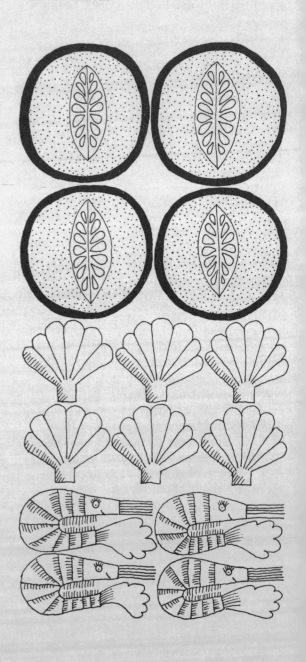

# Paella Valenciana

| | |
|---|---|
| 1 large roasting chicken | 2 small lobsters |
| 2 oz. butter | 24 prawns |
| 3 tablespoons olive oil | 24 shelled clams or |
| 1 garlic clove | mussels |
| 14 oz. long grain rice | 2 small Chorizo |
| 1 teaspoon saffron | sausages |
| 2 pints chicken stock | 1 large tin red |
| | pimentos |
| | salt and pepper |

▶ Cut a plump roasting chicken into pieces. Heat 2 oz. butter and 3 tablespoons olive oil in a large deep frying pan or a sauté pan with 1 crushed clove garlic. Sauté the chicken slowly until golden brown. Remove chicken and set aside.

▶ Add 14 oz. long-grained rice to the hot fat in the pan. Sauté until the rice is golden. Add 1 teaspoon saffron and 1½ pints hot chicken stock. Salt and pepper. Cook over a low heat uncovered until all of the liquid is absorbed, stirring occasionally with a wooden spoon so that it does not stick to the pan. The rice will be only partly cooked.

▶ Butter a Paella dish or an ovenware casserole. Put half the pieces of chicken in it. Cover the chicken with 1 small lobster cut into pieces, 12 prawns, 12 clams or mussels, 1 Chorizo sausage cut into thin slices and 2–3 diced pimentos. Cover with half the rice. Top the rice with the remaining chicken. Add the other lobster cut into pieces, 12 prawns, 12 clams or mussels, 1 Chorizo sausage sliced and 2–3 diced pimentos. Cover with the rest of the rice. Store in the refrigerator.

▶ To serve, pre-heat the oven and bake in a moderate oven 350°F, Reg 4, for 40 to 50 minutes. Add a little of the remaining chicken stock from time to time so that it remains slightly moist.

▶ Serve in the dish it was cooked in.

# Cold Cheese Soufflé

| | |
|---|---|
| 3 oz. grated gruyère cheese | 8 oz. chicken stock, fresh or cubes |
| 3½ oz. grated parmesan cheese | 2 tablespoons tarragon vinegar |
| ½ teaspoon Dijon mustard | 12 oz. double cream |
| 1 tablespoon gelatine | 1 pinch cayenne pepper |
| salt and pepper | 3 tablespoons breadcrumbs |
| | stuffed olives |

▶ In a bowl, mix well 3 oz. grated gruyère cheese, 3½ oz. parmesan cheese, ½ teaspoon Dijon mustard and 1 pinch of cayenne pepper. Salt and pepper to taste.

▶ Soften 1 tablespoon gelatine in 2 tablespoons of chicken stock. Let it stand 5 minutes. Heat the rest of the stock and dissolve gelatine in the hot stock. Stir in the cheese mixture. When well mixed, stir in 2 tablespoons tarragon vinegar.

▶ Whip 12 oz. double cream. Whip the cheese mixture. When frothy and light fold in the cream. Chill in the refrigerator until set.

▶ To serve, make a mound on a round plate with a ring of stuffed olives around the outer edge. Sprinkle with breadcrumbs browned in very little butter and cooled.

# 50

## MENU

*Stuffed Courgettes*

*Baked Tongue, Cumberland Sauce*

*Purée of Brussel Sprouts*

*Compôte of Apples and Lychees*

## Stuffed Courgettes

| | |
|---|---|
| 6 medium-sized courgettes | 1 teaspoon crushed dried oregano or basil |
| 1 large tin pilchards in tomato sauce | 2 tablespoons olive oil |
| 4 large tomatoes | 2 tablespoons wine vinegar |
| | 4 spring onions or 2 tablespoons chopped chives |

salt and freshly ground pepper

▶ Simmer 6 medium-sized courgettes, covered, until tender, about 6 to 8 minutes, in a small amount of boiling salt water. Shake pan to keep from sticking. Drain. Cool.

▶ When cold, cut in half lengthwise. Carefully scoop out centres, do not break shells. Chop finely, drain excess liquid. Remove the bones from 1 tin pilchards in tomato sauce. Mash finely with a fork. Add little by little the courgette pulp, to make a moist but not runny filling for the shells. Discard the rest if necessary. Fill the shells. Place covered in refrigerator.

▶ Peel, seed and chop finely 4 large tomatoes. Add 1 teaspoon crushed dried oregano or basil, 2 tablespoons olive oil, 2 tablespoons wine vinegar, salt and freshly ground pepper to taste, and thoroughly mix. Set aside in refrigerator.

▶ Chop finely the spring onions or chives and put aside in a plastic bag.

▶ To serve, arrange courgettes on serving dish. Mix the tomato sauce well and pour over. Sprinkle with chopped spring onions or chives.

# Baked Tongue

| | |
|---|---|
| 1 large tin ox tongue | 8 oz. breadcrumbs |
| 2 eggs | 3 tablespoons melted |
| 4 oz. plain flour | butter |

▶ Flour the tongue well and shake free of surplus. Coat with lightly beaten salted eggs and then immediately roll into the breadcrumbs, patting them well in.

▶ Butter the bottom of an oval roasting tin generously and place the tongue in it. Cover and put into the refrigerator.

▶ To serve, pour the 3 tablespoons of melted butter over the tongue and heat in a moderate oven 350°F, Reg 4 for about 20 minutes. If the breadcrumbs are not sufficiently brown, increase the heat for the last few minutes.

▶ Serve Cumberland Sauce separately.

# Cumberland Sauce

| | |
|---|---|
| 3 shallots or small onions | ¼ teaspoon made mustard |
| 1 orange | ½ teaspoon horseradish |
| 1 lemon | 1 pinch ginger |
| 5 tablespoons red-currant jelly | 1 pinch cayenne pepper |
| 1½ tablespoons wine vinegar | 1 pinch salt |
| 3 tablespoons port | |

▶ With a vegetable peeler peel 1 orange and 1 lemon in thin slices with none of the white adhering to them. Cut peel into very fine shreds. Mince or chop 3 shallots or onions very finely. Put into a saucepan with the shredded rind and a little water and boil for 15 minutes. Strain off water. Put back into saucepan. Add 5 tablespoons red-currant jelly—Bar le Duc, if possible—3 tablespoons port, 1½ tablespoons wine vinegar, ¼ teaspoon made mustard, ½ teaspoon horseradish and a pinch each of cayenne pepper, ginger and salt. Mix

well and boil for 5 to 10 minutes. Cool and put in a jar. This will keep indefinitely in the refrigerator in a tightly covered jar.

# Purée of Brussels Sprouts

| | |
|---|---|
| 2 packets frozen sprouts | ½ oz. butter |
| | chopped parsley |
| 2–4 oz. chicken stock | |
| | salt and pepper to taste |

▶ Cook 2 packets frozen sprouts according to the directions on the packet. Drain. Blend in a liquidizer with chicken stock, add more stock if it seems too thick. Add salt and pepper to taste and stir in ½ oz. butter.

▶ Reheat in a double boiler. Add more butter and stock if necessary. Serve with chopped parsley.

# Compôte of Apples and Lychees

| | |
|---|---|
| 6 cooking apples | ½ tablespoon lemon juice |
| 4 oz. granulated sugar | |
| 8 oz. water | grated rind of ½ lemon |
| | 1 tin lychees |

▶ Stir and boil in a saucepan until dissolved 4 oz. granulated sugar, 8 oz. water, ½ tablespoon lemon juice and grated rind of ½ lemon.

▶ Peel, core and cut into eighths 6 apples. Add the fruit slowly to the boiling syrup and simmer gently over low heat until somewhat translucent. Do not break up the slices by over-cooking and letting them become mushy. Set aside to cool.

▶ Drain 1 tin of lychees. Add to the apples and chill.

# 51

## MENU

*Asparagus Tart*

*Salmon Trout, Sauce Gribiche*

*Cucumber Salad*

*Chocolate Ice Cream with Grated Marrons Glacés*

## Asparagus Tart

| Pastry | Filling |
|---|---|
| 6 oz. plain flour | 1 packet frozen green |
| pinch of salt | asparagus |
| 4 oz. butter | 4 rashers bacon |
| 1 egg yolk | 4 eggs |
| 1–2 tablespoons single | 8 oz. double cream |
| cream | 1 pinch cayenne |
| | pepper |

▶ Put 6 oz. of plain flour mixed with a pinch of salt on a board. With a pastry cutter or 2 knives cut 4 oz. butter into the flour, until thoroughly mixed and crumbly. Add yolk of 1 egg and 1 to 2 tablespoons single cream. Mix with your hands to form a soft dough. Wrap in a damp cloth. Chill in refrigerator for at least 2 hours.

▶ Roll out to fit a 7-inch pie tin. Make a fluted edge with the crust that laps over by folding it back, and pinch it with the thumb and forefinger. Prick the dough a couple of times with the prongs of a fork after you have placed it in the tin. Bake blind in a pre-heated oven at 400°F–420°F, Reg 6–7, 12 to 15 minutes or until lightly browned. When cool, wrap in wax paper and store in a dry place overnight.

▶ Cook the asparagus according to the instructions on the box or cook 1 bunch of fresh asparagus if available. Drain and put aside to cool. Store in a plastic bag in the refrigerator.

▶ Dice 4 rashers of bacon. Cook until crisp in a very little oil or butter. Drain on absorbent paper. Store in a plastic bag in a dry cool place, not in the refrigerator.

▶ Next evening, before the guests arrive, beat 4 eggs well. Add 8 oz. double cream and a pinch of cayenne pepper. Beat again. Stir in the bacon. Place the asparagus on the bottom of the baked pastry. Pour over the egg and bacon mixture. Just before serving time bake in a pre-heated oven at 350°F, Reg 4, for 20 minutes or until set and golden.

## Salmon Trout

| | |
|---|---|
| 1 3-lb. salmon trout | ½ teaspoon mixed |
| 1 oz. butter | Italian herbs |

▶ Have your fishmonger prepare a 3-lb. salmon trout, preserving the head and tail but removing the skin.

▶ Mix 1 oz. butter with ½ teaspoon mixed Italian herbs. Fill the stomach of the trout with this mixture. Lightly salt the trout.

▶ Wrap the trout in slightly buttered aluminium foil, first folding in the head and tail ends and then the sides, one overlapping the other. Put it in boiling water. Reduce heat and simmer for 20 minutes. Let it cool in the water it was cooked in. Remove from the water when cool and store in the refrigerator until next evening.

▶ Serve with Sauce Gribiche and Cucumber Salad.

## Sauce Gribiche

3 hard-boiled eggs | $\frac{1}{2}$ pint olive oil
$\frac{1}{2}$ teaspoon salt | $\frac{1}{4}$ pint malt vinegar
1 pinch pepper | 4–5 chopped dill
1 teaspoon Dijon |    gherkins
   mustard | 2 tablespoons chopped
 |    capers
2 tablespoons of chopped mixed parsley, tarragon, chives

▶ Put the yolks of 3 hard-boiled eggs through a fine sieve into a bowl. Add $\frac{1}{2}$ teaspoon salt, 1 pinch pepper and 1 teaspoon Dijon mustard. Beat well with a wooden spoon. Add very gradually, beating constantly, $\frac{1}{2}$ pint olive oil and lastly $\frac{1}{4}$ pint malt vinegar.

▶ Cut the whites of 3 hard-boiled eggs into fine julienne strips.

▶ Chop finely the gherkins. Chop capers. Chop very fine parsley, tarragon and chives to make 2 tablespoons in all. Stir all of these ingredients into the egg mixture. Store in a jar in a cool place.

## Cucumber Salad

2 young green | $1\frac{1}{2}$ tablespoons malt
   cucumbers |    vinegar
5 tablespoons olive oil | $\frac{1}{4}$ teaspoon salt
 | $\frac{1}{4}$ teaspoon pepper
finely chopped dill and parsley

▶ Score lengthwise with the prongs of a fork 2 young green cucumbers. Be sure that they are firm and hard. Slice in paper-thin slices. Sprinkle with salt and pepper. Store in refrigerator.

▶ Put 5 tablespoons olive oil, $1\frac{1}{2}$ tablespoons malt vinegar, $\frac{1}{4}$ teaspoon salt and $\frac{1}{4}$ teaspoon freshly ground pepper into a bottle with a tight lid. Shake well. Store in a cool place but not the refrigerator.

▶ To serve, drain cucumbers. Put in a glass salad bowl. Shake the vinaigrette in the bottle. Pour over cucumbers. Sprinkle with finely chopped dill and parsley.

## Chocolate Ice Cream with Grated Marrons Glacés

3 egg yolks | a few grains of salt
4 oz. castor sugar | 2 teaspoons vanilla
12 oz. milk | 8 oz. double cream
2 oz. bitter chocolate | 5 oz. approx. chopped
 |    marrons glacés

▶ Beat 3 egg yolks. Gradually beat in 4 oz. castor sugar. Beat until thick and smooth.

▶ Scald 12 oz. milk; with a wooden spoon, stir into the egg mixture. Add 2 oz. of grated bitter chocolate. Stir until dissolved. Cook in a double boiler over hot, not boiling water, until the custard coats the spoon. Add a few grains of salt. Cool and chill in refrigerator for 10 minutes.

▶ Add 2 teaspoons vanilla and 8 oz. double cream, unbeaten. Pour mixture into a refrigerator tray and freeze.

▶ Serve in cups and top with pieces of marrons glacés, about 5 oz. in all. You can also top it with grated coconut.

# 52

## MENU

*Mussel Soup*

*Boeuf a la Mode en Aspic*

*Waldorf Salad*

*Caramel Bread Custard*

## Mussel Soup

| | |
|---|---|
| 3 quarts mussels | 2 egg yolks |
| 12 oz. dry white wine | 8 oz. double cream |
| 8 shallots | 1 pinch cayenne |
| 1 clove garlic | pepper |
| | salt to taste |

▶ Pick over 3 quarts of mussels, discarding any that are not firmly closed. Scrub each mussel under running water with a stiff brush. With a small knife, scrape off the beard which protrudes from one side of the closed shell. Soak them for at least ½ hour to degorge any remaining sand.

▶ In a large enamelled pan, bring 12 oz. dry white wine to a boil with 8 shallots and 1 clove of garlic finely chopped. Onions can be used if shallots are not available. Boil 3 to 5 minutes to reduce slightly. Drain the mussels and add to the wine. Cover tightly and cook over high heat for 5 minutes, shaking the pan to cook the mussels evenly. Strain, reserving the broth. Remove the mussels from their shells and return to the broth. Cool and store in a tightly closed container overnight in the refrigerator.

▶ Beat 2 egg yolks and stir in 8 oz. double cream. Cover and store in refrigerator.

▶ To serve, reheat the mussels in their broth. Add the cream. Cook over low heat until slightly thickened. Add salt to taste and a dash of cayenne pepper.

## Boeuf à la Mode en Aspic

| | |
|---|---|
| 4 lb. fillet beef (rib end) | 1 bottle Madeira wine |
| 8 carrots | or Marsala |
| 3 onions | 2 tablespoons lard or |
| 3 celery sticks | oil |
| 8 sprigs parsley | 3 tablespoons brandy |
| 1 sprig thyme | 1¾ pints beef stock |
| 1 bay leaf | 1 calves foot |
| 3 cloves | 3 tablespoons gelatine |
| 1 teaspoon salt | 2 egg whites |
| ¼ teaspoon pepper | watercress or parsley |
| 1 bottle dry Sauterne | for garnish |

▶ Place in the bottom of an earthenware casserole 2 carrots, 3 onions, 3 sticks of celery, 8 sprigs parsley, 1 sprig thyme, 1 bay leaf, and 3 cloves. Rub a 4 lb. fillet of beef (rib end) with 1 teaspoon salt and ¼ teaspoon pepper. Place it on the vegetables. Pour over 1 bottle dry Sauterne and 1 bottle Madeira or Marsala. The casserole must be just large enough for the meat to be entirely covered by the wine. Cover and leave for 24 hours.

▶ Remove the beef. Dry thoroughly. Heat the wine and vegetable marinade with only 1½ pints of the beef stock. You can use tins or bouillon cubes for this. Brown the meat carefully on all sides in 2 tablespoons lard or oil. Pour over 3 tablespoons warm brandy. Flambé. Put the meat in a heavy pan. Pour over the warmed marinade mixture. Add 1 calves foot split, and 6 carrots peeled but not sliced. Bring to a boil. Reduce heat, taste for seasoning and simmer for 4 to 5 hours until tender in the covered casserole.

▶ Take out and put aside beef and 6 carrots. Strain the stock. Cool and remove all of the grease.

▶ Dissolve 3 tablespoons gelatine in
$\frac{1}{4}$ pint cold stock. Let stand 5 minutes.
Add to the remaining stock. Beat 2 egg
whites until stiff, add to stock. Heat to the
boiling point, stirring constantly.
Remove from heat and let stand 10
minutes. Strain by pouring stock through
a piece of dampened cheesecloth or through
a sieve. Pour stock into a deep mould to
the depth of $\frac{1}{4}$ inch. Put mould and the
rest of the stock into the refrigerator.

▶ Cut the meat in slices of uniform size
$\frac{1}{4}$–$\frac{1}{2}$ inch thick. Slice carrots thin.
Place a layer of meat slices on the stiff
jelly in the mould. Pour over some of
the slightly jellied stock. Place a layer of
carrots on the meat, cover with jelly, then
alternate layers of meat, carrots and jelly;
the last layer must be meat. Put in the
refrigerator overnight.

▶ When ready to serve, dip mould in hot
water for several seconds. Run a palette
knife around the edge of the aspic. Turn
serving dish over mould, reverse, and give a
sharp jerk to unmould the aspic onto the
serving dish. Surround with watercress or
parsley. Cut into slices at the table.

## Waldorf Salad

| | |
|---|---|
| 5 cooking apples | $\frac{1}{4}$ lb. pitted dates |
| 4 sticks of celery | $\frac{1}{4}$ lb. shelled walnuts |
| 3 tablespoons lemon juice | 4 oz. mayonnaise (Menu 48) |
| 3 tablespoons sherry | 4 oz. sour cream |
| chopped walnuts to garnish | salt and pepper |

▶ Peel and core 5 cooking apples.
Quarter the apples and cut into thin slices
lengthwise. Marinate in 3 tablespoons
lemon juice and 3 tablespoons sherry.
Cut 4 sticks of celery crosswise in thin
slices. Cut $\frac{1}{4}$ lb. dates into shreds. Break
$\frac{1}{4}$ lb. shelled walnuts into small pieces.
Salt and pepper slightly. Mix with the
apples. Combine 4 oz. mayonnaise with
4 oz. sour cream. Pour over the apples.
Mix well. Serve in a glass bowl with a few
chopped walnuts sprinkled on top.

## Caramel Bread Custard

| | |
|---|---|
| 8 oz. granulated sugar caramelized | 4 eggs |
| 14 thin slices stale bread | $1\frac{1}{2}$ oz. sugar |
| 3–4 oz. butter | 8 oz. double cream |
| 20 blanched almonds | 8 oz. milk |
| 1 grated lemon rind | rum or brandy |
| | cream for serving |

▶ To caramelize mould put 8 oz. granulated
sugar into a heavy frying pan. Shake over
heat without stirring until melted and
golden brown. Remove from stove. Add
3 tablespoons hot water and stir to the
consistency of thick syrup. Pour into
mould and tilt back and forth until all the
surfaces of the mould are covered. Cut the
crusts from 14 thin slices of stale bread.
Soften 3–4 oz. butter. Spread them onto
both sides of the bread slices. Cut each
slice into 3 pieces and line the bottom of
the caramelized mould with them. Shred 20
almonds. Sprinkle some of the almond
shreds and a little grated lemon rind on
the bread. Repeat until the bread is used,
alternating the direction of the bread
slices for each layer.

▶ Beat 4 eggs until foamy, add $1\frac{1}{2}$ oz.
sugar and beat again. Add 8 oz. double
cream and 8 oz. milk. Mix thoroughly and
keep in refrigerator until next day.

▶ Next evening pour the egg mixture over
the bread in the mould and place the
mould in a pan filled with hot water. Bake
in a moderate oven 350°F, Reg 4 for
40 to 50 minutes. Remove from oven but
leave mould in the pan filled with hot
water.

▶ Before serving, unmould. Put a
little rum or brandy into the mould to
rinse out any remaining syrup and pour
over pudding. Heat a little additional rum
or brandy, light it and pour over the
pudding. Serve flaming, with cream if
desired.

# 53

## MENU

*Oysters on the Half Shell, Cocktail Sauce*

*Jellied Duck*

*Green Bean Salad*

*Melon Melba*

## Oysters on the Half Shell

9–12 oysters per person

▶ If you are an old hand at this and have the proper knife, you can open the oysters yourself just before serving. We suggest, however, that you have the fishmonger deliver them already opened. They keep very well in the refrigerator.

▶ Arrange them on cracked ice in a serving plate. You may place in the centre a small glass of cocktail sauce, but to really savour the flavour of an oyster a few drops of lemon juice are sufficient, so serve them with lemon wedges.

▶ For those that must:

## Cocktail Sauce

| | |
|---|---|
| 6 oz. chili sauce | juice of 1 lemon |
| 2 oz. prepared horseradish | dash hot pepper sauce |

▶ Combine all ingredients and chill.

## Jellied Duck

| | |
|---|---|
| 1 young duck | $\frac{3}{4}$ pint chicken stock |
| 6 oz. lean bacon | 1 onion |
| 6 oz. lean pork | 1 carrot |
| 12 oz. dry white wine | 1 sprig thyme |
| 2 bay leaves | $1\frac{1}{2}$ tablespoons gelatine |
| salt and pepper | parsley sprigs to garnish |

▶ Remove the skin from a young duck. Cut the duck into thin slices as long as possible. Mince together 6 oz. of lean bacon, 6 oz. lean pork and the duck's liver. Salt and pepper. Line a greased mould with only half the mixture. Cover with the slices of duck and top with a layer of the remaining bacon, pork and duck livers. Put 1 bay leaf in the centre of the mould. Pour over 6 oz. good dry white wine. Cover and bake for 2 hours in an oven at 250°F, Reg $\frac{1}{2}$. Cool.

▶ Simmer over very low heat the bones of the duck, $\frac{3}{4}$ pint chicken stock, 1 onion, 1 carrot, 1 sprig of thyme, 1 bay leaf and 6 oz. dry white wine, for 1 hour. Drain, reserve the stock and when cool strain it through a fine cloth. Chill, then remove all the grease.

▶ Soak $1\frac{1}{2}$ tablespoons gelatine in 2 oz. cold water, let stand 5 minutes. Reheat the stock to the boiling point. Remove from the heat. Combine it with the soaked gelatine and stir until dissolved. Put aside to cool and then place in the refrigerator until the gelatine is half set.

▶ Cut the duck pâté in $\frac{1}{2}$-inch slices. Arrange slices on a serving dish and pour over the half-set jelly. Put in the refrigerator until next day.

▶ Decorate with sprigs of parsley and serve with a bowl of Green Bean Salad.

# Green Bean Salad

| | |
|---|---|
| 3 lb. French green beans | 6 tablespoons olive oil |
| 4¾ pints boiling water | 2 tablespoons wine vinegar |
| 2 tablespoons salt | ¼ teaspoon salt |
| chives and parsley | ¼ teaspoon dry mustard |
| lettuce for serving | ½ teaspoon freshly ground pepper |

▶ Snip off the ends of 3 lb. French green beans. Wash in hot water immediately before cooking. Using a very large saucepan, boil 4¾ pints water and 2 tablespoons of salt. Drop beans, a handful at a time, into the rapidly boiling water. Then bring back to a boil on a high heat, and boil slowly, uncovered, for 10 to 15 minutes. Taste one bean after 10 minutes, it should be slightly crunchy. Drain beans in a colander, and run cold water over them. Spread on a cloth and pat dry. Put them in the refrigerator in a covered bowl until next day.

▶ Put 6 tablespoons olive oil, 2 tablespoons wine vinegar, ¼ teaspoon dry mustard, ½ teaspoon freshly ground pepper into a screw-top jar and shake until thoroughly blended.

▶ Chop finely enough chives and parsley to have 2 level tablespoons of each.

▶ Pour vinaigrette, chives and parsley over beans and mix thoroughly.

▶ Serve on a bed of lettuce on a serving dish.

# Melon Melba

| | |
|---|---|
| 1 large ripe melon | 12 oz. guava jelly |
| 8 oz. strawberry jam | 8 oz. sherry |
| 4 oz. greengage jam | juice of 1 lime or lemon |
| 4 oz. red-currant jelly | 1½ pints double cream |
| 4 oz. brandy | |

▶ Mix the jams, jelly and brandy, and heat thoroughly.

▶ Cut the melon into sections, taking care not to separate them entirely from the bottom, spread segments flowerwise and fill with Ice Cream Indonesian Manner.

▶ Pour the hot jam mixture over each portion when serving.

*Ice Cream Indonesian Manner*

▶ Melt 12 oz. guava jelly with 8 oz. sherry over a low heat. Add juice of 1 lime, or 1 lemon if lime not available.

▶ Whip 1½ pints double cream stiff, fold into the guava sherry mixture and pour into refrigerator trays. Freeze to a mush, remove from ice compartment, beat well, and refreeze until solid.

# 54

## MENU

*Courgette Salad*

*Prawn Pilaf*

*Blackberry Melon*

## Courgette Salad

| | |
|---|---|
| 6 medium-sized courgettes | 2 oz. wine vinegar |
| 4 oz. olive oil | $\frac{1}{2}$ tablespoon sugar |
| 1 level tablespoon minced onion | $\frac{1}{2}$ tablespoon chopped parsley |
| $\frac{1}{4}$ teaspoon salt | $\frac{1}{2}$ tablespoon chopped fresh basil |
| | freshly ground pepper |

▶ Wash and cut without peeling 6 medium-sized courgettes into $\frac{1}{4}$-inch slices.

▶ Heat 4 oz. olive oil with 1 level tablespoon minced onion. Add the sliced courgettes and sauté for 2 minutes over high heat. Reduce heat, sprinkle with $\frac{1}{4}$ teaspoon salt and cook briefly until just tender but not mushy. Do not let them brown. Remove with a perforated spoon to a glass serving dish. Cool.

▶ Add 2 oz. wine vinegar and $\frac{1}{2}$ tablespoon sugar to the oil remaining in the pan. Bring to a boil. Simmer for 1 minute and cool. Pour over the courgettes. Chill in the refrigerator until served.

▶ To serve, sprinkle with $\frac{1}{2}$ tablespoon each of chopped parsley and fresh basil. Dried basil can be substituted if fresh is not available.

# Prawn Pilaf

2½ lb. large fresh
  prawns
  or 3 packets frozen
  shrimps or prawns
1 lb. fish heads and
  trimmings
1¼ pints dry white wine
1¼ pints water
3 large onions
1 bay leaf
1 sprig thyme
6 sprigs parsley

1 clove garlic
1 celery stalk
½ tablespoon coarse
  salt
6 peppercorns
6 oz. olive oil
4 large tomatoes
12 oz. patna rice
½ teaspoon saffron

▶ Make a court bouillon with 1 lb. fish heads and trimmings, 1¼ pints dry white wine, 1¼ pints water, 1 onion peeled and quartered, 1 bay leaf, 1 sprig thyme, 2 sprigs parsley, 1 clove garlic, 1 celery stalk, ½ tablespoon coarse salt and 6 peppercorns. Bring to a boil, cover and cook over moderate heat for 40 minutes.

▶ Strain bouillon into another saucepan, bring to a rapid boil and plunge 2½ lb. prawns or 3 packets frozen shrimps or prawns into the boiling liquid. As soon as water reboils turn down heat and cook only until prawns turn pink. Measure out 1¼ pints court bouillon and set aside for rice. Cool prawns in the remaining bouillon. If fresh large prawns are used, shell and de-vein as soon as they are cool enough to handle and replace in the bouillon until needed. Frozen shrimps or prawns that are already cooked when bought do not, of course, need cooking again.

▶ Skin, seed and chop 4 large ripe tomatoes.

▶ Heat 6 oz. olive oil in large heavy saucepan and fry 2 thinly sliced onions until very lightly browned. Add 12 oz. dry rice and stir until rice is coated with oil and transparent. Reheat reserved bouillon to boiling and pour over rice. Add chopped tomatoes and ½ teaspoon saffron diluted in a little warm water and simmer until liquid is almost completely absorbed and rice is tender, but not mushy. Take off

stove and, when completely cool, mix in the prawns or shrimps. Set aside the remaining bouillon to baste when reheating, if necessary.

▶ Oil a deep ovenproof serving dish, pour in the prawn or shrimps and rice mixture, cover and chill.

▶ Reheat in slow oven, 335°F, Reg 3, covered with tin foil. Sprinkle with 4 sprigs finely chopped parsley just before serving.

# Blackberry Melon

3 melons
6 oz. castor sugar
1½–2 lb. blackberries

▶ Cut melons in two lengthwise, scoop out seeds, wrap the two halves of each melon, hermetically sealed, in aluminium foil or plastic wrap, and chill. Wash and clean blackberries, mix with 6 oz. castor sugar and chill. Tinned Morello cherries can be substituted if there are no berries in season. Pile the sugared fruit into melon halves just before serving.

# 55

## Cauliflower Rio Grande

| | |
|---|---|
| 1 large head cauliflower | 2 avocados |
| 6 tablespoons olive oil | 2 tablespoons lemon juice |
| 3 tablespoons wine vinegar | 1 clove garlic |
| $\frac{1}{2}$ teaspoon salt | 1 tomato |
| fresh ground pepper | chopped parsley |
| 3 oz. blanched almonds | lettuce leaves for serving |
| | salt and pepper |

▶ Cut off the stalk of 1 large whole cauliflower, remove green leaves, steam over boiling water for about 30 minutes. Do not overcook as it must still be firm. Cool. Store in refrigerator.

▶ In a jar with a screw cover, shake, until well mixed, 6 tablespoons olive oil, 3 tablespoons wine vinegar, $\frac{1}{2}$ teaspoon salt and freshly ground pepper. Pour over the cauliflower and put in the refrigerator in a covered bowl.

▶ Next evening, blend in a liquidizer 3 oz. blanched almonds, and the vinaigrette from the cauliflower. Peel 2 avocados. Add to the almonds in the liquidizer with 2 tablespoons lemon juice and 1 peeled clove of garlic. Liquidize again. Skin and remove seeds of 1 tomato, add to mixture and liquidize. Add salt and freshly ground pepper to taste.

▶ To serve, place chilled cauliflower on a bed of lettuce leaves. Pour over some of the avocado sauce. Serve rest of sauce apart in a bowl. The avocado sauce must be prepared no more than an hour or so before the dinner; it cannot be left overnight.

## Carbonnade Flamande

| | |
|---|---|
| 1 lb. lean pork fillet | 1 tablespoon brown sugar |
| 2 lb. chuck or rump beef | 6 sprigs parsley |
| 5 oz. butter | 1 sprig thyme |
| $1\frac{1}{2}$ lb. onions | 1 bay leaf |
| 4 cloves garlic | 4 oz. brandy |
| 8 oz. stock, fresh or cubes | dash Tabasco sauce |
| 1 pint lager beer | 8 oz. sour cream |
| | salt and pepper |

▶ Slice finely $1\frac{1}{2}$ lb. onions. Melt 3 oz. butter in a casserole. Add onion and mix well with the melted butter. Add 4 cloves peeled, mashed garlic. Cover casserole and simmer on low heat for $\frac{1}{2}$ hour, stir from time to time, so that the onions will brown evenly.

▶ Cut 1 lb. of lean fillet of pork and 2 lb. of chuck or rump beef into slices 4 by 4 inches and $\frac{1}{2}$ inch thick. Melt the remaining 2 oz. butter in a frying pan. Brown slices of meat, a few at a time. Add to the onions and mix well.

Heat 8 oz. stock in the same frying pan. Pour over the meat. Add 1 tablespoon brown sugar. Mix well. Season to taste with salt and pepper. Make a bouquet garni with 6 sprigs of parsley, 1 sprig of thyme and 1 bay leaf tied together. Put into a casserole.

Pour over 1 pint lager beer. Simmer for a few minutes on top of stove until hot. Cover and put in a pre-heated oven, 335°F, Reg 3. Regulate oven so that the liquid in the casserole continues to simmer slowly. Cook about $2\frac{1}{2}$ to 3 hours. If a fork pierces the meat easily, it is done. Correct seasoning and remove bouquet garni. Set aside.

Next evening reheat the Carbonnade slowly on top of the stove on an asbestos mat. Add a dash of Tabasco and 4 oz. of brandy, stir. Then stir in 8 oz. sour cream. Serve with Peruvian Potatoes.

## Peruvian Potatoes

| 10 medium-sized potatoes | 1 teaspoon cayenne pepper or Tabasco sauce |
|---|---|
| 4 oz. oil | |
| 5 thick slices stale bread | 2 tablespoons tomato purée |
| 2 onions | $1\frac{1}{2}$ teaspoons salt |
| | 5 tablespoons grated gruyère cheese |

Wash 10 medium-sized potatoes. Cook in their jackets. Skin and cut into largish cubes.

Soak 5 thick slices stale bread, crusts removed, for 5 minutes. Squeeze out all the water and crumble. In a large saucepan heat 4 oz. oil. Fry breadcrumbs in the hot oil until crisp and reserve the oil. Remove with a perforated spoon to absorbent paper. When excess grease is absorbed, store in a bowl until next day.

Peel and slice crosswise into thin slices 2 onions. Fry in the hot oil in which the crumbs were cooked, until golden brown. Stir in scant teaspoon cayenne pepper or Tabasco sauce and 2 tablespoons tomato purée, mix well. Add the potatoes, sprinkle with $1\frac{1}{2}$ teaspoons salt, stir carefully so that the potatoes do not break. When they are all well coated with the mixture store in a cool place until next day.

To serve. Stir in the breadcrumbs and reheat on moderate heat. Just before serving, stir in 5 tablespoons grated gruyère cheese.

## Prunes in Red Wine

| 1 lb. large prunes | 1 stick cinnamon |
|---|---|
| 16 oz. red wine | rind $\frac{1}{2}$ lemon |
| 8 oz. sugar | double cream |

Soak 1 lb. of large prunes in red wine overnight.

Boil prunes in the wine to which you have added 8 oz. sugar, 1 stick cinnamon, and the rind of $\frac{1}{2}$ a lemon. Cook until the prunes are soft. Remove them and take out the stones. Let the juice boil a little longer, until it is reduced in quantity and thickened. Place in refrigerator.

Serve very cold with double cream.

# 56

## MENU

*Smoked Trout, Celery Relish*

*Boiled Chicken in Mushroom Sauce*

*Swiss Roesti Potatoes*

*Frozen Oranges*

## Smoked Trout, Celery Relish

| | |
|---|---|
| 3 large smoked trout | 1 tablespoon |
| 8 sticks of celery | horseradish |
| 3 tablespoons olive oil | 1 lemon |
| 3 tablespoons lemon | salt and freshly ground |
| juice | pepper |

▶ Remove the heads and tails from 3 large smoked trout. Cut in half lengthwise from stomach to back and carefully remove the bones. Dust with freshly ground pepper and arrange in an oblong serving dish flesh-side down. Cover and put in refrigerator.

▶ Wash, string, cut in half lengthwise and then in very thin slice crosswise, 8 sticks of celery. Put in a plastic bag or container into the refrigerator.

▶ In a jar with a screw top, shake well 3 tablespoons olive oil, 3 tablespoons lemon juice and 1 tablespoon grated horseradish. Add salt and pepper to taste. Set aside.

▶ Cut 6 thin slices of lemon. Wrap in foil and keep to garnish the trout.

▶ Next evening, arrange the trout on a serving dish. Shake the vinaigrette vigorously and pour over the celery. Mix well and surround the trout with the celery. Garnish with lemon slices.

## Boiled Chicken in Mushroom Sauce

| | |
|---|---|
| 2 small chickens | 1½ lb. mushrooms |
| 4 onions | 7 tablespoons butter |
| 6 leeks | 2 tablespoons plain |
| 2 sticks of celery | flour |
| 6 carrots | 8 oz. single cream |
| 6 sprigs parsley | salt |
| ½ teaspoon peppercorn | pepper |
| ½ tablespoon salt | paprika |

▶ Place wing-tips, neck and giblets of 2 chickens into a pan large enough to hold the birds, with 6 carrots peeled and cut in quarters lengthwise, 6 well-washed leeks, 2 sticks of celery, 6 sprigs parsley and ½ teaspoon peppercorns.

▶ Cover with 1½ pints cold water. Bring to a boil cover and cook rapidly for 1 hour.

▶ Place a peeled whole onion inside each bird and tie legs and wings to body. Plunge into boiling stock, reduce heat and simmer gently until tender but not falling to pieces. Add ½ tablespoon of salt after ½ hour's simmering.

▶ Strain stock and cool chickens in it. When cold, carve chicken into serving pieces, take out ¾ pint stock, replace pieces of chicken in the remaining liquid, cover and chill overnight.

*Mushroom Sauce*

---

▶ Wash and slice 1½ lb. mushrooms and fry rapidly in 5 tablespoons butter with 2 finely chopped onions. Season with salt and pepper and put aside.

---

▶ In a saucepan cook gently 2 tablespoons butter with 2 tablespoons plain flour. Reheat reserved ¾ pint stock with 8 oz. single cream and gradually add to flour and butter. Simmer for 10 minutes, stirring constantly. Cool the sauce, mix the mushrooms and onions into it and chill.

---

▶ Next evening reheat the sauce in a double boiler and the pieces of chicken in their liquid over low heat. When both are very hot, take chicken pieces out of boiling stock, arrange them in a hot ovenproof serving dish and pour the mushroom sauce over them. Cover and keep hot in a low oven, 290°F, Reg 1.

---

▶ Serve with Swiss Roesti.

## Swiss Roesti Potatoes

---

2½ lb. old potatoes (preferably floury ones)
3 oz. butter      1½ teaspoons salt

---

▶ Wash and peel 2½ lb. potatoes. Grate them on a coarse grater, sprinkle with 1½ teaspoons salt.

---

▶ Melt 2 oz. butter in a frying pan and toss in half the grated potatoes. Press them down, then add the other half. Cover with a flat plate smaller than the frying pan, pressing it firmly on to the potatoes. Fry for 15 minutes.

▶ Turn them out on to the plate and then let them slide back into the pan, so that the uncooked half covers the bottom of the pan. Fry for a further 15 minutes. Put them into an ovenproof dish and keep in the refrigerator.

---

▶ Next evening reheat them in this dish on top of the stove, adding the other 1 oz. butter. Repeat the process of turning them so that they will brown more on both sides. Keep warm until serving.

## Frozen Oranges

---

| 6 large oranges or | pinch of salt |
|---|---|
|   more | 8 oz. double cream |
| ½ lemon | 8 oz. milk |
| 5–6 oz. castor sugar | fresh leaves |

---

▶ Cut off the tops of 6 large oranges. Save the tops. With a grapefruit knife cut around the rind to loosen the pulp. Scoop out carefully with a spoon. Put orange cups aside. Extract as much juice as possible from the pulp. You will need 8 oz.

---

▶ In a bowl, combine 8 oz. orange juice, juice of ½ lemon, 5–6 oz. castor sugar and a pinch of salt. Gradually stir in 8 oz. milk and 8 oz. double cream. Stir until sugar is dissolved. Pour into refrigerator tray and freeze until the outer edge is solid. Transfer mixture to a bowl and beat with a rotary beater until it is smooth. Fill the orange cups with mixture. Cover each orange with a piece of foil and freeze until firm.

---

▶ In the evening, remove foil, replace top of orange and serve on a plastic leaf if fresh leaves are not in season.

---

▶ If your freezing compartment is not large enough for the 6 oranges, freeze the mixture in a tray instead and fill the orange when you serve.

# 57

## MENU

*Greek Lemon Soup*

*Bobotee*

*Pears Zingara*

## Greek Lemon Soup

| | |
|---|---|
| 16 oz. real chicken stock | 5 lemons |
| 12 oz. single cream | 1 teaspoon monosodium glutamate powder |
| 1 tablespoon cornflour | 1 pinch cayenne pepper |
| 4 egg yolks | chopped parsley |
| salt and pepper to taste | |

▶ In a saucepan combine 16 oz. chicken stock, 12 oz. single cream. Heat over a low heat stirring constantly. Stir in 1 tablespoon of cornflour which has been dissolved in 1 tablespoon water. Cook until it thickens, stirring constantly. Do not let it boil.

▶ Beat 4 egg yolks. Gradually pour a little hot soup into them. Stir until thoroughly mixed. Stir this mixture into the soup. Cook for 2 minutes until thoroughly mixed and slightly thick. Remove from the stove. Add the juice of 4 lemons, 1 teaspoon of monosodium glutamate powder, a pinch of cayenne pepper, salt and pepper to taste. Chill overnight in the refrigerator.

▶ Serve very cold in small single cups, garnished with paper thin slices of lemon and chopped parsley.

## Bobotee

| | |
|---|---|
| 2 lb. cooked lamb | 10 blanched and shredded almonds |
| 1 thick slice bread | 3 oz. seedless raisins |
| 8 oz. milk | 2 tablespoons curry powder |
| 2 medium onions | 1 teaspoon sugar |
| 1 apple | 1 tablespoon lemon juice |
| 2 oz. butter | 2 eggs |
| mango chutney | |
| salt and pepper | |

▶ Chop coarsely 2 lb. cooked lamb.

▶ Soak 1 thick slice of bread, crusts removed, in 8 oz. milk. Squeeze dry the softened bread, reserving the milk. Mix bread with the meat.

▶ Slice 2 medium onions paper thin, lengthwise, not in rounds. Peel, core, and slice lengthwise 1 apple into thin slices. Fry onions and apple in 2 oz. butter. Remove from heat. Add 10 almonds shredded, 3 oz. seedless raisins, 2 tablespoons curry powder, 1 teaspoon sugar and 1 tablespoon lemon juice. Mix well. Stir in 1 beaten egg, add the meat and stir over heat for a few minutes. Salt and pepper to taste. Put in a well-buttered pie dish. Set aside in a cool place until next day.

▶ Beat 1 egg. Add the reserved milk. Keep in the refrigerator until next evening.

▶ To serve, pour egg mixture over the meat and bake in a slow to moderate oven 310–335°F, Reg 2–3 for 1 hour. Serve with Rice and mango chutney.

# Rice

12 oz. long-grained rice    1 tablespoon butter
1½ pints boiling water    juice of 1 lemon
½ tablespoon salt

▶ Slowly pour 12 oz. long-grained rice, not the pre-cooked variety, into 1½ pints of rapidly boiling water salted with ½ tablespoon salt. Stir once. Cook uncovered for 15 to 20 minutes. When the rice is not quite ready, drain in a colander and run cold water over the rice in the colander until thoroughly cold. Drain well, shaking the colander vigorously. Place in a well-buttered oven dish. Store covered in a cool place until next day.

▶ To serve. Pour over the juice of 1 lemon. Dot with bits of butter, 1 tablespoon in all. Place uncovered in a moderate oven 350°F, Reg 4 for about 20 minutes. Stir once during this time.

# Pears Zingara

6 pears    8 oz. water
6 large oranges    8 oz. red wine
1 lb. granulated sugar    2 tablespoons Grand Marnier

▶ Peel, core and cut in half 6 pears.

▶ Make a syrup by boiling ½ lb. granulated sugar and 8 oz. water for 5 minutes. Poach the halves of pears in this syrup until tender. Remove the pears to a serving dish. Cook the syrup until it is reduced to half its original volume. Pour over the pears.

▶ Peel 6 large oranges, cutting well into the fruit so that you slice off all the white membrane. Cut into segments.

▶ Make a second syrup by boiling ½ lb. granulated sugar and 8 oz. red wine for 5 minutes. Pour over the oranges and steep for 1 hour.

▶ Remove the orange segments from the wine syrup and place around the pears. Cook the syrup until slightly thickened. Add 2 tablespoons Grand Marnier. Cool. Pour over the pears and oranges and put in refrigerator until served.

# 58

## MENU

*Greek Hors d'Oeuvres*

*Pheasant Tart*

*Wine Mousse*

## Greek Hors d'Oeuvres

| | |
|---|---|
| 2 large cucumbers | 16 oz. (approx. |
| 1 teaspoon fresh | 3 cartons) plain |
|   chopped mint |   yoghourt |
| 1 clove garlic | 6 small tomatoes |
| 2 anchovies | 2 avocados |
| fresh ground pepper | 5 oz. green olives |
| 1 lemon | a few red radishes |
| | $\frac{1}{2}$ lb. cooked prawns |
| | 1 teaspoon ketchup |

▶ Peel $\frac{1}{2}$ a cucumber, cut in quarters lengthwise, remove seeds and chop very finely. Chop finely 1 teaspoon of fresh mint leaves (if not in season, use 1 teaspoon of mint sauce). Crush 1 clove of garlic and chop 2 anchovies. Beat 16 oz. plain yoghourt, add ketchup, fold in these chopped ingredients and season with freshly ground pepper. Pour into bowl and chill.

▶ Quarter 6 small tomatoes. Peel and cut $1\frac{1}{2}$ cucumbers and 2 avocados into cubes. Sprinkle the latter with lemon juice and if possible only prepare these just before the dinner to prevent blackening. Add prawns. Wash radishes, cut off leaves.

▶ Serve each vegetable, and the olives, in individual bowls or on an hors d'oeuvres plate, and pass the yoghourt sauce separately.

# Pheasant Tart

| | |
|---|---|
| 1 casserole pheasant | 2 medium onions |
| 4 oz. butter | $\frac{1}{2}$ teaspoon cayenne |
| 6 slices fat bacon | pepper |
| $1\frac{1}{4}$–$1\frac{1}{2}$ pints chicken | 1 teaspoon salt |
| stock, fresh or | 4 oz. dry white wine |
| cubes | 3 pairs frankfurter |
| 2 white cabbages | sausages |

1 oz. plain flour

▶ Melt 2 oz. butter in a large frying pan. Brown pheasant quickly, turning frequently to avoid burning.

▶ Chop 6 slices bacon, fry lightly and put into a flameproof casserole. Place pheasant on top of bacon and pour over $\frac{3}{4}$ pint chicken stock. Cover and cook very slowly over low heat on an asbestos mat for 1 hour, adding more stock if it gets too dry.

▶ In the meantime, remove 4 good outer leaves from the 2 cabbages. Put aside. Then quarter the remaining cabbage and remove cores. Cover the quarters with boiling water, let stand for 5 minutes, drain and shred finely.

▶ Chop and fry 2 onions in the remaining 2 oz. butter until golden brown. Season with $\frac{1}{2}$ teaspoon cayenne and 1 teaspoon salt, add the shredded cabbage, mix and continue cooking for 10 minutes on low heat.

▶ Put the cabbage, another $\frac{1}{2}$–$\frac{3}{4}$ pints of chicken stock and 4 oz. dry white wine into the casserole with the pheasant and bacon. Simmer slowly until the bird is tender (1 to 2 hours, depending on its age). Add three pairs frankfurter sausages for the last 20 minutes of cooking.

▶ Take out the sausages and the pheasant and remove the bones from the latter. Drain the cabbage in a colander. Press to collect as much stock as possible. Reserve this liquid. Place the cabbage in an ovenproof serving dish, preferably earthenware, and arrange the pieces of pheasant and the sausages on top.

▶ To make sauce, skim off 2 tablespoons of fat from the reserved stock, put into a saucepan over medium heat, stir in 1 oz. flour, gradually add the drained stock. Cook over low heat, stirring constantly until thickened. Moisten the contents of the casserole with half the sauce and cover with the 4 reserved cabbage leaves. Put aside until next day.

▶ Reheat next evening in a slow oven 335°F, Reg 3 for about $\frac{3}{4}$ hour. Serve any left-over sauce, reheated, separately.

# Wine Mousse

| | |
|---|---|
| 4 egg yolks | 3 tablespoons |
| | castor sugar |
| 1 pint dry Sauterne | |

▶ Beat 4 egg yolks until light with 3 tablespoons castor sugar, and gradually add 1 pint dry Sauterne.

▶ Pour mixture into top of a double boiler and heat *over* but not *in* almost boiling water, beating constantly with a wire whisk or rotary beater until thickened, foamy and almost doubled in volume.

▶ Fill individual cups with the mousse and freeze until needed.

▶ Serve with dry sweet biscuits.

# 59

MENU

*Polish Borscht*

*Vitello Tonnato*

*French Green Bean Salad,
Vinaigrette Dressing*

*Apricot Tart*

## Polish Borscht

| | |
|---|---|
| 3¼ pints beef consommé | 1 tablespoon tarragon vinegar |
| 6 medium-sized cooked beetroots | 3 dill gherkins |
| salt and pepper to taste | |

▶ Put 3¼ pints beef consommé into a large saucepan.

▶ Peel and grate 6 medium-sized cooked beetroots. Add to the consommé, bring to a boil on a medium heat and simmer for ten minutes; add the tarragon vinegar and strain through a fine sieve. Then store in the refrigerator.

▶ The next evening, reheat. Put the gherkins, sliced paper thin and cut into strips, into each cup of soup before serving.

## Vitello Tonnato

| | |
|---|---|
| 3 lb. loin of veal, topside preferably | butter |
| 1 sliced carrot | 1 sliced onion |
| 1 bay leaf | 6 peppercorns |
| green olives for garnish | salt |

| | |
|---|---|
| 1 large tin tuna fish in oil | 2 teaspoons juice of cooked veal |
| 1 large tomato | salt and pepper to taste |
| | juice of ½ lemon |

▶ Butter the loin of veal, place on tin foil, dust it with salt, add scrubbed and sliced carrot, 1 sliced onion, 1 bay leaf, 6 peppercorns.

▶ Wrap it in tin-foil and seal the ends.

▶ Cook for 2 hours in a heavy fireproof casserole in a hot oven 420°F, Reg 7; then test it. If juice runs a clear yellow with no trace of rosy colour it is done, otherwise continue cooking up to 20 more minutes.

▶ Reserve and strain the juice after cooking. Wrap again in the tin-foil and store in refrigerator until next day. Then cut the veal into slices, coat one side with the tuna fish sauce, re-assemble and cover with remainder of the sauce. Garnish with green olives.

*Tuna Fish Sauce*

▶ Skin and seed 1 large tomato, chop finely.

▶ Remove the tuna fish from the tin. Save the oil in the tin.

Mash the fish, add the chopped tomato and put the mixture into a bowl. With a wooden spoon stir in the oil from the tin drop by drop until you have a thick paste. Mix in the lemon juice. Use the veal juice to mix in, if the fish sauce is too strong.

## French Green Bean Salad

| | |
|---|---|
| 2 lb. beans | 4 teaspoons salt |
| | 3 pints rapid boiling water |

Trim and wash 2 lb. of beans. To keep the colour of the beans, drop them into the boiling salted water, a handful at a time. Boil uncovered for 10 to 15 minutes. Taste a bean, it should be tender but crunchy. Drain in a colander and immediately run cold water over them for 5 minutes.

Drain again and put them on a clean cloth, and pat dry.

Put the beans into a covered bowl. Place in the refrigerator until ready for use. Serve with Vinaigrette Dressing.

## Vinaigrette Dressing

| | |
|---|---|
| 2 tablespoons wine vinegar | $\frac{1}{4}$ teaspoon dry mustard |
| $\frac{1}{2}$ teaspoon salt | 6 tablespoons olive oil |
| freshly ground pepper | chopped chives and parsley |
| | 2 hard-boiled eggs |

Place all the ingredients except the oil, chopped herbs and hard-boiled eggs in a small screw-top jar. Shake well until thoroughly mixed. Add the oil, shake again and put aside until ready to use.

Just before serving the salad, shake the dressing well and pour over the beans. Sprinkle with the chopped chives and parsley, garnish with quarters of hard-boiled eggs.

## Apricot Tart

| | |
|---|---|
| 8 oz. butter | 1 tablespoon grated lemon peel |
| 4 egg yolks | 4 oz. sifted flour |
| 8 oz. castor sugar | 1 lb. fresh or dried apricots |
| | apricot jam |

With your electric mixer beat 8 oz. butter until creamy. Add 8 oz. castor sugar, gradually beating all the time. When very smooth and creamy, beat in the egg yolks, one at a time. Stir in the 1 tablespoon grated lemon peel, fold in 4 oz. sifted flour.

Lightly grease a baking tin with butter, sprinkle with flour, shake off excess. Pour the cake mixture into the tin to a depth of $\frac{3}{4}$ inch. Cover with halves of ripe apricots. If you use dried apricots, they must be soaked for 12 hours and then thoroughly dried.

Bake in a medium oven, 300°F, Reg 3.

Glaze top of tart with melted apricot jam before serving.

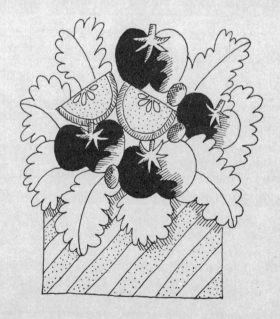

## MENU

*Smoked Salmon*

*Chicken Esterhazy*

*Austrian Risi Pisi*

*Raspberry Macaroon Bombe*

## Smoked Salmon

12 paper-thin slices smoked salmon
lemon wedges
black pepper
pumpernickel, rye bread or toast
butter

▶ Arrange 12 paper-thin slices of smoked salmon on a dish. Garnish with wedges of lemon.

▶ Have a pepper mill of black pepper on the table. Serve with thin slices of pumpernickel or dark rye bread spread with unsalted butter. Very thin slices of toast can replace the pumpernickel, if you prefer.

## Chicken Esterhazy

| | |
|---|---|
| 1 large chicken | 1 carrot |
| 4 tablespoons olive oil | 1 onion |
| 3 tablespoons wine vinegar | 3 sticks celery |
| | 3 tablespoons butter |
| salt and pepper | 3 tablespoons oil |
| 1 large onion | 1 tablespoon flour |
| 2 cloves garlic | $\frac{1}{2}$ lb. mushrooms |
| parsley, thyme and rosemary | juice $\frac{1}{2}$ lemon |
| | 2 tablespoons single cream |
| 2 bay leaves | |
| salt and pepper | |

▶ Cut a large chicken into 8 serving pieces. Reserve neck and back to make stock, and put the rest into a bowl. Pour over a marinade made of 4 tablespoons olive oil, 3 tablespoons vinegar, salt and pepper. Add 1 large onion and 2 cloves of garlic chopped, chopped parsley, thyme and rosemary. Mix well, marinate for 12 to 24 hours.

▶ Make the stock with 1 pint water, back and neck of chicken, 1 carrot, 1 onion, 1 bouquet garni (3 sticks of celery, 6 sprigs parsley, 1 sprig thyme and 1 bay leaf tied together with string). Simmer for 1 hour on low heat. Salt and pepper to taste. Add 1 chicken bouillon cube if stock is too weak and some of the marinade.

▶ Sauté the chicken in 1 tablespoon butter and 3 tablespoons oil for 15 minutes over a medium heat, pour on enough well-seasoned stock to cover the chicken and simmer very slowly until tender, adding more stock to keep it covered if necessary. This will not take long.

▶ Remove from the stove, put pieces of chicken aside, strain stock.

▶ Melt 1 level tablespoon butter, blend in 1 level tablespoon flour and stir in the strained stock. Cook until thickened, re-season if necessary. Add 2 tablespoons single cream and, when well mixed, pour over the warm chicken and put aside in a cool place.

▶ Cut off the stalks and wash thoroughly $\frac{1}{2}$ lb. mushrooms, drain, slice thinly with juice of $\frac{1}{2}$ lemon. Put in the refrigerator in a plastic container.

▶ Next evening cook the mushrooms in 1 level tablespoon butter for 5 minutes. Reheat the chicken in its sauce on a low heat and when hot add the mushrooms. Serve with Austrian Risi Pisi.

## Austrian Risi Pisi

| | |
|---|---|
| 2 tablespoons butter | 1 medium-sized tin of |
| 1 medium-sized onion, | peas |
| finely chopped | |
| 1 teaspoon salt | |
| 1 teaspoon paprika | |
| 6 oz. patna rice | |
| boiling water | |

▶ Melt the 2 tablespoons butter in a saucepan, add the finely chopped onion and rice and fry until the rice is slightly transparent. Put in the salt and paprika and pour sufficient boiling water over the rice to cover by $\frac{1}{2}$ inch. Cook covered for about 20 minutes.

▶ Fluff with a wooden spoon, adding the drained tinned peas. Keep in refrigerator and reheat in a moderate oven, 350°F, Reg 4, adding small pieces of butter and a little hot water if it seems too dry. This will take about 20 minutes.

## Raspberry Macaroon Bombe

| | |
|---|---|
| 1$\frac{1}{4}$ pints double cream | 1 packet frozen |
| 12 small macaroons | raspberries |
| 2 oz. kirsch | 3 tablespoons |
| | sweetened chocolate |
| | powder |

▶ Whip 1$\frac{1}{4}$ pints double cream until stiff.

▶ Crumble 12 small macaroons. Pour over 2 oz. kirsch and macerate for $\frac{1}{2}$ hour, then fold in $\frac{1}{3}$ of the whipped cream.

▶ Blend in the liquidizer 1 packet of frozen raspberries. Add castor sugar if they are not the sweet variety. Fold in $\frac{1}{3}$ of the whipped cream.

▶ Fold in 3 tablespoons sweetened chocolate powder and add the last third of the whipped cream.

▶ Fill the bottom of a mould with the macaroon mixture. Then pour over the raspberry mixture and lastly the chocolate cream. Cover the mould with foil and place in the freezing compartment for at least 4 hours or overnight.

▶ If Bombe has been left overnight, take it out of the freezing compartment and leave it in the refrigerator for at least an hour before serving. Turn out on a serving dish and serve.

# 61

## MENU

*Chopped Chicken Liver and Egg*

*Brisket of Beef and Butter-bean Casserole*

*Tomato Salad*

*Frozen Lemons*

## Chopped Chicken Liver and Egg

| | |
|---|---|
| ½ lb. chicken livers | 4 tablespoons grated |
| 1½ oz. butter | onion |
| 3 hard-boiled eggs | ½ teaspoon mustard |
| | 3 tablespoons sour |
| | cream |
| | sliced pumpernickel |
| | and butter |

salt and fresh ground pepper

▶ Lightly fry ½ lb. chicken livers in 1½ oz. butter.

▶ Blend in a liquidizer.

▶ Chop 3 hard-boiled eggs. Add to chicken livers with 4 tablespoons grated onion, ½ teaspoon mustard and 3 tablespoons sour cream. Blend again. Salt and pepper to taste. It must be light and fluffy. Add more cream if necessary. Store covered in refrigerator until used.

▶ Make a mound of the chicken liver on a plate and surround with thin slices of buttered pumpernickel.

## Brisket of Beef and Butter-bean Casserole

| | |
|---|---|
| 3 lb. brisket beef | 1 clove garlic |
| ¾ lb. dried butter- | 3 sticks of celery |
| beans | 3 sprigs parsley |
| 4½ pints water | sprig of thyme |
| 2 thick slices lean | 1 bay leaf |
| bacon | 2 teaspoons salt |
| 3 oz. coarse barley | ¼ teaspoon pepper |
| 2 carrots | 1 teaspoon ground |
| 1 onion | ginger |

▶ Soak ¾ lb. dried butter-beans in 4½ pints water overnight or for at least 8 hours.

▶ Parboil in boiling water for 10 minutes 2 thick slices of lean bacon. Drain, rinse with running cold water. Cut crosswise in ¼-inch strips.

▶ Bring to a boil in an ovenproof casserole a 3-lb. piece of a brisket of beef, the butter-beans and their liquid, the bacon strips, 3 oz. coarse barley, 2 carrots, an onion, a bouquet garni (3 sticks of celery, 3 sprigs parsley, a sprig of thyme and a bay leaf tied together), 1 clove of garlic crushed with 2 teaspoons salt, ¼ teaspoon pepper and 1 teaspoon ground ginger. Cover the casserole, reduce the heat and simmer for 40 minutes. Remove the carrots, the onion, and the bouquet garni. Cut the meat into serving pieces and return to the casserole. Cover and keep overnight.

▶ Next day, put the casserole in the oven, being very sure that it is tightly covered. Bake in a very slow oven, 250°F, Reg ½–1, for 5 hours. Serve in the casserole in which it was cooked.

## Tomato Salad

|  | *Dressing* |
| --- | --- |
| 6 tomatoes | 3 oz. tarragon |
| 1 bunch watercress |    vinegar |
|  | 1 tablespoon powdered |
|  |    mustard |
|  | 1 teaspoon salt |
|  | ⅔ cup olive oil |
|  | freshly ground pepper |

▶ Pour boiling water over the 6 tomatoes, drain, and peel them after 10 minutes, then chill for 1 hour in the refrigerator. Only when really cold, cut them into thick slices.

▶ Wash the watercress, drain and dry in a soft cloth. Chop off stems and place in the bottom of the salad bowl. Add the tomatoes. Mix the dressing in the usual way and pour over the salad.

## Frozen Lemons

| 8 oz. single cream | 8 oz. castor sugar |
| --- | --- |
| 8 oz. milk | 6 large lemons |

▶ Stir 8 oz. single cream, 8 oz. milk and 8 oz. castor sugar until the sugar is thoroughly dissolved. Pour into a refrigerator tray and freeze until the mixture is mushy.

▶ Remove to a bowl. Add the juice of 2 lemons. Beat well with a rotary beater. Pour into the refrigerator tray and freeze for 2 hours.

▶ Remove again to a bowl. Beat thoroughly. Return to freezer to harden.

▶ Cut the tops off 6 large lemons. With a grapefruit knife and a spoon remove all of the pulp and as much of the white membrane as possible without piercing the rind. Cut a paper-thin slice off the bottom of each shell so it will stand upright. Store in a plastic bag in the refrigerator until used.

▶ To serve, fill each lemon shell with the frozen cream. Piling it high. If any sort of leaves are available, serve each lemon on a leaf.

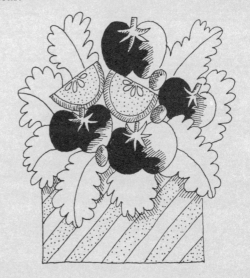

**62**

MENU

*Cucumbers in Sour Cream*

*Hounkiar Beyendi*

*Purée of Aubergines*

*Grand Marnier Fruit Cup*

## Cucumbers in Sour Cream

| | |
|---|---|
| 2 cucumbers | 4 tablespoons wine |
| 2 onions | vinegar |
| | $\frac{1}{2}$ pint sour cream |

salt and fresh ground pepper

▶ Soak peeled and thinly sliced cucumbers in iced water until crisp. Drain well.

▶ Slice, paper thin, 2 onions. Add to cucumbers, sprinkle with salt and freshly ground pepper. Pour over them 4 tablespoons wine vinegar and place in refrigerator.

▶ Drain when ready to serve and pour over them $\frac{1}{2}$ pint sour cream. Stir well with a spoon.

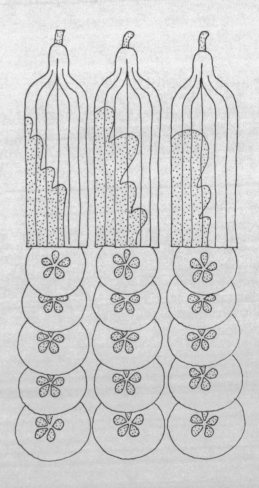

# Hounkiar Beyendi

| | |
|---|---|
| 6 thick veal escalopes | 6 oz. stock, fresh or |
| 3 tablespoons olive oil | cubes |
| 1 large onion | 1 teaspoon salt |
| 3 tablespoons tomato | 1 teaspoon paprika |
| purée | |
| 3 tablespoons ketchup | |

▶ Brown 6 thick veal escalopes slowly, 10 minutes each side, in 3 tablespoons olive oil. Season with 1 teaspoon salt, 1 teaspoon paprika. Remove to an ovenproof serving dish.

▶ In the same pan fry 1 large chopped onion until transparent. Add 3 tablespoons tomato purée, 3 tablespoons tomato ketchup, and 6 oz. stock. Mix well, cook for 5 minutes and pour over the escalopes.

▶ Reheat, covered, in oven at 335°F, Reg 3 for $\frac{3}{4}$ hour.

▶ In the Greek version $2\frac{1}{2}$ lb. of veal are cut into 2-inch cubes and fried with the chopped onion quickly until whitish, then the 3 tablespoons tomato purée, 3 tablespoons ketchup, 1 teaspoon salt, 1 teaspoon paprika are added and the 6 oz. of stock. The veal cubes are then stewed on a low heat.

# Purée of Aubergines

| | |
|---|---|
| 6 aubergines | 4 oz. single cream |
| 1 tablespoon butter | dash of Worcester |
| 4 oz. milk | sauce |
| | 1 tablespoon parmesan |
| | cheese (grated) |

▶ Wash the aubergines and place in a fireproof dish with a small quantity of water. Cover with greaseproof paper or a lid and bake in a moderate oven 350°F, Reg 4 until tender, about 40 to 45 minutes.

▶ Remove aubergines, wrap in a damp towel and let them stand for about 10 minutes to loosen the skins. Peel, place flesh in a bowl, add butter and beat with a wooden spoon until smooth.

▶ Heat milk and cream together over a low heat and add slowly to the aubergine mixture, stirring until the consistency is thick and creamy. Season to taste, add Worcester sauce and parmesan cheese, stirring continually. Place in a cool place until required.

▶ To reheat, place saucepan on an asbestos mat over a very low flame.

▶ Serve in a bowl, and serve the veal separately, either Turkish or Greek version.

# Grand Marnier Fruit Cup

| | |
|---|---|
| 4 oranges | 4 oz. castor sugar |
| 2 grapefruits | 3 tablespoons Grand |
| 1 small packet pitted | Marnier |
| dates | |

▶ To section oranges and grapefruits, cut off a small slice of the top of the orange or grapefruit. Place on a board cut-side up. With a sharp knife remove the rind and the white skin, cutting from top to bottom. When all is removed, slice off the bottom. Over a bowl so as to catch the juice, loosen the sections by cutting down along the membranes. Lift out the segments in one piece and remove any seeds.

▶ Cut in shreds 1 small packet of dates. Add to the orange and grapefruit sections. Add 4 oz. castor sugar, mix well. Pour over 3 tablespoons Grand Marnier. Place in refrigerator until served.

## 63

### MENU

*Peppers Monégasque*

*Grouse and Baked Beans*

*Rum Cake*

## Peppers Monégasque

| | |
|---|---|
| 6 sweet red peppers | 1 bay leaf |
| 6 medium-sized | 4 oz. olive oil |
| tomatoes | ½ teaspoon saffron |
| 5 oz. seedless raisins | 4 oz. white wine |
| 3 oz. black olives | 1 tablespoon brown |
| 12 very small onions | sugar |
| 3 sticks of celery | 1 pinch cayenne |
| 3 sprigs parsley | pepper |
| 1 sprig thyme | 1 teaspoon salt |
| | ¼ teaspoon pepper |

▶ Grill 6 sweet red peppers (green peppers can be substituted if red not available) over high heat (if on gas, over flame), until the skin blisters and blackens. Put immediately into cold running water. Peel off the blackened skin. Cut in halves lengthwise, remove the seeds and white membranes. Cut across into thin strips. Peel 6 medium tomatoes. Cut in quarters, remove the seeds and juice. Cut into small pieces.

▶ Prepare a bouquet garni by tying together 3 sticks of celery, 3 sprigs parsley, 1 sprig of thyme and 1 bay leaf. Soak 5 oz. seedless raisins in lukewarm water. Remove stones from 3 oz. black olives. Blanch and peel 12 very small onions. Heat 4 oz. olive oil in a saucepan. Add tomatoes, ½ teaspoon saffron diluted in a little warm water, the bouquet garni, 1 teaspoon salt and ¼ teaspoon pepper. Cook 20 minutes over a low heat.

▶ Remove bouquet garni. Put through a sieve or liquidizer. Add onions, drained raisins and olives to the tomato purée. Stir in 4 oz. white wine, 1 pinch cayenne pepper and 1 tablespoon brown sugar. Cook over low heat until the onions are tender, stirring occasionally. Add the sliced peppers. Cook 10 minutes longer. Cool and put in the refrigerator overnight.

▶ Serve in a glass salad bowl.

## Grouse and Baked Beans

| | |
|---|---|
| 1½ lb. dried butter- | 1 teaspoon dry |
| beans | mustard |
| 3 casserole grouse | 1½ teaspoons salt |
| 1-lb piece lean bacon | 2 tablespoons treacle |
| 9 small onions | |

▶ Wash and soak overnight 1½ lb. dried butter-beans. Next morning, drain. Clean and truss 3 casserole grouse. Cut a 1-lb. piece of lean bacon into 6 pieces. Score each piece in several places. Blanch in boiling water 10 minutes. Drain, rinse with cold water.

▶ Place the 3 grouse in a deep ovenproof dish. Dust with 1½ teaspoons salt. Put 9 blanched peeled small onions around them. Cover birds with the drained beans. Put the pieces of bacon scored side up into the beans. Make a paste of 1 teaspoon dry mustard, 2 tablespoons treacle and a little hot water to dissolve it. Pour over the

beans. Add enough water to cover the
beans and grouse. Close the lid tightly.
Bake slowly in a pre-heated oven at
300°F, Reg 1–2 without stirring for 4 to 6
hours. Add a little boiling water from time
to time so that the beans do not dry out.

▶ 15 minutes before serving remove the lid
and allow the beans to brown. Serve in the
same ovenproof dish. The grouse remain
whole but the meat falls from the bones.
If made 24 hours earlier bake for only
3–5 hours, keep tightly covered in a cool
place and bake the grouse for 1 hour before
serving.

## Rum Cake

| Crust | Filling |
|---|---|
| 9 oz. digestive biscuit crumbs (use Graham crackers if obtainable) | 4 eggs |
| | 12 oz. castor sugar |
| | 1 oz. plain flour |
| | 16 oz. single cream |
| 2 oz. icing sugar | $\frac{1}{2}$ tablespoon gelatine |
| 5 tablespoons melted butter | 2 tablespoons water |
| | $1\frac{1}{2}$ oz. grated bitter chocolate |
| | $\frac{1}{8}$ teaspoon cream of tartar |
| | 3 tablespoons dark rum |
| | 4 oz. double cream |

▶ Crush very finely the digestive biscuits by
rolling them with a rolling pin until you
have $1\frac{1}{2}$ teacups. Add 2 oz. icing sugar, mix
well. Stir in 5 tablespoons melted butter
until well blended. Pat into the bottom and
sides of a large pie tin. Bake in an oven
300°F, Reg 2 for 15 minutes. Remove from
oven and cool in the tin.

▶ Beat the yolks of 4 eggs. Add gradually
8 oz. castor sugar from the measured sugar,
beat until creamy. Stir in 1 oz. flour, blend
well. Pour over 16 oz. scalded single
cream. Cook in the top of a double boiler
over hot, not boiling water, stirring
continuously until it coats a wooden spoon.

▶ Soak $\frac{1}{2}$ tablespoon gelatine in
2 tablespoons water for 3 minutes. Add to
the egg mixture and stir until it dissolves.

▶ Take half the custard and add $1\frac{1}{2}$ oz.
grated bitter chocolate, stir until chocolate
is melted and custard is a uniform colour.
When cool add to the cooled biscuit pie
shell.

▶ Beat 4 egg whites until stiff. Beat in 4 oz.
castor sugar and $\frac{1}{8}$ teaspoon cream of
tartar.

▶ When the rest of the custard is cool
stir in 3 tablespoons dark rum. Fold in the
beaten egg whites, mix well. Spoon over
the chocolate custard.

▶ Whip 4 oz. double cream, cover the top
of the pie. Wrap in wax paper. Put in the
refrigerator for 24 hours.

# 64

## MENU

*Tomatoes Stuffed with Smoked Salmon Pâté*

*Gratin of Veal*

*Broccoli*

*Belgian Rhubarb Tart*

## Tomatoes Stuffed with Smoked Salmon Pâté

| | |
|---|---|
| 6 small tomatoes | 1 teaspoon grated |
| 1 cup of minced | onion |
| smoked salmon | 1 tablespoon lemon |
| 3 level tablespoons | juice |
| butter | 1 level tablespoon |
| 1 level tablespoon | chopped parsley |
| anchovy paste | salt and pepper |
| | watercress or parsley |
| | to serve |

▶ Cut off the tops of 6 small tomatoes. Carefully scoop out the pulp, seeds and juice. Season with salt and pepper. Chill.

▶ Mince enough smoked salmon to make 1 cup. Cream 3 tablespoons butter. Add 1 tablespoon anchovy paste, mix thoroughly. Add the salmon, 1 teaspoon grated onion, 1 tablespoon lemon juice and 1 tablespoon finely chopped parsley. Beat with a wooden spoon until everything is thoroughly mixed. Pour off any water which may have formed in the tomatoes, stuff them with the salmon mixture. Keep in the refrigerator until ready to serve on a bed of watercress, or parsley.

## Gratin of Veal

| | |
|---|---|
| $2\frac{1}{2}$-lb. boned leg of veal | 3 tablespoons dry white wine |
| 1 pinch of thyme | 1 pinch of cayenne |
| 2 rashers of bacon | pepper |
| 3 medium onions | 4 tablespoons single |
| 3 tablespoons brandy | cream |
| 4 oz. butter | 4 tablespoons grated |
| 1 oz. plain flour | gruyère cheese |
| 8 oz. milk | salt and pepper |

▶ Season $2\frac{1}{2}$ lb. of veal with salt and pepper and pinch of thyme.

▶ Melt 2 oz. butter in a heavy casserole, lightly brown the meat on all sides in the butter. Lay 2 rashers of bacon on top of the meat and secure with toothpicks.

▶ Peel and cut into thin slices 3 medium-sized onions; surround the meat in the casserole with the onions. Stirring the onions constantly, cook over high heat until golden brown. Reduce heat, put lid tightly on the casserole and cook over low heat for $\frac{1}{2}$ hour. Warm 3 tablespoons of brandy, light and pour flaming over the meat. Cover again and cook for $\frac{1}{2}-\frac{3}{4}$ hour longer or until meat is tender.

▶ Melt 2 oz. butter in a saucepan and with a wooden spoon stir in 1 oz. flour. Stirring constantly, cook for 2 minutes. Add 8 oz. milk. Stirring constantly, cook over low heat about 10 minutes until it thickens. Season with salt and pepper.

▶ Remove the meat from the casserole. Stir in 3 tablespoons dry white wine, and a pinch of cayenne pepper. Cook for a few minutes over high heat, stirring constantly. Remove from stove and pass the sauce through a fine sieve or liquidizer, then stir in the white sauce. Mix well. Add 4 tablespoons single cream and 2 tablespoons grated gruyère cheese. Mix well.

▶ Cut the meat in thin slices and put in an ovenproof serving dish. Pour over the sauce, place, covered, in the refrigerator until next day.

▶ To serve, sprinkle the remaining 2 tablespoons grated gruyère cheese over the meat. Reheat in a moderate oven, 350°F, Reg 4, for 20–30 minutes, raising the heat at the last minute to form a golden crust.

# Broccoli

2 packets frozen broccoli
2 oz. butter
1 level tablespoon breadcrumbs

▶ Cook 2 packets of frozen broccoli according to the instructions on the packet. Drain. Keep in a covered dish in the refrigerator.

▶ Crumble fine dry bread to make 1 level tablespoon breadcrumbs.

▶ To serve, reheat the broccoli in a steamer. Melt 2 oz. butter; when hot, stir in 1 tablespoon breadcrumbs, brown them slightly.

▶ Serve the broccoli in a dish with the melted butter and breadcrumbs poured over.

# Belgian Rhubarb Tart

| Pastry | Filling |
|---|---|
| 12 oz. plain flour | 1 lb. rhubarb |
| 8 oz. butter | 1 lemon |
| 3 oz. castor sugar | 1 large brioche— |
| 1 egg | 8 oz. |
| pinch salt | 3 oz. butter |
| | 8 oz. castor sugar |

▶ Make a mound of 12 oz. plain flour on a board. Make a large well in the centre of the mound, cut 8 oz. butter into small pieces, fill the well with this, then add 3 oz. castor sugar, pinch of salt, and 1 egg. With your hands quickly work the ingredients into a smooth dough. Form into a ball, wrap in a damp cloth and chill in the refrigerator for 1 hour.

▶ Wash and peel the 1 lb. of rhubarb. Pour over the juice of 1 lemon.

▶ Roll out the dough and line a 9-inch buttered pie tin.

▶ Cut an 8 oz. stale brioche (any rich sweetened bread may be used if brioche is not available) into thin slices. Cut slices in half and line the pastry shell with them. Melt 3 oz. butter, pour over the bread, sprinkle with 4 oz. castor sugar, cover with rhubarb, sprinkle with remaining 4 oz. sugar. Bake in a pre-heated oven at 450°F, Reg 8 for 10 minutes. Reduce heat to 350°F, Reg 4 for about 30 minutes or longer.

▶ Serve slightly warmed through, or cold.

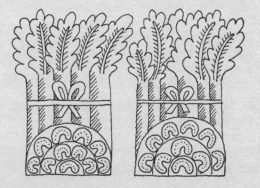

# 65

## MENU

*Crabmeat in Red Pepper Relish*

*Mediterranean Chicken Pie*

*Lettuce and Avocado Salad*

*Hedgehog Peaches*

## Crabmeat in Red Pepper Relish

| | |
|---|---|
| ¾ lb. crab, fresh or tinned | 5–6 heaped tablespoons red pepper relish (see recipe for Pepperoni Relish, Menu 33) |
| 6 tablespoons olive oil | |
| 2 tablespoons wine vinegar | |
| ¼ teaspoon salt | 2 hard-boiled eggs |
| ¼ teaspoon pepper | lettuce leaves |
| | chopped parsley |

▶ Flake and remove the membranes from ¾ lb. fresh or tinned crabmeat. Put in the refrigerator.

▶ Make a vinaigrette. Shake well in a jar with a screw top 6 tablespoons olive oil, 2 tablespoons wine vinegar, ¼ teaspoon salt, ¼ teaspoon pepper. Add 5–6 heaped tablespoons red pepper relish, or to taste, and set aside.

▶ To serve, shake vinaigrette, then pour over crabmeat. Mix well, using a fork. Serve on a bed of lettuce leaves, surrounded by slices of hard-boiled eggs. Sprinkle with a bit of chopped parsley.

## Mediterranean Chicken Pie

| | |
|---|---|
| 1 5-lb. roasting chicken | 16 oz. port |
| unsalted dripping | grated rind of 1 orange |
| 4 slices lean bacon, ¼-inch thick | 3 oranges |
| | ½ tablespoon lemon juice |
| 12 very small onions | 3 oz. butter |
| 1 lb. small mushrooms | 1 oz. flour |
| 4 hard-boiled eggs | salt to taste |
| 16 oz. chicken stock | |

| | |
|---|---|
| 1¼ lb. flour | 2 egg yolks |
| 8 oz. butter | 2–3 tablespoons light cream |
| | pinch of salt |

▶ Rub a 5-lb. chicken with soft, unsalted dripping. Place on a greased rack, in a roasting pan, uncovered, breast-side up, with the oven pre-heated to 450°F, Reg 8. Reduce heat immediately to 350°F, Reg 4. Baste frequently with the pan dripping and cook about 1 or 1¼ hours until nearly done. Remove the chicken and the rack, leaving the dripping in the pan. Cut chicken into serving pieces and place in a deep ovenproof pie dish.

▶ Cut across into ¼-inch wide strips 4 slices of lean bacon. Put in a saucepan, pour boiling water over them and simmer for 10 minutes. Drain, rinse with cold water and dry thoroughly.

▶ Blanch and peel 12 very small onions. Remove the stalks of 1 lb. small mushrooms. Wash mushrooms thoroughly, rinsing 2 or 3 times. Dry.

▶ In the fat remaining in the roasting pan cook the bacon, onions, mushrooms over high heat on top of the stove, until slightly brown. Remove from the pan and add to the chicken.

▶ Add 4 hard-boiled eggs, quartered.

▶ Skim the fat from the roasting pan and stir into the remaining liquid 16 oz. chicken stock, 16 oz. port, the grated rind of 1 orange, the juice of 3 oranges, and ½ tablespoon lemon juice. Heat over moderate fire.

▶ In a saucepan, melt 3 oz. butter, blend with 1 oz. flour and, stirring continuously, cook until slightly brown. Stir in the port mixture gradually. Simmer over moderate heat, stirring continuously until it slightly thickens, 5 or 10 minutes. Pour over the chicken in the pie dish and when cool put into refrigerator until next day.

*Pie Crust*

▶ Put 1¼ lb. flour in a bowl and with a pastry cutter or 2 knives cut 8 oz. butter into it. Add 2 egg yolks, a pinch of salt, and 2 or 3 tablespoons single cream. With your hand, knead the dough lightly so that it barely holds together. Put in a plastic bag in the refrigerator overnight.

▶ Next day, roll and pat out the dough on a floured board ¼ inch thick, to fit the top of the pie dish. Set it over the mixture in the pie dish and press it securely to the edges. Bake in a moderate oven, 350°F, Reg 4, 30 minutes or until crust is brown.

## Lettuce and Avocado Salad

| | |
|---|---|
| 2 heads lettuce | 2 tablespoons wine |
| 2 avocados | vinegar |
| 1 clove garlic | ½ teaspoon salt |
| 6 tablespoons olive oil | ¼ teaspoon pepper |
| | juice of 1 lemon |

▶ Discard outer leaves of 2 heads of lettuce. Wash remainder in cold water. Drain, shake well to remove all water. Wrap in a towel and store in the vegetable compartment of refrigerator.

▶ In a jar with a screw top shake vigorously 6 tablespoons olive oil, 2

tablespoons wine vinegar, ½ teaspoon salt, ¼ teaspoon pepper and 1 peeled clove of garlic. Put aside.

▶ Before dinner peel 2 avocados and cut into large chunks. Sprinkle with juice of 1 lemon, put aside. This should be done not more than 2 hours and preferably 1 hour before, so that the avocados will not discolour.

▶ To serve. Combine the lettuce and avocado in a salad bowl. Pour over the dressing after removing the clove of garlic. Toss the salad carefully.

## Hedgehog Peaches

| | |
|---|---|
| 6 fresh peaches | 5 oz. red-currant jelly |
| 16 oz. water | 1 teaspoon lemon juice |
| 4 oz. granulated sugar | ¼ lb. blanched |
| | almonds |

▶ Prepare a syrup of 16 oz. water and 4 oz. granulated sugar. Cook until sugar dissolves and syrup is clear.

▶ Pour boiling water over 6 ripe peaches. Let them stand 5 minutes. Drain. Cool them by running cold water over them. Carefully remove the skins.

▶ Poach peaches immediately in the hot syrup for 8 to 10 minutes. Remove from syrup to cool.

▶ Cut ¼ lb. blanched almonds into slivers. Stick the slivers into the peaches. Put in a container with a cover. Pour over syrup and put in refrigerator until 1 hour before dinner.

▶ Before serving, melt 5 oz. red-currant jelly with 1 teaspoon lemon juice, 1 tablespoon of peach syrup. If too thick, add a little water, heat and pour over the fruit arranged on a serving dish with raised sides.

# 66

## MENU

*Sweet and Sour Beans*

*Magyar's Gulyas, New Potatoes*

*Roquefort Balls in Aspic*

## Sweet and Sour Beans

| | |
|---|---|
| 2½ lb. French green beans | 3 tablespoons sugar |
| ¼ lb. lean bacon | ½ pint cider vinegar |
| ½ oz. butter | salt |
| 2 onions | |

▶ Wash and string 2½ lb. French green beans. Cut as preferred or leave them whole if they are small.

▶ Drop the beans a handful at a time into a large pan containing 6 or 7 pints of rapidly boiling salt water, ½ teaspoon salt for each pint of water. Bring back to a boil and cook for 10 to 15 minutes until tender. Drain and cool.

▶ Remove the rinds and chop finely ¼ lb. lean bacon. Fry in ½ oz. butter. Add 2 onions previously minced, cover and cook over medium heat for 5 minutes. Stir in 3 tablespoons sugar and ½ pint cider vinegar. Simmer for 10 minutes. Cool. Pour over beans, mix well and chill in refrigerator overnight.

▶ To serve, reheat in the top of a double boiler and serve in a hot vegetable dish.

## Magyar's Gulyas, New Potatoes

| | |
|---|---|
| 3 lb. beef (chuck, shin or flank) | 1¼ pints mixed beef and chicken stock made of cubes |
| 3 lb. onions, coarsely chopped | 1 lb. tomatoes peeled, seeded and chopped |
| 1 oz. lard | 1 medium-size green pepper, seeds and ribs removed |
| ½ tablespoon salt and a pinch of pepper | |
| 3 tablespoons sweet Hungarian paprika | 1½ lb. very small new potatoes |

▶ Cut the meat into 1-inch thick slices, remove all fat and cut slices into 1-inch cubes. Peel and chop coarsely 3 lb. of onions. Melt 1 oz. lard in a heavy casserole. Add onions and cook over low heat until they are soft. Stir in, off the heat, 3 tablespoons paprika and $\frac{1}{2}$ tablespoon salt. Add meat and 8 oz. stock, bring to the boil. Partially cover the casserole. Turn heat down and simmer for 1 hour or more until the meat is almost tender. If meat is getting dry add more stock. (You ought to have plenty of gravy, but as different kinds of onions give different amounts of juice, you may have to add more stock.)

▶ Now remove the meat and strain the gravy. Return both to the casserole, add chopped pepper and tomatoes. Taste for seasoning. Cook over medium heat for 25 to 35 minutes, again partially covered. When tender let it cool and store in refrigerator.

▶ Cook $1\frac{1}{2}$ lb. of small potatoes in their skins in plenty of water.

▶ Next day skim any fat off the surface of the Gulyas. Peel potatoes and mix into the Gulyas. Reheat in the evening slowly on top of the stove.

## Roquefort Balls in Aspic

| | |
|---|---|
| $\frac{1}{2}$ lb. Roquefort cheese | 16 oz. sherry flavoured |
| 4 oz. butter | tinned consommé or |
| $\frac{1}{4}$ teaspoon pepper | 2 tablespoons of aspic |
| | powder, diluted |
| | in 16 oz. water and |
| | 1 tablespoon sherry |
| | celery and tomatoes |
| | to garnish |

▶ Put $\frac{1}{2}$ lb. Roquefort cheese through a fine sieve. Cream 4 oz. butter until smooth. Beat in the Roquefort and $\frac{1}{4}$ teaspoon pepper. Form into balls the size of a walnut. Pour 8 oz. of the aspic on the bottom of a ring mould and let it set in the refrigerator. When set, place the Roquefort balls on the aspic in the mould. Pour over the remaining aspic. Place in refrigerator overnight. To serve, unmould onto a serving dish and decorate with sticks of celery and tomatoes cut lengthwise in eighths.

## MENU

*Indonesian Salad*

*Saupiquet with Ham Montbard*

*Cherry Croquemtouffle*

## Indonesian Salad

| | |
|---|---|
| 2 oz. long-grained rice | 1 tablespoon lemon |
| 1 tinned lobster | juice |
| 1 green pepper | $\frac{1}{4}$ teaspoon salt |
| 3 shallots or small | $\frac{1}{4}$ teaspoon pepper |
| onions | $\frac{1}{4}$ teaspoon curry |
| 3 tablespoons olive oil | powder |
| | chutney |

▶ Cook in a large amount of boiling water 2 oz. long-grained rice. Cook 15 to 20 minutes, stirring occasionally until done. Drain in a colander.

▶ Immediately run cold water over it until rice is thoroughly cold. Let it drain in the colander until completely dry. Cut 1 tinned lobster into smallish pieces. Wash, remove the seeds and white membrane from 1 green pepper. Chop coarsely. Peel and chop 3 shallots, or small onions. Mix it all with the rice.

▶ Make a dressing by shaking in a jar 3 tablespoons olive oil, 1 tablespoon lemon juice, $\frac{1}{4}$ teaspoon salt, $\frac{1}{4}$ teaspoon pepper, $\frac{1}{4}$ teaspoon curry powder.

▶ It is better to prepare everything beforehand and mix salad and dressing just before serving.

▶ Pour over the rice and with a fork mix well. Serve heaped on a nest of green leaves. Decorate with pieces of chutney.

## Saupiquet with Ham Montbard

| | |
|---|---|
| 1 2-lb. tin Danish ham | 2 sticks of celery |
| 2 onions | 8 sprigs parsley |
| 2 carrots | 1 sprig thyme |
| 3 oz. butter | $\frac{1}{2}$ bay leaf |
| 1$\frac{1}{2}$ pints veal stock or | $\frac{3}{4}$ pint single cream |
| tinned consommé | 3 tablespoons brandy |
| 8 oz. Chablis wine | 1 packet frozen peas |
| 1 oz. plain flour | 1 medium tin |
| | mushrooms |
| | cooked new potatoes |
| | or rice |

▶ Slice thinly 2 peeled onions and 2 peeled carrots. Melt 1 oz. butter in a pan large enough to hold a 2-lb. tinned Danish ham. Add the onions and carrots and stir until the vegetables are well coated with the melted butter. Place the ham in the pan with the vegetables. Pour over 1$\frac{1}{2}$ pints hot veal stock (tinned consommé can be substituted) and 8 oz. Chablis (a similar type of white wine can be substituted). Add 1 bouquet garni (2 sticks celery, 8 sprigs parsley, 1 sprig thyme, and $\frac{1}{2}$ bay leaf tied together). Simmer over low heat until the vegetables are done, about $\frac{1}{2}$ hour. Remove the ham and reduce the stock by one-third. Strain the stock.

▶ Melt over low heat 2 oz. butter. Add and blend 1 oz. flour. Add the hot strained stock and, stirring constantly, cook until the sauce is smooth and thickened. Cool and store in the refrigerator.

▶ Wrap the ham in aluminium foil or plastic and store in the refrigerator.

▶ Next day reheat the sauce in a double boiler. Add $\frac{3}{4}$ pint single cream and 3 tablespoons brandy. Blend well. Add 1 packet frozen peas, cooked according to instructions on the packet. Drain and slice 1 medium tin mushrooms. Add to the cream sauce.

▶ Cut the ham in slices and arrange the slices to overlap in a shallow ovenproof serving dish. Pour over the sauce. Place the dish in a pan of hot water. Reheat in a medium oven 335°F, Reg 3 for $\frac{1}{2}$–$\frac{3}{4}$ hour.

▶ This is delicious accompanied at table with tiny steamed new potatoes or rice.

# Cherry Croquemtouffle

| | |
|---|---|
| 1 lb. flour | $\frac{1}{2}$ tablespoon kirsch |
| 10 oz. castor sugar | 1 large tin cherries |
| 1$\frac{1}{2}$ teaspoons baking powder | scant 3$\frac{1}{2}$ oz. ground almonds |
| 3 eggs | jug of double cream |
| $\frac{3}{4}$ lb. butter | |

▶ Sift 10 oz. flour, 6 oz. sugar and 1$\frac{1}{2}$ teaspoons of baking powder into a bowl. Make a mound of the flour with a well in the centre. Beat 3 eggs. Pour into the well with $\frac{1}{2}$ tablespoon kirsch and 4 oz. melted butter. Mix well with your hands.

▶ Butter a pie tin. Pat the dough into the bottom of the pan to form a crust. Cover this dough with stoned cherries.

▶ Put 5 oz. plain flour, scant 3$\frac{1}{2}$ oz. ground almonds and 4 oz. sugar in a bowl. Cut $\frac{1}{2}$ lb. butter into small lumps. With a pastry cutter or 2 knives, cut the butter into the flour mixture until it has the consistency of large crumbs. Cover the cherries with this mixture. Cook 30 to 40 minutes in a pre-heated medium oven, 350°F, Reg 4. It should be golden brown on top. Remove from tin. Cool.

▶ Serve cold, accompanied by a jug of double cream.

# 68

MENU

*Tomato Ring Mould with Avocados*

*Curry of Lamb*

*Lime Mousse*

## Tomato Ring Mould with Avocados

| | |
|---|---|
| 18 oz. tomato juice | 2 oz. gelatine |
| 1 pinch sugar | 3 tablespoons cold |
| 1 tablespoon grated | water |
| onion | 16 oz. tinned beef |
| 1 bay leaf | consommé |
| 1 level teaspoon dried | salt to taste |
| sweet basil | 2 avocados, peeled |
| 1 tablespoon | and stoned |
| Worcester sauce | 2 packets of frozen |
| juice of 1 lemon | prawns |

▶ Simmer 18 oz. tomato juice, 1 pinch sugar, 1 tablespoon grated onion, 1 bay leaf, 1 level teaspoon dried sweet basil, for 5 minutes. Strain.

▶ Dissolve 2 oz. gelatine in 3 tablespoons cold water. Let stand 5 minutes. Add to strained tomato juice. Stir until gelatine is dissolved.

▶ Combine tomato juice with 16 oz. tinned beef consommé, 1 tablespoon Worcester sauce and juice of 1 lemon. Season to taste with salt. Pour into a wet ring mould. Chill overnight in refrigerator.

▶ To serve, unmould on a serving dish. Arrange slices of avocado across the ring. Fill centre with unfrozen prawns.

## Curry of Lamb

| | |
|---|---|
| 1 medium-sized leg of | $\frac{3}{4}$ lb. pumpkin cubes |
| lamb | $\frac{1}{2}$ lb. seedless raisins |
| 4 oz. curry powder | 1 fresh coconut or |
| 6 onions | 2 tablespoons of |
| 2 cloves garlic | desiccated coconut |
| 4 oz. butter | infused in a cup of |
| 2 tablespoons | boiling water |
| cooking oil | 2 tablespoons Bovril |
| 4 large cooking | juice of 1 lemon |
| apples | 4 hard-boiled eggs |
| 2 tablespoons | chopped peanuts |
| chopped parsley | mango chutney |
| 2 tablespoons | salt to taste |
| chopped celery | |

▶ Ask the butcher to skin, bone, and remove all fat from a medium-sized leg of lamb. Cut lamb in 1-inch cubes. Put 4 oz. curry powder on a sheet of greaseproof paper. Roll the meat in it and knead until all the curry powder is absorbed.

▶ Peel and chop fine 6 onions and 2 cloves of garlic.

▶ In a large pan melt 4 oz. butter and 2 tablespoons oil, add the onions and garlic, cook until they are golden yellow. Add the meat. Stir until well mixed. Cook for 10 minutes over a moderate heat.

▶ With an ice pick bore holes in the 2 eyes of a fresh coconut. Pour the milk from the coconut over the meat, plus enough hot water to cover. If using desiccated coconut infusion, strain off the liquid and pour over meat.

▶ Peel, core and chop 4 large cooking apples. Chop celery and parsley to have 2 tablespoons each. Stir into the meat.

---

▶ Remove the seeds and stringy portions of a large slice of pumpkin. Peel and cut into small cubes to have ¾ lb. Add to the meat, with ½ lb. seedless raisins.

---

▶ Stir in 2 tablespoons Bovril and the juice of 1 lemon. Cover and cook over low heat, stirring occasionally, for 1½ hours. Cool. Store overnight in a cool place.

---

▶ To serve, reheat on top of the stove over low heat, stirring from time to time. The curry must be cooked a day in advance and reheated. Serve with plenty of rice (Menu 57), bowls of grated fresh coconut, coarsely chopped hard-boiled eggs, finely chopped peanuts and mango chutney.

# Lime Mousse

| | |
|---|---|
| 4 egg yolks | ¾ oz. gelatine |
| 8 oz. sugar (castor) | 3 tablespoons warm water |
| ¼ teaspoon salt | |
| 4 oz. fresh lime juice | 6 egg whites |
| ½ tablespoon grated rind of lime | 8 oz. double cream |
| | toasted almond slivers |

▶ Tear a piece of greaseproof paper long enough to go round a 2¼-pint soufflé dish. Fold it in half lengthwise and oil 1 side. With the oiled side in, wrap the paper around the soufflé dish, leaving it to extend for 4 inches above the rim. Secure it with Scotch tape.

---

▶ Beat 4 egg yolks. Add 4 oz. castor sugar and ¼ teaspoon salt. Beat until creamy. Stir in 4 oz. fresh lime juice. Put mixture in the top of a double boiler and, stirring continuously, cook over hot but never boiling water, until it is slightly thickened. Remove from the heat and stir in ¾ oz. gelatine dissolved in 3 tablespoons warm water and let stand for 5 minutes. Stir in ½ tablespoon of the grated rind of lime. Stir until the gelatine is completely dissolved. Cool.

---

▶ Beat 6 egg whites until very stiff. Gradually beat in 4 oz. castor sugar until they hold definite peaks. Stir into the lime mixture when nearly set. Beat 8 oz. double cream until it holds a shape. Fold into the lime mixture. Pour into the soufflé dish and chill overnight in the refrigerator.

---

▶ To serve. Remove the paper collar from around the soufflé dish. Press toasted shreds of almonds around the sides of the soufflé extending above the dish.

## MENU

*Eggs Soubise*

*Burgundian Jellied Fish Slices*

*Jemima's Salad*

*Coffee Hedgehog*

## Eggs Soubise

| | |
|---|---|
| 6 eggs | 9–10 oz. single cream |
| 1 tablespoon vinegar | 1 egg yolk |
| 1 lb. onions | 1 pinch of cayenne |
| ¾ teaspoon salt | pepper |
| 2 oz. butter | |
| 1 oz. flour | |

▶ Cook 6 eggs in boiling water with
1 tablespoon vinegar for 6 minutes. Run
under cold water to cool. Drain and put
aside.

▶ Peel 1 lb. of onions. Slice crosswise in
thin slices. Cook in ¾ pint boiling water
with ½ teaspoon of salt for 15 minutes.
Drain, reserving the cooking water. Put
through a fine sieve or blend in a liquidizer.

▶ Melt 2 oz. butter in a saucepan. Add
1 oz. flour and with a wooden spoon
stir until smooth. Add 8 oz. of the reserved
water from the onions, stirring constantly.
Add 8 oz. single cream, ¼ teaspoon salt and
a pinch of cayenne pepper. Cook 5 minutes,
stir in the blended onions and 1 beaten egg
yolk with 1 tablespoon of cream. Cook
5 minutes. Set aside to cool, stirring
occasionally. Put a little cream over the
top to keep a crust from forming, and
store in the refrigerator overnight.

▶ Next day, peel eggs and reheat in a
steamer. It will only take 5 minutes. Reheat
the sauce in a double boiler over hot
water, not boiling.

▶ To serve, put the eggs into individual
ramekins and pour the sauce over them.

## Burgundian Jellied Fish Slices

| | |
|---|---|
| 16 oz. red Burgundy | 1 lb. fish bones and |
| 16 oz. water | trimmings |
| 1 carrot | 6 thick slices fish, |
| 1 onion | hake, halibut or |
| 1 teaspoon salt | haddock (3 lb.) |
| 10 peppercorns | ½ lb. whitefish |
| 1 bay leaf | 1 leek |
| 2 whole cloves | 1 egg |
| 1 sprig thyme | 1½ oz. gelatine |
| 6 sprigs parsley | |
| 3 sticks of celery | |

▶ Pour 16 oz. wine and 16 oz. water into
a large saucepan with a cover.

▶ Peel and slice 1 carrot and 1 onion, and
add to saucepan with 1 teaspoon salt,
10 peppercorns, 1 bay leaf, 2 whole cloves,
1 sprig thyme, 6 sprigs parsley, 3 sticks of
celery and 1 lb. fish bones and trimmings.
Bring to the boil and cook this stock
covered for 40 minutes on low heat.

▶ Place 6 thick slices of the hake, halibut
or haddock in a casserole and strain
the boiling wine stock over the pieces. Bring
to a boil, reduce heat to minimum and
barely simmer for 10 minutes. Remove the
slices carefully and place on folded cloth.
Set aside.

▶ Chop ½ lb. of whitefish, the white part
of 1 leek and add to the stock with
1 slightly beaten egg white and 1 crushed
egg shell. Bring to a boil, lower heat and
continue cooking slowly for 5 minutes.

▶ Remove the casserole from heat and let stand undisturbed for 20 minutes in a warm place. During this time carefully remove skin from fish slices and arrange them in a deep glass serving dish. Strain the stock through a fine sieve lined with cheesecloth into a clean saucepan and reheat. Soften 1½ oz. gelatine in a cup of warm red wine, stir the mixture into the hot clarified stock and cool. When cold but not yet jellied, pour over the fish and put into refrigerator overnight.

## Jemima's Salad

| | |
|---|---|
| 1 cos lettuce | 4 tomatoes |
| 2 avocados | 1 level tablespoon |
| 1 level tablespoon red | grated carrots |
| radishes, diced | 2 tablespoons peeled |
| a little watercress | and sliced cucumbers |
| | |
| 2 tablespoons cider | 1 teaspoon honey |
| vinegar | 1 or 2 tablespoons |
| ½ teaspoon salt | chopped tarragon |
| 6 tablespoons olive oil | and parsley |
| pepper to taste | ½ teaspoon mustard |
| | powder |

▶ Remove stalks and outer leaves of the cos lettuce and wash each leaf. Cut the large leaves into half. Chop the 4 tomatoes. Peel the 2 avocados and chop them into ½-inch cubes, add the 1 level tablespoon carrots, 1 level tablespoon radishes, diced, 2 tablespoons peeled and sliced cucumbers and the watercress. Pour the dressing over and mix well.

### Dressing

▶ Take a small bowl. Mix well the 2 tablespoons cider vinegar, 1 teaspoon honey, ½ teaspoon salt, ½ teaspoon mustard powder. Now add 6 tablespoons olive oil and freshly ground pepper to taste. Stir until well blended and add the herbs.

## Coffee Hedgehog

| | |
|---|---|
| 2 tablespoons instant | pinch salt |
| coffee | 6 eggs |
| ¼ pint water | 1 teaspoon vanilla |
| 3 tablespoons castor | extract |
| sugar | 8 oz. double cream |
| 4 tablespoons dark | 18 double sponge |
| rum | fingers |
| 8 oz. butter | 3 oz. blanched |
| 8 oz. icing sugar | almonds |

▶ Dissolve 1½ tablespoons of the instant coffee and 2 tablespoons castor sugar in ¼ pint hot water, add 4 tablespoons rum and set aside.

▶ Cream 8 oz. softened butter with 8 oz. icing sugar and a pinch of salt until light and fluffy. Beat in one by one 3 whole eggs and 3 egg yolks, ½ tablespoon instant coffee and 1 teaspoon vanilla.

▶ Whip 8 oz. double cream stiff and fold into butter-egg mixture. If too liquid, place in refrigerator for a short time until it reaches a good spreading consistency.

▶ Split sponge fingers and arrange 9 halves, three by three, flat-side down on an oval dish. Moisten with ¼ of the rum-coffee syrup and spread a little less than ¼ of the butter cream. Repeat 3 times. Spread the cream on all sides as well as on top of the last layer of moistened sponge fingers. Place in refrigerator uncovered until the cream is sufficiently set to cover with aluminium foil without damaging the loaf. Keep refrigerated.

▶ Cut 3 oz. blanched almonds in halves lengthwise, brown lightly in moderate oven, 350°F, Reg 4, and put aside ready to decorate loaf before serving.

▶ Just before guests arrive, stick the roasted almond slices vertically into the top of loaf. Keep cold until ready to serve.

# 70

## MENU

*Chicken Waterzoi, New Potatoes
or Rice*

*Lemon Tart*

## Chicken Waterzoi

| | |
|---|---|
| 2 small roasting chickens | 1 teaspoon salt |
| water | 5 oz. butter |
| 3 chicken bouillon cubes | 1 oz. plain flour |
| 1 veal knuckle | 2 tablespoons single cream |
| 3 carrots | 3 egg yolks |
| 7 leeks | 12 oz. double cream |
| 7 sticks of celery | pinch of nutmeg |
| 1 onion | |
| 2 cloves | |
| a few peppercorns | |

▶ Place 2 small roasting chickens breast-side down in a large enamel pan. Put 1 veal knuckle, 3 peeled whole carrots, 3 leeks, 3 sticks of celery and 1 onion studded with 2 cloves around the chicken. Pour over enough water to cover chickens, adding 3 chicken bouillon cubes. Add 1 teaspoon salt and a few peppercorns. Simmer, uncovered, on a moderate heat until chickens are tender, test with a fork. Take out chickens. Continue to simmer chicken stock on a very low heat for 1 hour. Strain and pour back over chicken.

▶ Cut 4 leeks, white part only, and 4 sticks of celery into fine strips 2 inches long. Melt 2 oz. butter in a saucepan. Add leeks and celery, mix well with the butter. Cover and cook for 15 minutes on a very low heat. Do not let them brown. Pour over a ladle of the stock and continue cooking on low heat for $\frac{1}{2}$ hour. Set aside.

▶ Melt 3 oz. butter, mix in 1 oz. plain flour. Cook for 5 minutes, stirring continuously with a wooden spoon. Add 1$\frac{1}{2}$ pints strained chicken stock. Continue stirring and cook over low heat until it thickens. Film with 2 tablespoons single cream to prevent skin from forming. Put aside.

▶ Beat 3 egg yolks. Stir in 12 oz. double cream. Put, covered, in the refrigerator.

▶ Next day, skin chickens, carve into serving pieces, discarding backs, and reheat in the chicken stock. Reheat celery and leeks. Stirring continuously, reheat the white sauce in a double boiler.

▶ Pour chicken sauce into the leek and celery mixture. Add the beaten yolks and cream mixture and, stirring, cook for 5 minutes but do not boil. Add a pinch of nutmeg. Correct seasoning. It will not be a thick sauce as it is to be eaten as a soup. Keep hot in a double boiler or over hot water.

▶ To serve. Drain the chicken. Place the pieces in a soup tureen and pour over sauce. Serve at the table in soup plates.

▶ In Belgium, this is always served as a soup and main course, at the same time. It can be accompanied by steamed new potatoes or Rice (Menu 57).

## Lemon Tart

| Pastry | Filling |
|---|---|
| 6 oz. plain flour | 4 eggs |
| $\frac{1}{4}$ teaspoon salt | 1 lb. castor sugar |
| 6 oz. butter | 4 oz. water |
| 1–2 tablespoons iced | 2 oz. melted butter |
|    water | 4 small lemons |
| | pinch of salt |
| | pinch of nutmeg |

▶ Sift $\frac{1}{4}$ teaspoon salt with 6 oz. plain flour. Put on a board, make a well in the centre and put into the well 6 oz. slightly softened pieces of butter. Add the iced water. With your hands work the centre ingredients into a paste. Work in the flour, knead dough lightly until the ingredients are well blended. Form into a ball, put into a plastic bag, chill overnight in the refrigerator. Next day roll out the pastry and line a 9-inch buttered pie tin. Chill till ready to bake the tart.

▶ Beat 4 eggs slightly, stir in 1 lb. sugar, 4 oz. water and 2 oz. melted butter, stirring after you add each ingredient. Add pinch of salt and nutmeg.

▶ Grate the rinds of 2 small lemons, then remove all the white pith. Cut into very thin slices, removing any pips. Cut 2 more small lemons, leaving the rind, into very thin slices. Add grated rind and lemon slices to egg mixture and pour into the uncooked pastry shell.

▶ Bake in a moderate oven 350°F, Reg 4 for $\frac{1}{2}$ hour. This can be baked the day before, but if possible bake it just before the guests arrive and serve it slightly warm.

# 71

## MENU

*Michael's Salade Niçoise*

*Spare Ribs, Barbecue Sauce, with Baked Potatoes*

*Giselle's Apple Pudding*

## Michael's Salade Niçoise

| | |
|---|---|
| 1 cos lettuce | 6 tablespoons olive oil |
| 1 small cucumber | 2 tablespoons wine |
| 1 large green pepper |    vinegar |
| 4 small tomatoes | 1 egg yolk |
| 4 hard-boiled eggs | $\frac{1}{2}$ teaspoon Dijon |
| 1 avocado pear |    mustard |
| 1 medium tin tuna | $\frac{1}{2}$ teaspoon salt |
|    fish | $\frac{1}{4}$ teaspoon pepper |
| 4 fillets of anchovies | 1 tablespoon chopped |
| |    basil |

▶ Prepare the salad in advance by separating and washing the leaves of 1 head cos lettuce. Rinse several times. Dry the leaves by letting them drain in a colander. Roll in an absorbent towel or paper and store in refrigerator to crisp. Peel 1 small cucumber, wrap in plastic. Wash and cut off the top of 1 large green pepper. Cut in half, remove seeds and cut away white membrane, cut lengthwise. Put in a plastic container. Peel and cut into quarters 4 hard-boiled eggs; put in a plastic container. Cut 4 small tomatoes in quarters and put in a plastic container. Store all of these in the refrigerator until the time to make the salad.

▶ Put in a jar with a screw top 6 tablespoons olive oil, 2 tablespoons wine vinegar, 1 egg yolk, $\frac{1}{2}$ teaspoon Dijon mustard, $\frac{1}{2}$ teaspoon salt, $\frac{1}{4}$ teaspoon pepper. Shake well and store in a cool place until serving time.

▶ Towards the evening arrange the salad in a salad bowl. Cut the leaves of the cos lettuce into smaller pieces and put into bowl. Add the cucumber cut into cubes, the green pepper cut into strips, the quartered eggs and tomatoes. Flake a medium-size tin of tuna fish into large pieces. Cut 4 anchovy fillets into halves. Peel and cut in thick strips 1 avocado pear. Add to the green cos lettuce in the bowl. Sprinkle with 1 tablespoon finely chopped fresh basil. If not in season dried basil can be used. Set aside in the refrigerator until serving time.

▶ To serve. Shake the salad dressing in the jar until well mixed. Pour over the salad in the bowl. Toss gently and serve.

## Spare Ribs with Barbecue Sauce

| | |
|---|---|
| 18 4-inch-long spare | 1 teaspoon paprika |
|    ribs | 1 pinch sage |
| 3 tablespoons olive oil | 2 oz. brown sugar |
| 2 oz. chopped onion | $\frac{1}{4}$ pint chilli sauce |
| 2 cloves garlic | 4 oz. hot water |
| $\frac{1}{2}$ teaspoon dry | 2 tablespoons |
|    mustard |    Worcester sauce |
| 1 teaspoon oregano | 2 tablespoons |
| 1 teaspoon thyme |    tarragon vinegar |
| $\frac{1}{2}$ teaspoon ground | 2 tablespoons lemon |
|    coriander |    juice |

▶ Ask your butcher to cut spare ribs into 4-inch lengths, 18 in all.
Keep ribs in an ovenproof serving dish.

## Barbecue Sauce

▶ To make barbecue sauce, heat 2 tablespoons olive oil in a saucepan. Add 2 oz. finely chopped onions to the hot oil and cook 5 minutes. Add 2 finely chopped cloves of garlic. Cook 1 minute longer. Away from the heat, add $\frac{1}{2}$ teaspoon dry mustard, 1 teaspoon oregano, 1 teaspoon thyme, $\frac{1}{2}$ teaspoon coriander, 1 pinch sage, 1 teaspoon paprika, and 2 oz. brown sugar. Mix well. Stir in $\frac{1}{4}$ pint chilli sauce, 4 oz. hot water, 2 tablespoons Worcester sauce, 2 tablespoons tarragon vinegar and 2 tablespoons lemon juice. Mix well and simmer on low heat for 10 minutes. Stir occasionally so that it does not stick to the pan.

▶ 1 hour before dinner bake the ribs in a pre-heated moderate oven, 350°F, Reg 4. When ready to serve, brown under a grill. Reheat Barbecue Sauce and serve separately.

▶ Baked Potatoes (Menu 40) make a good accompaniment for this dish.

## Giselle's Apple Pudding

| | |
|---|---|
| 6 cooking apples | $\frac{1}{4}$ teaspoon salt |
| 6 oz. sugar | 2 oz. butter |
| 1 lemon | 6 oz. single cream |
| 5 oz. plain flour | double cream for serving |

▶ Peel, core and cut into quarters 6 cooking apples. Add the grated rind of 1 lemon to 6 oz. sugar. Mix well. Butter an ovenproof pudding dish. Place apples on bottom of dish. Sprinkle with sugar. Place in a very hot oven, 450°F, Reg 8. Bake for 10 minutes. Remove from oven.

▶ Sift 5 oz. plain flour with $\frac{1}{4}$ teaspoon salt into a deep bowl. With a pastry cutter or 2 knives, cut 2 oz. butter into the flour. Gradually stir in 6 oz. single cream to make a soft, almost liquid dough. Pour over the apples. Bake in a pre-heated oven, 300°F, Reg 2, for 30 minutes.

▶ Serve cold accompanied with a jug of double cream.

# 72

## MENU

*Canadian Prawns*

*Cold Roast Turkey, Pecan Stuffing*

*Belgian Endive and Roquefort Salad*

*Cranberry Ice Cream*

## Canadian Prawns

| | |
|---|---|
| 3 ½-lb. packets frozen prawns | 8 oz. double cream |
| 2 oz. butter | 4 oz. Dijon mustard |
| 1 oz. plain flour | 2 tablespoons parmesan cheese |
| 8 oz. milk | salt, pepper to taste |

▶ If the prawns are raw, cook 3 packets according to instructions on the packet. Remove shells if necessary.

▶ Melt over low heat 2 oz. butter. Stir in with a wooden spoon 1 oz. flour. Blend over low heat. Cool slightly. Stir in 8 oz. hot milk. Cook over low heat until thick and smooth.

▶ Mix well 8 oz. double cream and 4 oz. Dijon mustard. Stir into the white sauce. Mix thoroughly. Salt and pepper to taste.

▶ Butter lightly an ovenproof serving dish. Pour in ½ of the mustard sauce. Arrange a layer of prawns on top. Cover with the rest of the mustard sauce. Cover and store in the refrigerator.

▶ To serve, sprinkle with 2 tablespoons grated parmesan cheese. Dot with a few bits of butter. Bake in a hot pre-heated oven, 420°F, Reg 7, for 15 minutes. Serve immediately.

## Cold Roast Turkey, Pecan Stuffing

| | |
|---|---|
| 1 6-lb. turkey, ready trussed | unsalted butter |
| | salt and pepper |

*Stuffing*

| | |
|---|---|
| 3 medium onions | 6 oz. shelled pecan nuts (or walnuts) |
| 3 oz. butter | |
| 4 thick slices stale bread | 4 hard-boiled eggs |
| | 6 tablespoons chopped parsley |
| 8 oz. milk | |
| 6 oz. chopped cooked ham | ¼ lb. liver sausage |
| | 4 oz. brandy |
| salt and freshly ground pepper to taste | |

▶ Stuff the bird just before roasting. Rub it well with softened unsalted butter. Salt and pepper the bird only when it has browned. Place on a greased rack, breast-side up, uncovered in a roasting pan. Put in an oven pre-heated to 450°F, Reg 8. Reduce heat immediately to 350°F, Reg 4. Baste frequently with pan drippings. Cook until tender. Allow 25 minutes to the lb. Remove from oven. Cool. Wrap in silver foil and store in refrigerator.

▶ To serve, carve the bird, place on the serving dish surrounded with spoonfuls of the stuffing. Serve with Belgian Endive and Roquefort Salad.

## Pecan Stuffing

▶ Peel and chop 3 medium onions finely. Chop turkey liver.

▶ In a saucepan melt 3 oz. butter. Add the onions and turkey liver. Simmer for 10 minutes on medium heat, stirring from time to time. Do not let it brown.

▶ Remove the crusts from 4 thick slices of stale bread. Soak in 8 oz. milk. Squeeze out carefully until dry. Crumble.

▶ Chop fine, enough cooked ham to make 1 cup or 6 oz. Shell and chop fine 6 oz. pecan nuts or walnuts. Peel and chop fine 4 hard-boiled eggs. Chop fine enough parsley to make 6 tablespoons. Mix all together in a bowl. Add the onions and bread. Mix well. Add $\frac{1}{4}$ lb. liver sausage chopped into small bits. Mix again. Season to taste with salt and freshly ground pepper. Moisten with 4 oz. brandy.

## Belgian Endive and Roquefort Salad

| | |
|---|---|
| 8 leaves of chicory per person | $\frac{1}{4}$ teaspoon salt |
| | $\frac{1}{4}$ teaspoon pepper |
| | scant 3 oz. roquefort cheese |
| | 2 oz. vinegar |
| | 2 tablespoons sherry |

▶ Cut off the root ends of chicory. Wash them. Dry them well. Roll in a cloth and store in the vegetable compartment of the refrigerator.

### Roquefort Dressing

▶ Blend in a liquidizer 2 oz. vinegar, 2 tablespoons sherry, $\frac{1}{4}$ teaspoon salt, $\frac{1}{4}$ teaspoon pepper and scant 3 oz. roquefort cheese. Store in a cool place.

▶ To serve. Cut the chicory into 2-inch sections. Mix the dressing again and pour over the chicory leaves.

## Cranberry Ice Cream

| | |
|---|---|
| 1 lb. fresh cranberries or equivalent in tinned cranberries | 2 oranges |
| | 8 oz. double cream |
| 8 oz. water | |
| $\frac{3}{4}$ lb. sugar (castor) | |

▶ Cook 1 lb. fresh cranberries with 8 oz. water until soft. Mash through a sieve or blend in a liquidizer. Add $\frac{3}{4}$ lb. castor sugar and the juice of 2 oranges. Cool. Pour into refrigerator tray. Freeze with freezing unit at high for 20 minutes.

▶ Whip 8 oz. double cream. Fold into the slightly frozen cranberry mixture. Mix well. Return to the refrigerator tray. Freeze until firm then turn down the freezing unit to normal.

# Recipe Index

Menu numbers are given after each entry.

# MAIN COURSES

## MEAT

*Beef*

Beef Tongue, Boiled   17
Boeuf à la Mode (Beef in Aspic)   52
Boeuf Bourguignon   35
Boeuf Miroton (French stew)   29
Boeuf Strogonoff (Russian beef stew)   2
Braised Beef (Austrian)   42
Brisket of Beef   61
Carbonnade Flamande (Flemish, braised)   55
Chili con Carne (Mexican, minced)   21
Gulyas, Magyar's (Hungarian stew)   66
Roast Beef, Cold   8
Rumpsteak Esterhazy (Hungarian)   38
Spare Ribs   71
Spiced Beef   14

*Lamb*

Bobotee (South African curried lamb)   57
Curry of Lamb   68
Gigot à la Cuillère (French peasant's leg of lamb)   44
Hounkiar Beyendi (Turkish stew)   62
Lamb Stew, Greek   18
Lamb Stew, Turkish   5
Lamb Pie, Roumanian   31
Ruth's Lamb in Aspic   11
Tongue, Baked (Old English recipe)   50

*Pork and Ham*

Cold Honey Pork   6
Chops in Cider   25
Ham Chablis (hot)   19
Jambon Persille (in aspic)   40
Meat Loaf, The Emperor's   24
Muscovite Selianka (pork chops in sauerkraut)   23
Saupiquet with Ham Montbard (ham and artichokes)   67

*Veal*

Braised Veal Chops in Aspic   4
Gratin of Veal   64
Gulyas (Hungarian stew)   33
Meat Loaf, The Emperor's   24
Moussaka, King's (Greek, minced)   34
Paprika Veal Schnitzel (Hungarian)   10
Surprise Salad (calves brain)   45

Sweetbreads, Suprême of   27
Veal Pepperonata   16
Vitello Tonnato (cold Venetian veal)   59

## POULTRY

*Chicken*

Boiled Chicken   56
Brunswick Stew   46
Chaud-froid of Chicken   22
Chicken San Remo   30
Chicken Esterhazy (stew)   60
Cold Fried Chicken   36
Jellied Chicken Loaf   43
Magyar Chicken (Hungarian)   26
Mediterranean Chicken Pie   65
Moroccan Chicken (fried)   3
Paella Valenciana (Spanish, chicken, fish and rice)   49
Simla Chicken Curry   39
Waterzoi (in soup)   70

*Turkey*

Cold Roast Turkey   72
Hot Steamed Turkey   9

*Duck*

Cider Duck   41
Cold Roast Duckling   15
Jellied Duck   53

*Game*

Grouse and Baked Beans   63
Hare, Saddle of   32
Peasant Partridge   48
Pheasant Tart   58
Pheasant Normandy   12

## FISH

Burgundian Jellied Fish Slices   69
Crabmeat and Cucumber Salad   47
Fish Chowder Logan Version   1
Lobster Clarence   20
Prawn Pilaf   54
Salmon, Poached   37
Salmon Trout   51
Seafood Risotto   7
South American Fish, Clarita's   28
Swedish Fish Pudding   13

# DESERTS

# General Index

Acapulco cocktail, 21
Alexander's nut cake, 27
Allspice, 5, 46
Almonds: and cheese cake, 35; and lettuce soup, 3
Anchovies, 11, 58, 71: anchovy eggs, 23; paste, 18, 64
Andalusian soup, 36
Apple(s), 3, 12, 23, 39, 41, 57, 68: and lychees, 50; aspic, 2; poached in cider, 45; pudding, 33, 71; sauté, 41
Apricots: dried, 24, 59; jam, 59; tart, 59
Artichokes: fried stuffed, 35; hearts, 27, 33, 42; vinaigrette, 30
Asparagus: cold soup, 7; tart, 51; tips, 13; vinaigrette, 20
Aspic: apple, 2; boeuf à la mode, 52; braised veal chops in, 4; Guacamole, 48; lamb in, 11; Roquefort balls in, 66
Aubergines, 34: purée, 62
Austrian fried potatoes, 42
Austrian marrow, 5
Austrian risi pisi, 60
Avocados, 21, 48, 55, 58, 68, 71: and cottage cheese, 10; mousse, 37; slices, 9; with grapes, 32

Bacon, 8, 10, 12, 14, 17, 23, 25, 29, 35, 44, 48, 53, 58, 61, 64, 65
Barbecue sauce, 71
Barbara's golden syrup delight, 36
Barley, 61
Basil, 15, 30, 31, 50, 54, 68, 71
Beans: baked beans and grouse, 63; bean sprout and corn salad, 34; broad beans, 46; butter-beans, 61, 63; cold green bean soup, 31; French green bean purée, 18; green bean salad, 53, 59; haricot beans, 44; lima beans, 46; red beans, 21; sweet and sour beans, 66; white bean purée, 44
Beef: boiled, 29; braised, 42; brisket of beef and butter-bean casserole, 61; chuck, 55, 66; cold roast, 8; fillet, 2, 52; flank, 66; heel of round beef, 14; minced, 21; rump, 55; rump-steak Esterhazy, 38; shin, 66; sirloin, 8; spare ribs, 71; spiced, 14; topside, 35, 42 *See also* Boeuf
Beef consommé, 27, 30, 40, 59, 68
Beef stock, 15, 17, 29, 30, 38, 42, 52, 66
Beetroot, 59: Russian salad, 11
Bel Paese cheese, 5
Belgian rhubarb tart, 64
Biscuit Tante Marie, 29

Blackberry melon, 54
Black-currant ice, 22
Bobotee, 57
Boeuf Bourgignon, 35
Boeuf à la Mode en Aspic, 52
Boeuf Miroton, 29
Boeuf Strogonoff, 2
Bombe Baur au Lac, 38
Borscht, Polish, 59
Bouillon, 14, 32, 70: chicken, 5; court, 28
Bovril, 31, 68
Brie cheese, 5
Brioches, 64
Broccoli, 64: salad, 4
Brunswick stew, 46
Brussels sprouts: purée, 50; steamed, 12
Burgundian jellied fish slices, 69
Butter-bean and brisket of beef casserole, 61

Cabbage: purée, 35; red, 2; salad, 6; white, 48, 58
Caerphilly cheese, 23
Cakes: cheese and almond, 35; cherry, 9, 42; chocolate, 16, 19; Malakoff, 37; nut, 27; rum, 63
Calvados, 12, 41
Calves brain, 45
Calves foot, 14, 52
Camembert cheese, 5
Canadian prawns, 72
Capers, 11, 14, 17, 21, 25, 38, 51: juice, 13
Caramel custard, 15
Caramel bread custard, 52
Caramel oranges, 48
Caraway seed, 6, 23, 29
Carbonnade Flamande, 55
Carrots: cream of carrot sauce, 9; cream of carrot soup, 40; fried, 3; salad, 8
Casaba melon, 49
Cauliflower, 45: Rio Grande, 55
Celeriac: in sauce remoulade, 25; salad, 16
Celery: and tomato salad, 22; relish, 56
Chablis, 67
Charlotte Française, 12
Cheddar cheese, 4, 8, 23, 41, 64
Cheese: Bel Paese, 5; Brie, 5; Caerphilly, 23; Camembert, 5; Cheddar, 4, 8, 23, 41, 64; cheese and almond cake, 35; cold soufflé, 49; cottage, 10, 18, 35; Double Gloucester, 23; Gorgonzola, 18; Gruyère, 12, 49, 55; mock soufflé, 8; parmesan, 15, 19, 34, 35, 36, 42, 49, 62, 72; Pont l'Evéque, 5; Roquefort, 5, 66, 72; Stilton, 23; Viennese Sacher, 18; Wensleydale, 23
Cherries, 7, 24: cake, 9, 42; Croquemtouffle, 67; glacé, 2

xii

## 37

*Avocado Mousse*
*Poached Salmon, Sauce Mousseline*
*Cucumber Salad*
*Malakoff Cake*

## 38

*Halibut Salad*
*Esterhazy Rumpsteak*
*Noodles in Brown Butter*
*Bombe Baur au Lac*

## 39

*Yoghourt Prawn Soup*
*Simba Chicken Curry*
*Rice and Green Pepper*
*Pineapple Water Ice*

## 40

*Cream of Carrot Soup*
*Jambon Persillé*
*Baked Potatoes, Salad Pitoeff*
*Junket, Kissel Sauce*

## 41

*Gnocchi*
*Cider Duck*
*Sauté Apples*
*Honey Mousse*

## 42

*Artichoke Hearts au Gratin*
*Braised Beef*
*Austrian Fried Potatoes*
*Cherry Cake*

## 43

*Oeufs Mollets Portuguaise*
*Jellied Chicken Loaf*
*Fennel Salad*
*Date Pudding*

## 44

*Tuna Fish Santa Barbara*
*Gigot à la Cuillère (Seven-hour Leg of Lamb)*
*Purée of White Beans*
*Oranges in Red Wine*

## 45

*Everybody's Fish Soup, Garlic Croutons*
*Surprise Salad*
*Apples Poached in Cider*

## 46

*Hungarian Liver Sausage Loaf*
*Brunswick Stew*
*Virginian Frozen Plum Pudding*

## 47

*Senegalese Soup*
*Crabmeat and Cucumber Salad*
*Pears Baked in Cream*

## 48

*Guacamole Aspic*
*Peasant Partridge*
*Caramel Oranges*

## 49

*Ginger Melon*
*Paella Valenciana*
*Cold Cheese Soufflé*

## 50

*Stuffed Courgettes*
*Baked Tongue, Cumberland Sauce*
*Purée of Brussels Sprouts*
*Compôte of Apples and Lychees*

## 51

*Asparagus Tart*
*Salmon Trout, Sauce Gribiche*
*Cucumber Salad*
*Chocolate Ice Cream with*
*Grated Marrons Glacés*

## 52

*Mussel Soup*
*Boeuf à la Mode en Aspic*
*Waldorf Salad*
*Caramel Bread Custard*

## 53

*Oysters on the Half Shell, Cocktail Sauce*
*Jellied Duck*
*Green Bean Salad*
*Melon Melba*

## 54

*Courgette Salad*
*Prawn Pilaf*
*Blackberry Melon*